Wendy Sand Eckel

Educating Tigers

AmErica House
Baltimore

First printing

Cover design: Carolyn White

ISBN: 1-893162-57-5
PUBLISHED BY AMERICA HOUSE BOOK PUBLISHERS
www.ericahouse.com
Baltimore

Printed in the United States of America

Dedication:

To Elizabeth and Madeline whom I love more than I thought possible and whose beautiful souls and pure hearts have already begun to enrich this world.

To Jeff, for your unwavering love, support and encouragement, and without which I never would have persevered.

And, to Mom, for your daily emails full of love and support. You never doubted me for a minute.

Foreword

Pursuing help for a dyslexic child is a bit like falling down the hole in Alice's "Wonderland." The experience of identifying a learning disability is a surreal one for most parents and is often filled with many unexpected twists and turns with teachers, educational diagnosticians, tutors, psychologists, psychiatrists, social workers, speech/language pathologists and neurologists. The varied perceptions and comments from other parents in the community after a diagnosis are also quite surprising, and at times, isolating.

Wendy Eckel's book *Educating Tigers* is so unique -- as she has woven her wisdom as the real-life parent of a delightful, dyslexic child into a fictional account about one family's attempt to deal with their child's learning needs. Eckel's knowledge and experience as a social worker in family practice lends a professional, as well as a personal slant to her descriptions of how all of the relationships in a family change when a child is diagnosed with a learning difference.

At last there is an entertaining, fictional story available to parents about these rather harrowing experiences. *Educating Tigers* is a long-awaited book about a crisis which is faced by about 20% of our population. Wendy and her husband, Jeff, are survivors of their trip in to "Wonderland"; optimism leaps off the pages. Other parents in this same predicament will easily relate to the Cunningham family in this story as they attempt to emotionally survive this arduous and complicated process of securing an appropriate educational program for their dyslexic child.

Educating Tigers is a must read for parents of dyslexic children and for the professionals who are in the business of helping families to cope with these issues over the long run, with compassion and a sense of humor.

Fran Bowman, Ed.D.
Educational Specialist
Bowman Educational Services
Columbia, MD

Having just returned to work following the birth of my second child, a colleague, noticing my exhaustion, asked me what lesson Tiger was in my life to teach me (social workers are known to ask these questions of one another). I remember thinking it odd to be asked to define Tiger's existence in such a way. But, feeling obligated to answer her, I said something about patience or endurance. After all, I was raised in Ohio and above all else, we are taught to be nice.

Now, more than seven years later, with the perspective of having lived through difficult times, I would answer her much differently. Because there are many lessons about living and love, and most particularly, ourselves, those of us who become parents can learn.

For me, the most profound knowledge came when I realized Tiger would require a part of me I had never intended to share.

But there is much for everyone to learn from my Tiger, some of it obvious, some of it disturbing, but all of it worth learning.

Preschool

I sipped the remains of my cooling coffee and as my motor began to run at last I hummed an old song from the sixties. Max claims it is abnormal for a Steppenwolf song to enter an adult mind as frequently as it does mine. He thinks it says something about the pathology of my subconscious. It's my theme song, I explained to my husband. And most likely why I use (overuse, Max would say) the metaphor of a motor when trying to make sense of things.

Jamie stood in the kitchen, patiently waiting to leave for school. Her symmetrical golden braids rested on her backpack. I looked over at her just as her newly acquired, wire-rimmed glasses caught the reflection of the morning sun. I smiled. "It must be hard to start your first year of middle school in glasses."

"Not really. Besides, I just remember your promise: Contacts next summer."

"If..." I coached.

"If I'm responsible all year with my glasses."

I kissed her on top of her head. "Exactly. But that's never been much of a problem for you now, has it?" I poured a second cup of coffee into my commuter mug and turned off the coffee maker. I scanned the kitchen for a lit burner, open breadbag or forgotten container of milk. "We're out of here," I said to Jamie as I swept up my coffee and brief case.

For instance, families are like motors. When working properly they hum along, each part functioning separately but in tandem with the others. However, when one part malfunctions, each interconnected part is affected, causing the entire motor to perform poorly. Max will give me this much. He likes the family metaphor even though he tends to think of himself more as the high-test gasoline than a laboring machine part.

I started toward the garage and was surprised when Jamie didn't follow. I stopped and looked over my shoulder. "Coming?"

"Aren't we forgetting something?" Jamie asked calmly.

"Are we?"

"What is this, *Home Alone Four*?"

"I thought Tiger was already in the van. Don't tell me she's not."

"Okay, I won't, but she isn't."

My heart sank. The morning routine is a motor that is highly susceptible to breakdowns. One misfire can cause a chain reaction that impacts the rest of the day.

"Okay, Plan B. Carry this stuff into the van and open the garage door. Take my keys and put them in the ignition." Jamie's eyes widened. "Go!" I ran from room to room and finally found Tiger in the infrequently used living room intertwined on the sofa with Baxter, our Labrador.

"There you are!"

Tiger looked up, her large, brown eyes as droopy as the dog's. "Baxter doesn't want me to leave him. He gets lonely."

I resisted the urge to start firing commands. "I know he does, sweetie." I reached for her arm and she allowed me to pull her out from under the dog. Her cotton tee shirt was wrinkled from Baxter's weight but there was no time for us to negotiate a change of clothes. I gave Baxter a perfunctory pat on the head and gently pointed Tiger in the direction of the kitchen.

"Wait," she said as she rolled out of my hands and skipped back to the dog who was watching her movements intently. Tiger kneeled before him and kissed him tenderly on the nose. She picked up his velvety ear and whispered, "I love you, boy." Baxter whimpered sadly. "Don't worry, we'll be back before you know it."

"Tiger --"

"Coming."

Max has concluded that I think in terms of motors because my father sold cars. He owned a dealership, I corrected. A General Motors dealership, Max had added, as if that made it less significant. But Max was raised in a wealthy Washington suburb by a trust-funded mother and a successful father. He thought about things differently. He suggested there were a lot better songs from the 60's to choose from. Perhaps. All I know is that the first time I felt my motor running I was dancing with my girlfriends in a middle school gymnasium and being admired by a particularly exciting boy. It was the first time I had felt joy since my father's death.

"Jamie," I said as the trees flew by the windows. The lane to the Chesapeake Day School was wooded and narrow. "I didn't know there was ever a three."

"Three what?"

"*Home Alone Three.*"

"I hate those movies," Tiger interjected. "They're so violent."

I smiled at her word choice. "We're coming up on the tree. Tell me if you see them."

Tiger craned her neck to see out of the van window. The sun blinked through the trees and she waited patiently for the clearing that gave way to the first view of the Severn River. The nest sits in a towering old oak at the edge of the river bed and on a lucky morning we can catch the sun reflecting from the glowing white

10

heads of a pair of bald eagles. "Well?"

"Not today," Jamie said. "They must be out hunting."

"I doubt it," Tiger said with confidence.

Jamie looked over at her sister. "Why?"

"Because," Tiger said as she continued to look out the window, "Bald Eagles are scavengers. They would rather steal prey from other hunters like ospreys. They only hunt if there isn't anything to steal."

"No way!" I said.

"Yup."

"Well, I love them anyway," Jamie said.

"Me too," I added. "I love them because they are breathtakingly beautiful."

"And I love them because," Jamie hesitated, "because they mate for life."

"What about you, Tig?" I asked.

Tiger sat quietly for a few moments and then said in a serious voice, "I love them because they survived even though they were almost extinct."

I rounded the circle in front of the Chesapeake Day School a little too quickly. Jamie slid open the door and hopped out of the van as soon as I came to a stop. "Bye, Mom," she sang sweetly, and waited for her sister. School. This was her element: Books and book covers, sharpened pencils and zippered pencil cases, friends, rules and praise. Jamie loved school and school loved her. She stood with her backpack on one shoulder and waved to a nearby friend.

"Bye, Jamie. Have a great day," I called and turned to look at Tiger. She hadn't moved toward the open door. "Let's not be late today," I said, trying to sound cheerful.

"What's today?" Tiger asked quietly.

"Monday." I looked at her as if to ask why but she was looking down at her hands.

"That's all?" she said, her voice barely audible through the silky, brown hair veiling her face. I studied Tiger. She looked small and vulnerable. I had hoped that by the second grade I would stop having a pit of worry in my stomach every morning.

"Come on, Tiger, everyone's waiting behind Mom!" Jamie whined from outside the van. She was shifting her weight from hip to hip as she watched her schoolmates filing into school ahead of her. "Tiger--" Jamie ducked her head back into the doorway to cajole her younger, slower sister out of the van. But Jamie's face softened when she saw Tiger's misery. "Do you want me to tie your shoe real quick?" she said with empathy more befitting an adult than a girl of eleven.

"No thanks, I can do it," Tiger said in resignation and slid out of the van at last, dragging her backpack behind her.

"Bye," I called. "I love you!"

11

"Love you, too!" Jamie said as she slid the heavy door closed with a bang. She put her hand on Tiger's small back and gently, but firmly, hurried her toward their school.

I waved to the head mistress who greeted Jamie and Tiger as they walked through the tall pillars marking the school's entrance. She stood there every morning, rain or shine, and greeted each child by name. Her presence was comforting and gave the appearance that someone was at the helm, in charge, ensuring the school ran safely and smoothly.

Jamie smiled brightly at her principal, but Tiger kept her head down, her untied shoelace flapping between her shoes. Velcro®, I thought. But Max had insisted Tiger would never learn to tie her laces properly if her shoes had Velcro® fasteners.[1]

Too impatient to pursue Tiger, the head mistress greeted the next child and my heart sank when I compared her response to Tiger's. She was a petite girl who stood erect, shoes neatly tied, hair combed tightly into small, even pigtails, and dressed in a pleated skirt and matching sweater that Tiger would never consent to wear. The head mistress' stern face lit up as she leaned down to hear the girl's animated conversation.

I looked away and eased out of the line of cars, continuing around the circle and rounding an overgrown clump of boxwoods that scratched the van as I passed. Their musky fragrance wafted in through my open window. I should come out to the school some Saturday and prune those aging beauties, I thought, before the parents with the expensive cars threaten to have them removed. Parents have influence in private schools which is why Max and I were thrilled when he was invited to serve on the board of trustees this year. His liberal approach to education was needed to offset the overzealous, more conservative set of parents.

It had been an unexpected decision for us to choose a private education for our children. Max and I had always staunchly defended the importance of public education. But that was before Jamie's insufferable kindergarten year in an overcrowded classroom that focused more on crowd control than education. And so, reluctantly, we had concluded that we couldn't sacrifice our children for our beliefs and enrolled Jamie, and now Tiger, in the Chesapeake Day School.

And I am surprised how much I love this school. The classrooms are located in a stately, old farmhouse with a tall flag pole centered in the clump of boxwoods. The breeze from the nearby river keeps the flag flapping reliably. It's a beautiful, pastoral setting, a rare pocket of serenity in this increasingly hectic part of the world that is wedged between the growing sprawl of Washington and Baltimore. There

---

[1] VELCRO® is a registered trademark of Velcro Industries B.V.

are times, while waiting for Jamie and Tiger at the end of a school day, when I have welled with tears, happy tears, at the sight of the safe, confident children filing into the buses and cars, the friendly teachers guiding them.

I edged the van I swore to never own through the brick gates and waved to the familiar faces I passed, some looking dwarfed by the size of the Suburbans they were maneuvering, others giving their children last minute instructions in the rear view mirrors of their Volvo station wagons. Once away from the school I sighed and picked up my coffee. My worry for Tiger lingered and I debated in my mind what was bothering her. A friend? It couldn't be. Tiger was a loyal and trustworthy companion. Her teacher? No. She was as kind and gentle as Tiger.

I knew I was nearing work when I passed a pair of jogging midshipmen, clad in their Naval Academy sweats, their footsteps falling in sync to an unheard cadence. And I realized I needed to focus more on my driving when I almost nudged a few Maryland state workers who were well within their allotted crosswalk. It was time to switch gears. This was Monday, much to Tiger's disappointment, and one of my long days at work. I wouldn't arrive home until after seven o'clock and our faithful sitter of eight years would pick Jamie and Tiger up from school. Maybe I would talk with Max tonight about Tiger. Maybe he had some insight into the source of her uncharacteristic melancholy. I pulled into my designated parking space and slipped into my cream-colored blazer.

"I see Baxter's been riding in the van again," Leslie called from behind me. Leslie was another family therapist at the private psychiatric hospital that employed us both. I smiled and rolled my eyes at her. Leslie approached me looking beautiful as usual in a green, silk dress with coordinating blazer, expensive shoes, matching purse and delicate, gold jewelry. Her blonde hair was cut and colored in an up-to-date style and I envied her flawless appearance.

I looked over my shoulder at the back of my jacket. "Great! Can you believe this? I have a therapy session with the family from hell this morning, military father, spit-shine shoes. The last thing I need is to look as if my Labrador slept on my suit."

"Well, did he?"

"You know the scary part is I'm not really sure."

Leslie smiled and began picking the stubborn, black hairs from my jacket. When she finished she turned me around by my shoulders and smiled down at me from her five-foot, eleven-inch height. "Okay, let's have a look." She expertly fluffed the layers in my hair. "There," she said as she looked down at my black skirt and tights. "You look great. Cute outfit. You can really pull off those shorter skirts. I'm all legs when I wear them."

"Thanks. I'll take what I can get, but cute isn't quite the look I was shooting for. This Colonel is supposedly in charge of top secret interrogations at the

13

Pentagon. You know the type, specially trained to intimidate people." Leslie laughed. "He could probably undergo days of bodily torture and starvation without showing a single emotion." I looked up at Leslie. "It's days like this that I wish I were taller."

Leslie slipped her arm through mine as we walked toward the brick institution. "Somehow I think you'll do just fine, Katie."

"Thanks," I said, squeezing her arm. "So, you're looking untidy as usual. How was your weekend?"

"Quiet," she said softly. "Too quiet."

"Not good."

"No, it isn't," she said halfheartedly.

"I wish you would have come over. You know you're always welcome, if not expected."

Leslie chuckled. "I probably should have. How are my darlings?"

"Well, one of your darlings is enjoying her return to school."

"And Tiger?"

I looked up at Leslie as the automatic glass door opened. The autumn sun sat low in the sky and glared into my eyes. I saw a trace of the dreaded aura of a migraine and quickly looked away. "Let's just say she's still adjusting."

Betty handed us each a stack of pink message forms and greeted us cheerfully from her perch behind an elegant, new reception desk. The hospital was redecorating with the intent of attracting wealthy patients who could pay the pricey fees when their insurance companies refused, an all too frequent occurrence in this era of Managed Care. But Betty looked out of place behind the expensive desk with her wiry gray hair, polyester blouse and loose knit pants. We stopped and scooped up handfuls of M&M's from the cut glass jar she kept faithfully filled.

"Oh, Katie," Betty sang. She was sporting a devilish grin. Leslie and I leaned in closer to listen. "Your nine o'clock has been in the lobby since eight!" she whispered loudly. "And I don't think he's moved a muscle!"

I rolled my eyes at Leslie and we stifled our laughter as we ducked into the elevator. "Thanks, Betty," I called through the closing doors.

"Anytime, ladies," she called back, her laughter sounding more like a cackle, a permanent condition from a lifetime of smoking.

I said good-bye to Leslie on the second floor, which housed the adolescent chemical dependency unit. Her office was on the third floor, east wing, adult psych. My keys clanked importantly as I opened the door to the locked unit where staff and patients were easily distinguished by the presence of an official ring of keys.

After checking in with the nurses on the weekend's activities, I poured a cup of coffee and hurried down the long corridor to my office, marveling at how the interior decorators had managed to coordinate this entire unit in various textures and

14

shades of forest greens and burgundy. The expensive carpet still smelled new and I appreciated the little multicolored flecks of color that concealed my inevitable coffee spills as I juggled my belongings down the hall each morning.

I slipped into my office and closed the door. It was my favorite time of day, alone, in my neat and organized space, surrounded by my favorite things, some personal, some whimsical, some declaring my legitimacy as a family therapist, and some to comfort those that come to me for help.

I kicked off my shoes, rested my stockinged feet on my desk and took a deep, relaxing breath. Thoughts of Tiger kept floating up to my consciousness but it was time to plan for my session with the Colonel. And although he and his alcoholic son were about to be summoned to my office, I was not afraid of how things would go. I could feel the adrenaline do its work as I planned my agenda.

There were many in my profession who avoided chemical dependency, what with the high rate of relapse, the ongoing sense of crisis, but I felt energized by it. I would have six weeks with the Colonel and his son in which I would try to help them work through the immediate crisis, educate them about chemical dependency and move them to a place where they could function in a way that encouraged communication and supported sobriety. Every patient and family were a new challenge, a new motor in need of a tune up (sometimes a complete overhaul), inevitably with an underlying secret or undisclosed family dysfunction. My role as mechanic required me to dig and prod, respectfully, and to clean out the built up residues so they could begin to heal. For most, healing requires letting go of their denial that a problem exists and of the illusion of an ideal, perfect family. After that, real change could begin.

The morning passed quickly, as was usually the case in this fast-paced, crisis-oriented hospital. The Colonel had shown some vulnerability and surprised both his son and me when he reached over and spontaneously hugged him at the end of the session. His son was visibly shocked at this uncharacteristic display of affection and despite a desperate attempt not to, cried.

After the session I rushed to team meeting in order to discuss each patient's treatment plan with the rest of the staff and then to my daily group therapy session with the adolescents. The Colonel's son was eager to talk about his father and received a lot of support and encouragement from the other patients. The Colonel's inability to express affection provided us with a theme for the group and enabled the others to share similar problems and experiences.

After group I poured yet another cup of coffee and plopped down into a chair by the nurses' station. I took one sip and scowled at the bitter taste.

"That's been there all morning, honey," Dolores, the charge nurse, said dryly.

She was standing behind the medications counter.

I smiled, embarrassed at how I must have looked. "I didn't see you there."

"I don't know how you could miss me, dearie!" she said sarcastically. Dolores had fifteen years of sobriety and was respected for her candor and sought after for her hugs. She was a large woman, but carried herself with a controlled, self-confident manner. She looked at me kindly over the top of her half-moon glasses. An occasional gray wiry strand had recently begun to appear form her otherwise short, brown hair, but she seemed to be accepting this with grace as she did everything else.

I smiled at Dolores and put my coffee down on the table next to me. It was in my favorite mug that pictured a Sandra Boynton animal hanging on to the top of a long stair case. The fading letters said, "Congratulations, you made it!" It had been a gift from my mother when I graduated from Social Work school. "Maybe I'm taking that new report about the benefits of caffeine a little too seriously."

"I don't think that sludge you just swallowed had many health benefits."

"No, I think you're right. Why don't I go and make a fresh pot." I pushed myself up out of the newly upholstered chair.

"Oh, by the way, Miss Katherine, you got a call from that hoity-toity school you're sending your kids to."

"Are they okay?" I asked.

"No emergency, honey, or you know I would have interrupted you in group. They said to call when you're free."

"Thanks, Dolores." I patted her affectionately as I walked past. "I appreciate you taking the message from my hoity-toity school."

The large, bold-faced clock, identical to the one I had watched endlessly in elementary school, was at one-o'clock when I arrived at the Chesapeake Day School.

"Sorry you had to leave work," Shelly, the school receptionist, said sincerely. "But Mary didn't want to wait to talk to you." Mary Peterson was Tiger's second grade teacher and Shelly could read the concern on my face.

She rolled her office chair away from her computer and over toward the reception counter. She leaned forward and crossed her arms. Shelly loved the insider information her job provided. "I don't think it's any big deal, Katie, I just saw Trisha on the playground and she looked fine. She was playing a great game with the other kids. They were pretending to be tigers in the jungle. It was really cute."

"Sometimes I wonder if she takes her nickname a little too seriously."

Shelly laughed. "Really, Katie, I would have heard if it was something

16

serious." She smiled reassuringly.

Although I sensed Shelly's privileged information status could as easily work against me as for me, I allowed myself to be comforted and sat down in the chair designated for visitors. I greeted several friendly teachers and parents as I waited for Mary.

As time passed I checked with the hospital from my cellular phone and learned that Betty had successfully rescheduled my appointments. Leslie had agreed to take over my family education group in case I didn't get back in time and had gently reminded me that I owed her one. I picked up a dated women's magazine that was buried under a scattered stack of school brochures and absentmindedly flipped through the well-read pages. As I perused page after page of make-up ads I wondered if perhaps I should wear more lipstick, or at least update my palette, or maybe at forty it was time for an "age-defying" moisturizer. At last I arrived at a page with text and was intrigued to find an article claiming to have condensed the art of parenting into ten simple lessons. This should be good, I thought to myself. These "authorities" make it seem so easy, suggesting parents only need to follow a few simple guidelines to raise the perfect child. But the title had my interest, parenting was my expertise, at home and in my work, and I was curious to read the latest best seller's spin on the topic.

Ten *Lessons* in Becoming the *Parent* Your *Children* *Need* and *Deserve*

Lesson One:
Humility

Lesson Two:
Empathy

Lesson Three:
Extending the Family

Lesson Four:
Fathering

Lesson Five:
Advocacy

Lesson Six:
Trusting Your Instincts

Lesson Seven:
Sacrifice

Lesson Eight:
Acceptance

Lesson Nine:
A Healthy Marriage

Lesson Ten:
The Importance of Siblings

Lesson One:
Humility

The first lesson in parenting is humility.
Parenting requires adults to realize
children are separate individuals, with their own ideas,
personalities and destinies.
It is humbling for parents to acknowledge,
and accept,
that their child won't become the person they
had expected or planned for.
A child's uniqueness will display
itself in the most unexpected ways.

    "I think Trisha should return to first grade," Mary said. We were sitting across from each other in second grade-sized desks.

"What?" I asked. "Mary, for goodness sakes! What are you talking about?"

"There is something wrong with her. I think she has some sort of learning disability."

"Mary," I said, trying to stop my voice from cracking. "Slow down, here. First grade? We talked about this last spring." I paused, trying not to panic. "Everyone said she was too mature to repeat a grade. That's why we had her tutored all summer. You were there, you agreed!" I wiped away a tear, embarrassed to be crying in front of a teacher. How could I tolerate the Colonel's penetrating stare for more than an hour, but cry within two minutes of Mary?

"I assumed Trisha would have made some progress this summer with all that tutoring, but it seems I was mistaken. Most of the other children are reading chapter books and Trisha struggles with every word. I'm sorry to have to tell you this," she said stiffly, "but she doesn't belong in my classroom. We think you should have her tested." Mary primly adjusted the cardigan that was clasped around her shoulders and avoided my eyes.

I stared at Mary's unfriendly face. The tears spilled from my eyes. "Mary, come on, this is Tiger! She is anything but learning disabled." My voice cracked. "Sure she'd rather sit in a mud flat than at her desk, but that's what makes her so unique. She's a budding scientist, a naturalist, and refreshingly different!" I fished in my oversized bag for a tissue. The tears were blurring my vision and I tried to use the lull in the conversation to regain my composure. But Mary had an agenda and impatiently handed me a box of tissues from her desk. The square box was decorated in a Noah's Ark theme and it occurred to me how violent that story is and how it must terrify children. This is what happens when you displease authority, they don't let you on the boat and leave you to drown.

Mary cleared her throat and I reluctantly pulled a tissue from the box and sighed. "Of course I want to know if there's a problem with Tiger. Did something happen today?"

"As a matter of fact, yes. Trisha was hiding out in the coat room this morning. School had already begun when Shelly found her just standing in there. When she brought her back to class I told Trisha that she would have to stay in for morning recess as a consequence." My heart ached at the thought of Mary chastising Tiger in front of her classmates. "And not five minutes later, she disappeared again, when it was time for reading partners. I sent Kristin in to look for her and sure enough, she was back in the coat room. This time I escorted her directly to Mrs. Larson's office and she suggested I call you in for a conference."

The tears returned as I listened to Mary speak so harshly about my gentle, sweet Tiger. What was happening? This was my loving, safe school in a farm house with a ten-year-old Labrador wandering the halls. And Mary had been so kind to Jamie. I had been looking forward to Tiger's year with her. I had been sure Tiger would respond to her warmth and patience. But the person before me conveyed neither. "Okay," I said, my voice barely audible. "Thank you for letting me know. I guess I can schedule some sort of testing. Where's Tiger now?"

"Trisha is in art and she's fine. Although she's been given extra homework for her misbehavior." Mary stood, clutching an unrelated stack of papers. She had delivered her message. This was my problem now, to fix without her help.

I looked up at her from my cramped perch behind the desk and felt ridiculously small. I stood quickly to meet her eyes. "There has to be an explanation. Tiger wouldn't hide in the coat room just to defy you. She's not that kind of child. You know that, Mary."

"Frankly, I don't know that," she said defensively. "And whether or not Patricia has displayed this behavior in the past, the point is, she's doing it now, in my classroom, and I simply can't condone her behavior, nor can I allow it to set a bad example for the other students."

"Patricia! I asked you the first day of school to please call her Tiger, or at least Trisha. She hates to be called Patricia, she's too much of a free spirit to be called by her formal name."

"Perhaps you should be more worried about Trisha's performance in school than about her free spirit.'"

My eyes narrowed as I looked at Mary. "Does Mrs. Larson agree with this?"

"Yes. Frances Larson backs her teachers and she agrees with me completely," Mary said, taking a step back from me, and it appeared, the problem. "Patricia is not fitting in and is taking my time and attention away from the other children. It simply can't continue." I waited for Mary to say more, to say she understood or was sorry, or that she would try to engage Tiger, or help her in some way. The silence was deafening. I had learned in my training to use silences, let them speak, they were often more powerful than words. But this silence was unbearable. No words of comfort or compassion were forthcoming from Mary Peterson today. "The children will be back any minute."

"Of course, I'll be going. I wouldn't want to disrupt the class anymore than we already have." I put my bag on my shoulder and dabbed my eyes with the saturated tissue. Mary cleared her throat quietly. I searched her face for a glimmer of understanding or reassurance that Tiger would be all right. But Mary's delicately lined face was frozen. I shivered involuntarily, turned quickly away and left.

"Tested? For what?" Max shouted through the static of my phone. "This is outrageous! I'm calling Frances Larson. She's way out of line here."

"Max, Mary said Tiger might have a learning disability," I said, trying to sound strong, but the words fell to the pit of my stomach like rocks. Learning Disability. I felt nauseous. I buzzed down the oversized window to get some air. "They found her hiding in the coat room this morning, and even after Mary punished her, she went right back in there."

"Jesus, Katie, that doesn't sound like Tiger. She's one of the most cooperative kids in that school. All she wants to do is please everyone. Someone must have done something to her."

"That was my first reaction, too, that she had a reason to be in there, but all Mary could do was complain about her behavior and how she doesn't want her in second grade."

"That's it, I'm calling Frances."

"Maybe you should wait until we've had a chance to talk. I can't even think yet. Will you be home at a reasonable hour? That's a request, you know, perhaps a demand."

"I don't know, Katie, I just got off the phone with the president of the Chesapeake Bay Foundation. They want to go ahead with their lawsuit against the State for failing to enforce the EPA laws. It's a huge case and this place is already hopping."

"That's great, Max," I said, not ready to change the subject.

"Right, well, anyway, I'll try to get out of here as soon as I can, no promises, but I'll do my best. I'm still going to call Frances Larson. I'm on the board, for Chrissakes, we give more money to that school than, well, I don't know, but she has some explaining to do."

"Do what you have to, but let's not make any fast moves. Ask her questions, don't threaten her with a lawsuit," I pleaded.

"You really think I'm a hothead, don't you, Katie?"

"Actually, I think we're both hotheads, but let's not go there, we need to focus on Tiger. I'm an emotional wreck. I'm just going to sit here and stare at this big tree until school lets out. Could you call Lois and tell her I don't need her today?"

"Can't you do that, Katie? I don't know her number." Max's voice revealed his desire to get on with his day. He was a social man with an engaging sense of humor. One of his favorite lines when we were out with friends was how he operated on a "need to know" basis with his wife. "Katie tells me only what I need to know, where we're going, when to show up and what to wear." Apparently our babysitter's phone number didn't fall into his "need to know" category. Eight years and she wasn't in his rolodex.

"Max, this meeting was really upsetting, I'm a mess and I'm worried about Tiger seeing me this way. I don't want her to know what Mary said, at least not yet. I really need your help tonight. Please try to make it home early. Please? I think I may actually be begging you."

"I'll try, I promise. Hang in there, Katie. There's nothing wrong with our Tiger. There may be something wrong with that school, but not our Tiger. I love you, babe."

"Me too."

Watching the children board the bus that afternoon provoked tears of a different kind. I felt as if I were looking at them through different lenses. The children looked strangely vulnerable, the teachers as if they had the potential to do harm. I tried to shake these thoughts but couldn't. Had it all been an illusion -- this feeling of security abut our informed choice, this ideal, better school? What else had I missed?

I scrutinized Tiger's face when she finally emerged from the school. She looked tired and I could see stains from lunch on her "Save the Whales" tee-shirt. At least her shoes were tied. I was relieved to see her chatting with a little boy from her class. She looked normal and happy and I began to feel better.

Frances slid open the van door and ushered Jamie and Tiger inside. She stuck her small, aging face in and smiled. "Hello, Katie, looks as if the dog has been riding in the van again."

Ha, ha, I thought to myself. "Frankly, Mrs. Larson, I'm sorry to say I think the girls bring this home from your black Lab."

Frances laughed too loud. It wasn't really very funny.

22

"Let's go, guys." I had no desire to make small talk with this woman, let alone bear her subtle criticisms. I couldn't look at her I felt so betrayed.

"Where's Lois, Mom?" Jamie asked innocently. "Why are you here? I mean, it's nice to see you and all, but doesn't Lois pick us up on Mondays?"

"I had a meeting at school this afternoon so I decided to take the rest of the day off. Would you close the door, sweetie, so I can get going?" Jamie slid the door shut and I accelerated too quickly. My tires let out a squeal as the van lurched forward. Jamie was pushed back into her seat. "Sorry," I said, embarrassed. I drove through the gates and was relieved to finally be away from there. Jamie sat forward again, her shoulder strap tight across her chest.

"As I was saying, Mom," Jamie continued. "Lois makes us homemade pizza on Mondays, and she doesn't make us eat a vegetable."

"Well, I'm glad you enjoy Lois so much but you're stuck with me tonight. How about we all go out for pizza?"

"With Daddy?" Tiger finally spoke.

"No, not tonight. He's working on a big case, but he promised he would try to be home early. You should ask him about the case, Tiger, he's suing the State so they will do a better job protecting the Bay."

"That's nice," Tiger said. She was clearly not interested in why he wasn't going to be home for dinner, just that he wouldn't be.

"Hey, Tiger," Jamie said, leaning her chin on the back of Tiger's seat. "Why did I see you in Mrs. Larson's office this morning?" My ears perked up at this question and I silently thanked Jamie for asking it instead of me.

"She just wanted to talk to me about being late for morning news, that's all."

I was surprised when Jamie didn't question her further, but after a moment, I looked in the rear view mirror and saw them whispering to each other. Jamie nodded knowingly and they fell silent. That was it. No more discussion.

"Why were you late, Tiger? We got to school in plenty of time." I couldn't stand letting it go at that. I wanted to be let in on the secret.

"I was having trouble with my backpack again. I don't think this is a very good one. Kristin's is really neat. I'm going to ask her where she got it."

I glanced back at Tiger. Is that what she was doing? There had to be more to it than that. "Was Mrs. Larson angry with you, honey? Isn't that a big deal to be sent to her office?"

"Geez, Mom!" Jamie interrupted protectively. "Let it go. Tiger didn't do anything wrong."

I started to defend myself until I heard Tiger say so softly it was almost inaudible, "I don't feel like going out for pizza tonight. Can we just go home?" She was staring out the window.

"Sure, Tiger," I said. "It's okay, honey. I'm sure Mrs. Larson wasn't angry

23

with you. Maybe I'll try my hand at homemade pizza tonight. And no vegetable, unless you count black olives as a vegetable."

The rest of the trip home was uncomfortably quiet, no discussion about the eagles, and if anyone held their breath past the old cemetery at the end of the lane, they didn't say so. As soon as I pulled into the garage, both girls ran into the house, bypassing a wagging Baxter, and upstairs into Jamie's room. The door closed behind them with a deliberate bang.

Under any other circumstances I would have been thrilled to be home early on a Monday afternoon and able to spend time with Jamie and Tiger. We live in a cozy, old cape cod house with white clapboard siding, black shutters and a newly remodeled kitchen. It is everything I have ever wanted in a house, with its intimate size and comfortable furnishings. The kitchen, as in any good house, is where people gather. It is framed by tall, white painted cabinets and warm, wood floors. The small breakfast nook is enlarged by colonial sized windows that welcome the southern exposure sunlight and warm the entire room in the afternoons. We kept the cozy size of the kitchen when we renovated and updated only the cabinets and appliances. Max had been equally involved in its design. He loves to cook and uses it to relieve stress. He finds comfort in the formulas and order of cooking and claims that, combined with the opportunity for artistic expression, it is the perfect metaphor for this life. I try not to dwell on the obvious differences in our life themes: a sputtering motor versus gourmet cooking.

At the heart of the kitchen is a large, butcher-block island, surrounded by several tall, ladder-back chairs, and capped by an iron pot rack filled with my baskets and Max's expensive cookware. Tiger and Jamie often perch there after school, nibbling on apples from a large, ceramic fruit bowl while I prepare dinner and empty out lunch boxes. I love to make a cup of tea and busy myself while they work and chatter. It's the most precious time of the day and when I learn what they're really thinking and feeling, how their days have gone, what their worries are, conversations you could never hope for by direct questioning, but only through parallel activity.

After changing into my favorite leggings and a tee-shirt, I sat at the island, waiting for Tiger and Jamie to emerge. I could hear Jamie's radio and muffled voices through the floorboards. I distractedly petted Baxter, but even he sensed the change in his family's mood and sauntered over to the carpet in the adjoining family room and collapsed with a loud sigh. It was too quiet. I went upstairs. "What are you doing?" I called through the door.

"Nothing," Jamie answered.

"Don't forget to do your homework."

"Mom! Go away. I mean, please go away."

"Don't you want a snack?" I could hear footsteps and then Jamie's face

24

appeared through a narrow crack in the door. I smiled when I saw her. "Hi!"

"Mom, this is what Tiger and I do after school on Mondays. We come up in my room and talk and play and do homework. And Lois stays downstairs and makes dinner and plays with Baxter."

"She does?"

"Yes, she does. That's the routine," Jamie said in a pseudo patient voice. "Comprende'?"

"All right," I said reluctantly. "I certainly don't mean to be disruptive."

I pulled some cookbooks down from the shelf in search of a pizza recipe. I sat at the island and flipped through the pages. The recipes were a blur to my preoccupied mind and it felt as if the noiseless, inert kitchen was shouting at me. I looked up from the book and spied a bottle of white wine on the counter and debated briefly whether or not to indulge in a glass.

I leaned into the tall back of the stool and enjoyed the sensation of the smooth, buttery wine traveling down my throat. I tried to make sense out of my disquieting thoughts from my meeting with Mary. Maybe I'd overreacted. There wasn't anything wrong with Tiger. Maybe Mary has been teaching too long and has become too rigid. She just doesn't know how to teach to Tiger's creativity and uniqueness and that's making her uncomfortable. And the latest in parenting advice says children learn to read when they're developmentally ready. Don't hurry your children, instead, offer them the skills needed to learn to read. The fluency comes when they're ready, and all children catch up by the third grade. This was only the beginning of second grade. Perhaps Mary isn't up on the latest research. She certainly has a very traditional classroom. Jamie had loved its order and clear expectations, but it isn't surprising that Tiger finds it too constraining. She was the kind of child who needed to keep moving. Just yesterday morning I had called her for breakfast only to find her bed empty, covers rumpled at the foot of the bed. After searching the house I had finally found her riding up and down the street on her bike, still in her pajamas. When she came into the house, she hopped up onto her chair, began peeling an orange and explained that she had just "needed a ride."

My thoughts and the wine were beginning to ease my discomfort and, after pouring a second glass, returned the cookbooks to the shelf and dialed Papa John's pizza.

By eight-thirty Max had not arrived home and I was moving through the evening routine in a daze. Although the mellowing effects of the wine had long since turned to fatigue, I knew I had to stay conscious long enough to get Jamie and Tiger settled in bed. I knocked on Jamie's door and she yelled for me to wait. She had just gotten out of the shower and her maturing body had brought a new modesty along with it. Respecting her privacy I waited patiently for her to grant my entry. Meanwhile, Tiger sprinted by, dropping her wet towel at my feet.

"In my day we called that streaking," I said as I followed her into her bedroom. Baxter walked over to her and began licking the water from her little body. She rarely dried herself after her bath and now sat shivering on the braided rug covering the polished, wood floor.

"Can you get me some PJ's, Mom?" she asked through chattering teeth.

"They're in the drawer right next to you. And please don't let Baxter lick you, he'll dry out your skin."

Tiger ignored me and laid down on Baxter. I groaned at the thought of the dog hair clinging to her wet skin. I picked up her towel, hung it on the doorknob and pulled her favorite pajamas, covered in faded rain forest animals, out of her drawer. She struggled with the pants due to her wet legs while I tried to brush her tangled hair.

"Stop it, Mom!" She complained. "I can do it."

"You say that, Tiger, but then you never do," I complained back.

"Gee, thanks. You don't think I can do anything," she accused and then picked up her pajama top, marched past me into her sister's room and closed the door behind her. I waited to hear Jamie protest about the unannounced entry, but it was quiet. The unused brush was still in my hand. Baxter stood in front of me, panting heavily in my face, hoping to be next in line for some attention. He stood, waiting stubbornly, while droplets of saliva rolled down the sides of his mouth and onto my lap. His hot breath increased my agitation and I turned away from him. "Go lie down, Baxter." I was relieved when he turned away, at least someone was listening to me tonight. "Good, boy," I said, as he proceeded over to Tiger's bed, helped himself to one of her many stuffed animals and swaggered slowly out the door.

The wet circles of dog saliva were beginning to soak through my leggings. I looked up at Tiger's Winnie the Pooh clock, eight forty-five and not a word from Max. I sighed and decided to think about it later.

As I knocked on Jamie's door again it occurred to me how much of my evening had been spent standing outside her closed door. This time I entered without waiting for permission. Jamie and Tiger were both sitting up in Jamie's bed. Jamie was reading a magazine and Tiger was playing with a family of plastic horses.

"Well, at least you're in bed and I can stop following you two around," I said. "But why are you in Jamie's bed, Tiger?"

"She's sleeping here tonight," Jamie announced.

"Is that all right with you, Jamie?" I asked, surprised.

"Why wouldn't it be?"

"Well, I'm not sure. I'm really tired." Jamie rolled her eyes at the irony of my statement.

"When's Daddy coming home?" Tiger asked wistfully, maneuvering the "daddy" of her horse set.

"That's a good question," I said, not trying hard enough to conceal my frustration with their father.

"You're mad at him, aren't you," Jamie stated accusingly.

"Yeah, a little. I had hoped he'd be home by now." I sat down heavily on the end of her full sized canopy bed.

Jamie looked at me warily from over the top of her magazine. "You said yourself he has a big, important case. He can't help it if he has to work late. His job is very important."

"I know, Jamie, but it's hard when he says he's coming home at a certain time and then doesn't." Silence. She had no interest in why, she just didn't want me to be angry with her father. I looked at Jamie and sighed. "You could at least take my side."

Jamie studied me. "You always say we're not supposed to get involved."

"Ah, excellent point. Oh well. Was there something you needed to talk to Daddy about, Tiger?" I asked, feeling the need to change the course of the conversation. Maybe she would finally tell me why she had really been lingering in the coat room.

"No. I just like it when everyone's home. Baxter!" she called, patting the bed with her hand. "Time for bed, sweetie, come on!" Baxter loped in to the room with animal stuffing all over his mouth. I had forgotten about his abduction of the stuffed animal.

"Baxter!" Tiger shrieked. "Mommy, he shredded Myrtle the Turtle! How could you let him do that?" She jumped out of bed and grabbed what remained of Myrtle, tears streamed down her face.

"It's okay, Tiger," Jamie said, climbing out of bed to comfort her. "We'll sew him up. He'll be okay." Jamie flashed me an angry look. She knew I should be the one comforting her sister, but my hesitation had forced her to jump in when she had found her sister's grief to be unbearable. "We'll play a vet game tomorrow after school and Myrtle can be the patient."

She began scooping up the scattered, white puffs of stuffing. "Baxter didn't mean to do it, Tiger, he's just a puppy. Grab some tissues and we'll make a bed for Myrtle out of Baxter's reach."

Baxter watched them, puzzled. I grabbed his collar and walked him out the door, I was glad to have a scapegoat for what was clearly my negligence. I was guilty according to the good Samaritan law. I had witnessed the crime and done nothing.

Tiger allowed Jamie to comfort her and together they had wrapped Myrtle's remains in toilet paper and made a bed for him on some folded bath towels. "Now,"

27

I said. "Shall we try again?" And just as they had finally returned to bed, we heard his voice.

"Hey, family! Where is everybody?"

"Daddy's home!" Tiger squealed and ran out of the room. Jamie flashed me a quick smile and ran after her. Baxter, who had managed to saunter back into the room without me noticing, was close behind Jamie, shoving her into the wall as he tried to pass.

At team meeting the next morning Dolores announced that Danny, the Colonel's son, had been disruptive during the night and after breaking several rules and verbally assaulting a nurse, was placed in isolation.

"Pat had a real time with him," Dolores continued, shaking her head. Pat was the night nurse and had given Dolores a report at shift change that morning.

"That's too bad," I said, glad to have the opportunity to brainstorm about Danny and the Colonel. "There's obviously more to that family than meets the eye. Ain't that a surprise," I added. Everyone chuckled.

"Pat told him you might want to talk to him this morning, Kate. She gave him a writing assignment, but warned him that you may want to add to it."

"Sure, Dolores, I'll talk to him. I wonder what got into him."

"I saw the Colonel at family education last night," Rob said. "I think he's a drinker." Rob was an addictions counselor on the unit. He was forty-five years old and had been sober for the last ten. He had started drinking and smoking at the age of twelve, and although he had very little formal education, he was the best counselor on the unit. He could connect with the adolescents in a way that was neither condescending nor too familiar, and he could detect an alcoholic easily after the first meeting.

"Really?" I said with interest. "Well, Danny was certainly unnerved by his father's affection yesterday."

"Have you done a family history yet?" Rob asked. Everyone on the unit was aware that ninety percent of our patients had a history of alcoholism somewhere in their family, and we were all of the belief that this was most likely true for the other ten. This fact alone had given my job as family therapist more significance. It was common sense that returning a chemically dependent child to a home where there was alcoholism was a waste of time and money. We depended on families to support sobriety, and no one can spot hypocrisy faster than an adolescent.

"Not yet," I replied. "But it all fits: High pressure Pentagon career, always working late, traveling, top secret stuff, too, which kept him disconnected from the family. Mom divorced him a year ago and moved to the Midwest with her new husband and Danny's two younger brothers. Danny chose to stay with Dad so he wouldn't have to change schools for his last two years in high school. Has Danny said anything in group about the Colonel drinking? Any mention of violence at home?" I asked Rob.

"Nope," he said. "But Danny can drink. And I'd bet money the Colonel had been nipping at his own bottle before he came to group last night."

"So you'll look into that, Kate?" Dr. Tripp asked abruptly. We turned to look at the psychiatrist. "I've got Danny started on Prozac for the depression. Are we finished discussing Danny? Because I have another appointment."

"By all means, Doctor Tripp," Rob said slowly, emphasizing the "pp" in Tripp. He looked at him with an intensity that conveyed his strong feelings about Dr. Tripp's role on the treatment team. As the psychiatrist, he had authority over the treatment plan, and yet he knew very little about chemical dependency and spent the least amount of time with the patients. Medicating patients with antidepressants was an ongoing controversy between doctors and counselors, but the hospital catered to the psychiatrists. They brought in the patients, and, in turn, the revenue.

I looked at Rob and winked sympathetically. He rolled his eyes and sighed heavily. Despite his slight frame and hardened exterior, there was something sexy about Rob. His intensity and passion for his work were inspiring. He could describe in detail the first day he took a drink, the way the whiskey burned in his throat and how he felt warm all over. "I was an alcoholic from that first day," he had said. "From the day my uncle handed me a glass of Jack Daniels and dared me to drink it."

"Shouldn't you check in with him this morning, Doctor Tripp?" Dolores asked, revealing her surprise that he wouldn't.

"Well, no, Dolores, not this morning, it sounds as if you're handling his behavior appropriately."

Dolores reddened. Her years of AA (Alcoholics Anonymous) had taught her to speak her mind. She was frequently heard telling patients to "get honest" and Dr. Tripp's detached treatment style was making her visibly uncomfortable.

"I'll look into the family history, Doctor Tripp," I said. "I'm sure you agree that if his father is drinking, then Danny's sobriety is at risk when he returns home." Dr. Tripp, who had already begun to stand up, looked at me warily. "Certainly this morning's discussion has given us some insight into Danny's behavior. I'll be sure to let you know what we discover."

"Yes, of course, Kate. Let me know what you find out," he said, snapping his briefcase shut and scurrying out the door.

Dolores and Rob looked at each other and then me. They knew arguing with Dr. Tripp was a waste of their time and that the best way to work with him was to use his authority and medications when needed to enhance our treatment goals. And since Dr. Tripp wasn't needed to do either for Danny, it was best to let him go.

29

"Well, let me ask you this," he said gently. "What if she did have a learning disability? How would you feel about that?"

Rob had caught me off guard. I was so busy denying the possibility that I hadn't thought about it that way. "I would be shocked. I mean, don't learning disabilities run in families? There isn't anything like that in either of our families. Don't get me wrong, my family has more than its share of dysfunction, just never in academics. And practically everyone in Max's family went to an Ivy League school! That couldn't be it. I mean I knew my children would have problems, but never in school. I assumed that was the one thing that would come easily for them." I looked up at Rob. "Well, I guess I answered your question. I don't know, Rob, what should I do?"

"Now, I wouldn't know, Katie, my dear, I come from a family of drunks so it was no surprise when I turned out to be a drunk. But, shit, honey, a learning disability doesn't mean she's retarded."

"No, of course not. I know that. I don't know what I think. Dolores, you're awfully quiet, what do you think?"

"I think you have to take care of yourself, maybe pray about it," she said, patting my hand. "You'll know what to do, honey, you're a good mama. Just take it one day at a time."

I thanked them both for their help and support and retreated to my office. I sat at my desk and thought about Tiger. What has she been hiding from me? I closed my eyes and saw her face as I had in the rear view mirror yesterday afternoon. She had looked so old, so burdened. Rob was right, again, I had been so wrapped up in my own feelings, my anger at her teacher, my denial of a problem, that I hadn't thought enough about what she might be experiencing. I was the kind of mother who fought for her children, the mother of a Tiger, no less, and yet, somehow I had missed the fact that one of my cubs was suffering. I put my head on my desk, indulging in a few minutes before my next session. I laid there for longer than I had expected, thinking about Tiger and how to help her. When I lifted my head there was a stretch of squares indented across my cheek from my watch, my foot was asleep and my intercom was blinking, but I still had no idea how to help Tiger. A social worker, no less, who had been known to hand resource numbers to homeless people in lieu of spare change. But I had nothing in my bag for Tiger. A tear slipped out of my eye as I stood and buzzed Betty that I was ready for my next family.

31

Lesson Two:
Empathy

A better parent can remember how it felt to be a child.
When parents are able to step into their children's shoes
they will see the world differently.
They will remember how it felt to be smaller.
They will remember how big the world seemed.
They will remember how it felt to be afraid of the dark
and of the unknown.
They will remember how it felt to be powerless
in a world of bigger people.

Max arrived home at a reasonable hour that night but the angry exchange of the night before hung over us like a dark cloud. We were seated around the pine table in the breakfast nook, finishing our chicken stir fry in silence. I was pushing a piece of dry chicken around on my plate, finding my attempt at a healthy meal to be unappetizing, and was surprised when Max stood up to get a second helping. He scraped the wok clean, grabbed a loaf of sourdough bread, and came back to the table. We were all unusually quiet which made the scrape of his chair seem even louder as he scooted up to the table.

"Max, the floors."

Max was wiping the inside of his bowl with a piece of bread and looked up at me in surprise. "What did you say?"

"We just had the floors refinished. You should pick up your chair, not scoot it."

Max looked at me and furrowed his brow. I immediately regretted scolding him. Tiger looked between us nervously. Max returned to his bowl. "Seems I can't do anything right around here."

I considered a reply but thought better of it. But the echo of his negative words hung in the air and the absence of conversation filled the room with a heavy tension.

Jamie was the first to react. She started by making faces at Tiger but she was making designs with the food on her plate and failed to notice. Next she tried to

32

rouse Baxter, but he remained planted under Tiger's chair, his ears and eyes alert for a stray piece of chicken. Finally, in desperation, she picked a fight with me.

"Do I have to take a shower tonight, Mom?" She asked in a whine more befitting a much younger child.

"Please, Jamie, you're eleven, could you please try and sound like it?"

"Oh, thanks, Mom! I ask you a simple question and you immediately come down on me." She stood up, slamming her chair into the newly-painted wainscoting, walked dramatically to the sink and threw her plate in with a loud clang. She looked nervously into the sink, but when she realized it hadn't broken, she continued. "Nobody seems to care that I got and 'A' plus on my geography test today or that Mrs. Everhard asked me to be class representative to the student government. Mom just sits there and waits for a chance to come down on me. You expect perfection. I can't even talk right to suit you!" With a theatrical flair she turned and began to march toward the stairs.

"Just a minute, young lady," Max boomed. He was taller and broader than all of us combined and the room vibrated with his voice. "Just where do you think you're going?"

"To my room," Jamie said, sounding a little less sure of herself.

"Not until you apologize to your mother." Max smiled, expecting approval from me. He knew I believed parents should support each other, the "united front" I was always pushing for. But Max's entry into the discussion enabled me to gain some perspective and I regretted reacting so quickly to Jamie's bait. This was her honorable, albeit misguided, attempt to distract her family from their worries by putting the focus onto herself.

"Max," I whispered. "Let her go."

"Let her go? No way! Not after the way she's behaved. Jamie Marie, come back here right now," he commanded.

Jamie put the tip of her hair nervously in her mouth and considered her choices. Her pride was at stake and although I dreaded her outbursts, I admired her loyalty to her sister and her desire to unite her parents. She flung her long, golden hair behind her shoulders and stood bravely before her father. "Why doesn't she have to apologize to me?" She crossed her arms tightly in front of her.

"Because she's the mother."

"Oh, nice answer, Dad! Since when are you guys dictators? I guess Hitler didn't have to explain his behavior, either, people just killed everybody because he told them to! So now you guys can just make arbitrary rules and Tiger and I have to do it just because you say so?"

"Something like that, yes," Max said with a slight grin that only served to enrage Jamie.

"Well, you may not realize it, Dad, but this is a democracy! We kicked the dictators out. You treat us like we're slaves without a vote. Maybe Tiger and I will just go on strike, how about that?" Jamie looked nervously at Tiger, trying to enlist her support, buy Tiger had slid under the table and was on top of Baxter again.

I could see that Max was gaining steam, nothing stimulated him more than a good debate. And I knew from experience that he and Jamie could go on arguing for hours.

"Wait a minute," I interrupted. They both looked at me in surprise. "Time out. Or should I say, order in the court?" Max smiled and Jamie rolled her eyes. "I agree, Max, that Jamie's outburst is unacceptable, but I'm sorry I was grumpy with you, Jamie. I overreacted because I'm worried about other things. I'm sorry. You do need to take a shower, not because I'm hung up on rules, but because you're eleven with hormones raging and that's just how it goes."

Jamie reddened at my mention of hormones. Max looked at me with disappointment in his eyes. There was an awkward silence.

"What are horn-phones, Mommy? And why does Jamie have them?" Tiger asked from under the table.

We all looked down at Tiger. "Horn-phones? What are you talking about, Tiger?" Jamie asked impatiently.

"Tiger," I said quickly. "Hormones, you know, remember the book I read to Jamie and you this summer about how our bodies change? Hor-mones."

"No, I don't remember," she said quietly.

I looked at Tiger and could see she was embarrassed by her misunderstanding. I was trying to think of something comforting to say, but Max had moved on and was making a joke, which was his way.

"Hormones are what put hair on you chest, Tig, so watch out! Jamie's got them raging and we should all run for cover!"

Tiger was still lost, but Jamie, relieved the argument was over, saved us again by acquiescing. "Okay, I'll take a shower, buy only if I can watch TV afterwards."

"That remains to be seen," I replied distractedly. I was studying Tiger, trying to read her thoughts, but she seemed to be miles away.

Jamie marched up the stairs at last and Max returned to his cooling dinner and launched into a discussion about the Chesapeake Bay Foundation lawsuit. Any other night I would have been interested in his new case, asking questions and appreciating his enthusiasm. Max and I enjoyed discussing our jobs with one another, but with my lingering anger and concern for Tiger, I couldn't listen in the way he was accustomed.

Max looked up when I didn't contribute to the conversation and stopped talking. He wiped his mouth and picked up his bowl. "I'll clean up," he said, as he stood, careful that his chair didn't scratch the floor. Neither of us spoke as I scooped up Tiger and carried her upstairs to her own shower.

I had managed to soothe Jamie's ruffled feathers and Tiger's tired brain without event and they were both asleep, again, in Jamie's bed. I came downstairs in my slippers and curled up on the sofa in the family room with my current novel. Max was sitting in the overstuffed chair watching the Orioles game with a beer in his hand. The kitchen was dark and Baxter lay at his feet. I sat quietly for a few moments but couldn't concentrate on my book. It was a slow starter and I hadn't gotten involved in the plot or found a character I cared about yet. They all seemed too perfect and it annoyed me. I looked over at Max. "Don't you think we should clear the air before Jamie drives us both crazy?" Max continued to watch the television. "You know what her outburst was about tonight, don't you?"

"It was about taking a shower," he said sarcastically and continued to stare ahead. "But since you're the resident therapist, why don't you enlighten me on what it was really about, and why you deliberately undermined me when I tried to help."

"You're certainly being helpful now, though, aren't you? Both of our children are a mess and you're picking a fight with me! You know Jamie absorbs tension like a sponge, she was just trying to distract us from our anger with one another by getting us to focus on her. She knows we'll come together on parenting, well, at least most of the time."

"Now how do you know that?" Max turned to look at me. "Christ, Katie, you're always analyzing things. I feel like I'm a paragraph behind. Why can't Jamie just have a tantrum because she's eleven? And if she was trying to bring us together, I don't think it worked." After an awkward silence Max clicked off the television. "Okay, I agree we need to talk about the children, but first let's clear the air and stop grinding away at each other. Why did you come down on me so hard last night? I told you on the phone I had a potential for a late night."

"I know, but you promised that you would try! And I really needed you. There's always a good reason why you can't come home at a reasonable hour and, for the most part, I don't complain. But every case is bigger than the last and even though you try to not be late, sometimes your good intentions aren't enough. Oh," I said in frustration. "I guess what's really bothering me is that I was the mother from hell last night. I just couldn't stop thinking about my meeting with Mary, and the implications for Tiger, for all of us! I really needed a partner but you weren't there."

Max looked thoughtful. "I'm sorry it was so hard for you, Katie, please know that I did my best to be here. I thought I was doing all right by getting home at eight-thirty. The kids were still awake."

He was being understanding and reasonable and I was relieved. I could feel my anger begin to dissipate at last. "It's over now," I said softly. "I guess I'm angry at myself for not handling things better than I did. Do you know I drank two glasses of wine? And then I was so tired and grumpy it was unforgivable."

"God, woman! You're so damn hard on yourself. Of course you were upset. Let's just get through this. None of it is our fault. We either have a lousy teacher on our hands or a kid with a problem or both. Let's stop blaming ourselves, or worse, blaming each other." I looked over at Max and he smiled slowly, his eyebrows slightly raised, awaiting my reaction. God, he was handsome, with his dark, wavy hair and sparkling blue eyes. He was wearing a worn pair of khaki pants and a faded denim work shirt with the sleeves partially rolled up exposing his strong forearms. "So, truce? Are we okay?"

Max could still make my knees weak when he looked at me that certain way and I had to look away to avoid his penetrating gaze. "I guess I should schedule some testing for Tiger. I don't know what else to do. The school gave me a list of psychologists who were qualified to do educational testing. I'll check around the hospital and see who's good. God, a psychologist! I have to take my kid to a psychologist!" I looked back at Max. He was still looking through me and I squirmed. He put his beer down and walked slowly behind the sofa. He slid his large hands down into my shirt and I dropped my book.

It wasn't long before we lay quietly, attempting to squeeze under the throw that had rested on the back of the sofa and was intended more for decor than warmth. "Don't move," Max said and hopped up and ran into the dark kitchen. The light from the refrigerator illuminated his glistening, naked body. He waved toward the window, "Hello, Mrs. Steiner!" grabbed two cold beers and sprinted back to the family room. He climbed under the inadequate blanket and handed me a beer. "Cheers!" He clinked his bottle against mine and took a long sip. "Here's to making up." Max grinned mischievously and put his arm around me. He clicked on the television just in time for us to see Cal Ripken hit a double in the bottom of the eighth inning. "Katie?"

"Hmm?"

"Do you think it's a good idea for Jamie to be taking that government class?"

The following morning I was able to schedule an appointment for Tiger with Dr. Susan Chartwell on Friday. Apparently Dr. Chartwell had a cancellation and was able to see Tiger sooner than usual. Part of me was relieved to get the process underway, but the other, more irrational part, was worried that someone with an appointment available so soon might not be very competent.

Once I confirmed the appointment, I had to clear the time off with our unit director, Warner Burke. He was a strange, unlikable man, and Rob had confided in me his suspicions about his drinking. Although I'd never had concrete evidence that he had a problem with alcohol, there were times when he would get a wild look in his eyes, usually after lunch, and he was infamous for making inappropriate comments to the women in the hospital. The irony of a man with a drinking problem managing a chemical dependency unit was not lost on us.

He came to us from an Atlanta affiliate when the hospital reorganized along with redecorating. The units were now run by a matrix system of management which was confusing to a practical, linear thinker like me. The worst change was I no longer made my requests to the head of the social work department, a soft-spoken woman who I trusted and admired and who had been with the hospital for years. She was busy these days trying to justify her existence. My vacations and holidays were now at the mercy of Warner Burke.

Warner was recently divorced and had referred to himself as a "Georgia Boy" his first day on the job. Although he occasionally appeared at rounds where he would inevitably say something unsuitable in his attempt to be chummy with the doctors, his primary role was manager, which kept him busy and away from the daily operations of the unit. He had a lot of pressure from the hospital to keep the unit full, preferably with a waiting list, so, much to my relief, my contact with him was minimal.

I knocked on his door even though it was partially open. He beckoned me in and greeted me in an overemphasized southern draw. "Why, Miss Katie, to what do I attribute this rare visit from our esteemed social worker?"

"I hope I'm not disturbing you, Warner. Do you have a minute?"

"Why, of course," Warner said smiling. He gave me a quick once over with his eyes. It was his customary greeting. I walked over to the chair in front of his desk, tugged at my skirt and sat down. "I need to take a personal day on Friday and I just wanted to clear it with you. My daughter has a doctor's appointment in Baltimore and it looks as if it will take all day."

"Doctor's appointment? Well, now, didn't you take off most of Monday? It was at the last minute, if I recall, and without pre-authorization."

"No. I mean, yes, or, well, not really. I was called away and..."

"And didn't I see Miss Leslie from adult psych covering for you? Of course, Leslie is always a pleasure to see around here, but I wouldn't want to cause a problem with the other unit directors, borrowing their professional staff and all."

"It wasn't a problem, Warner. Leslie and I have always covered for each other. The whole social work department helps each other out in that way."

"Who's covering for you on Friday?" he asked. He was leaning so far back in his chair the springs began to creak from the tension.

"I've managed to schedule all my family meetings earlier in the week, Rob will cover my adolescent group, and that's all I have. Friday is my short day, Warner. I don't think it will inconvenience anyone or take away form the patients."

"Rob's a counselor with his own responsibilities. Besides, twice in one week is unacceptable. The hospital is cracking down on us these days, what with

Managed Care and all. I guess their tender stock holders aren't getting rich enough, quick enough. They expect a lot from me but what they seem to forget is alcoholism is out of fashion these days, not much media attention. Depression is more in fashion. Besides, you're a full time worker and every resident has to have at least one family therapy session a week. They get billed for it so they better have it. And even if you don't have any sessions, that time should be used for public relations and soliciting referral sources."

"I'm aware of that, Warner." I was getting annoyed. I had no interest in sharing his burdens. I had enough of my own. We looked at each other evenly, neither of us breaking our gaze. I knew Warner had a hard time getting along with me. He was more comfortable with submissive or flirtatious women. My northern abruptness usually left him searching for his charms. But I had enough on my mind and had no interest in taking care of his fragile ego. "Well, gee, Warner," I rose to leave, "this has been fun. Thanks for your time."

"Are we finished?" Warner leaned forward in his chair and looked at me over the top of his round, MBA-style glasses with an unfriendly smile.

"What?"

"I don't recall authorizing your request. Personal days are meant for funerals, not doctors' appointment. Frankly, I think you're going to have to take leave without pay. That's the only way I can justify allowing you to be gone again for personal reasons."

"Warner! Leave without pay? What are you talking about?" I was trying in vain to conceal my anger.

"Now, I thought I explained that," he said slowly. "The hospital administration? Do you recall that part of our conversation?"

I crossed my arms and glared at him. "Warner --"

"You seem to have missed the fact that I said you could take Friday off. You just won't get paid for it, that's all. Oh, don't look at me that way. You don't need the money anyway with that hotshot lawyer for a husband." He grinned at his attempt at humor but seemed to realize he'd gone too far. "I think we're finished. You can either take Friday off without pay or come in and work like the rest of us." He looked down at the papers on his oversized desk.

I shook my head in disbelief. I stared at the balding circle on the top of his head, imagining clever things to say to him, but I knew he had won. I sighed in defeat, ran my hands through my hair and left in silence.

It was time to talk to Tiger.

I tried in vain to say good-bye to Lois when I arrived home that evening. It was already dark and I was exhausted, but she was a social person who loved to chat.

38

After spending the afternoon with children, she was always enthusiastic to tell me about the day, but I just couldn't muster the energy for light conversation with Lois tonight. I dropped my bags from the grocery store on the counter and walked her to the door.

"Oh, I forgot to tell you," Lois said as she pulled on her jacket. "Tiger slipped off her bike today and scraped her knee."

"Slipped?" I asked. I was holding the door open for her, a less than subtle hint that I was ready for her to go.

"That's right. She just slipped off. That's when she scraped her knee. But it was just a little scrape, and I told her, Tiger, you just have to get up, dust yourself off, and thank the Lord you didn't scrape both of them!'" Lois announced proudly. She was an optimist to a fault.

"Is she all right?"

"Oh, she's fine!" Lois replied sounding hurt that I thought she might not be. "You know you're children are safe and well fed when they're in my care. Why, taking care of children is the most important work in the world. And I take my job very seriously."

"I know that, Lois. I really do." And we pay you pretty well for it, too, I thought to myself. I kept my hand on the doorknob.

Lois gathered up her belongings. "Well, I guess I'll see you tomorrow, then."

"That's right, we'll see you tomorrow," I said as she at last walked out the door. Baxter loped after her, disappointed she was leaving. She kept Baxter well fed too. I waved to her and once she was safely on her way, stepped back inside.

As soon as she was gone I felt guilty that I'd hurried her. I knew how lucky I was to have her in our lives. Without her, nothing would work. I kicked off my shoes but picked them up again when I heard Baxter coming in the door. He was a sweet dog but a shoe abductor and since none of us had ever successfully trained him, I usually took the path of least resistance and eliminated his opportunities. I glanced at the mail but knew I was putting off my talk with Tiger. What was I afraid of? This was Tiger, my baby. I grabbed my shoes and headed up the stairs.

I found Jamie sprawled on her bed talking on the phone. She waved and continued to talk. I waved back and quietly closed the door. There were days when I regretted buying Jamie her own phone and worried that it kept her away from the family. But Max insisted that she was turning twelve and needed her own space. He had reminded me that most of her classmates had televisions and computers in their rooms and that a phone was the least we could do. Another drawback to the privilege of private school.

I continued down the hallway to my room and pulled on a faded pair of jeans and a well- worn cotton shirt. I washed my face and enjoyed the sensation of the cool water on my face. It was obvious that Lois had either gotten bored or bothered by my cluttered house and had washed the towels in my bathroom and hung them neatly on the rack. They were fluffy from the dryer and I lingered in the soothing warmth. No matter how I tried I could never make our house look as neat and orderly as she did.

I knocked softly on Tiger's door and stepped inside. She was sitting on the window seat in one of her two dormer windows, surrounded by stuffed animals, and had them involved in an elaborate make-believe game. I smiled when I realized she'd dressed them in the doll clothes my mother had given her for her birthday. While my Aunt Matty sent Jamie and Tiger science kits and microscopes, my mother sent dolls. And when she discovered the Pleasant Company she began to give Jamie and Tiger an American Girl doll on each birthday. Jamie treated each doll with care, but Tiger was more likely to toss them in her closet and put her stuffed animals in the colonial beds and beautiful clothing.

"Hey, Tig," I said softly as I closed the door and came into her room. "Looks like a good game."

"Hi, Mommy. I didn't know you were home. Is Lois still here?"

"Nope. She went home, much to Baxter's chagrin. How many biscuits did she give him tonight?"

"About a million!" she said laughing. "She calls them cookies. She just asks him if he wants a cookie and gives him one. She doesn't even make him sit or shake or roll over. Me and Jamie think she spoils him, but at least she keeps him out of our rooms so he doesn't chew everything up."

"Oh, well, maybe if he gets fat he'll stop eating shoes and stuffed animals. That reminds me, how's Myrtle?" I sat cross-legged on her rug, close to where she was sitting. I was glad she was talking openly and I didn't have to force a conversation.

"He's okay, I guess. Lois sewed him up and Jamie and I played a game where he was in the hospital and we had all the other animals come to visit and stuff. But then Jamie got bored and went into her room. I was sort of mad she quit our game. It was really fun."

"Mm. I'm sorry. Where's Myrtle?" I asked as I stroked one of her animals. It was an amazingly soft, droopy-eared do and I hugged it as we talked. There were stuffed animals everywhere in Tiger's room. She had a full-sized bed, yet there was barely enough room for her little body. Max was always threatening to throw some of them out, particularly after trying to navigate through Tiger's room in the dark after arriving home late at night. But I would remind him that although we didn't like the clutter, they were our child's belongings and we had no right to get rid of them. The lawyer in him would eventually find it impossible to deny his children their property rights and would leave the menagerie undisturbed.

"He's over there on my dresser. His nose is gone, though, we can't find it. I

40

think Baxter chewed it up."

"There's a good chance of that, now, isn't there?" I agreed. Tiger's room was painted a warm, sunny yellow. She had chosen the color herself when I had agreed to take down the ducks and lambs wallpaper from her babyhood. As much as she had wanted a more grown-up room, she had worried about her old wallpaper. She was sensitive to the notion of discarding something because it wasn't useful anymore. But after much negotiation, I agreed to save some of the wallpaper and put it into a memory book and she and I were free to update her room together. There were yellow and white striped valances and white shutters on her windows, and a pale lavender comforter embroidered with small yellow and white flowers rested on her four poster bed. A happy stream of jungle animals was stenciled along the top of her walls and, of course, a poster of a beautiful tiger centered prominently over her bed. It was a warm and cheerful room that reflected her personality and I loved to sit in it with her.

"Mommy," Tiger said without looking up.

"What, honey?" I was surprised she was changing the subject, I was the one with the agenda.

"Mrs. Larson gave me a note to give to you. I'm pretty sure it's about me. I looked at it and saw my name on it. Jamie read it and told me not to worry."

"Where is it, Tig?" I was shocked that she would have sent a note home with Tiger. It struck me as extremely unprofessional. Of course Tiger would read it. "Can I see it?"

"It's over there," Tiger said, pointing to a crumpled piece of paper on the floor. I picked up the note and read silently, careful not to show any emotion on my face.

> *Dear Mr. and Mrs. Cunningham,*
>
> *It should be brought to your attention that Patricia is not meeting expectations for a second grader. She is not reading and her writing is illegible. She is also refusing to talk in class and is not turning in her homework. I would like to schedule a conference with you and her teacher as soon as possible. In the meantime, we would like you to make arrangements to have Patricia tested for psychological and/or learning problems.*
>
> *Sincerely,*
> *Frances Larson, Headmistress*
> *Chesapeake Day School*

"This should have bee sent through the mail. Why, it isn't even on letterhead!"

"What, Mommy?" Tiger asked, confused.

I looked up at her. "I'm sorry, honey, I'm just a little surprised Mrs. Larson sent this home with you."

"Am I going to have to go back to first grade?"

"Now where on earth did you get that idea?" Obviously Tiger was more aware of recent events than I realized. "No one is sending you back to first grade. You are far more mature and well-behaved that the other children in your class. They could all learn from you how to be a friend and treat other people."

"That's not true, Mommy. I'm not as well behaved as the other kids. I forget stuff and... and... I don't do anything as well as the other kids! You just don't know it."

"Everyone is good at something, Tiger. No one is better that anyone. You know that copy of the Declaration of Independence in Daddy's office, 'All people are created equal.'"

"I knew you wouldn't get it," she said, putting her head down on her small knees.

"Get what, honey, tell me? What don't I get? I want to get it," I pleaded.

"I'm stupid, okay!" she yelled. "Everyone knows it but you!"

My heart ached as I looked at her face. "That is one thing I will never know," I said, and Tiger moaned in frustration, her pencil-straight bangs bounced as she flopped her head back on to her knees. "But I can hear that you are having a hard time and I want to help you, honey. I think I can help. And if I can't, we'll find someone who will."

"The only way you can help is by never making me go to school again," she said desperately.

I inched over to Tiger and gently stoked her arm. She didn't resist, so I continued to touch her. Tiger was an extremely sensitive child, inside and out. She loved to be touched and close to others. She breast-fed well past twelve months of age and had always been easy to comfort with touch. As an infant she would stop crying as soon as I picked her up and held her, the closer the better.

Much to my relief, Tiger finally crawled off the window seat and into my arms. She curled up into a ball and let me rock her. I held her for a long time. "I love you no matter what, Tiger," I said soothingly. "Whether you get 'A's in school or 'Z's, no matter what you do. There is nothing you could ever do that could make me stop loving you. And whatever it is you're facing, you don't have to face it alone any more." Tiger remained silent but I could feel her small body begin to relax in my arms. I nestled my face in her hair and breathed her in, the faint scent of shampoo, the freshness of her skin.

"Mom!" Jamie yelled form the kitchen. "You better come down here!"

Tiger picked her head up, bumping the bridge of my nose. "It's Jamie!" she said as she ran out the door. I could still feel the warmth from her body in my arms and felt saddened by her abrupt departure. It seemed that ever since I had two children, the private, special moments were too infrequent, and inevitably interrupted by the other child.

"Mom!" they called in unison. Despite the urgency in their voices, I was moving slowly. I followed the sound of the commotion only to find that Baxter had eaten an entire package of raw ground beef, one package of mozzarella cheese and was halfway through the ice cream that was melting all over the counter. I had completely forgotten about the groceries. I looked at the mess and then at Baxter.

"There goes dinner!" Jamie said in an amused voice.

"You said you wanted him to get fat, Mommy!" Tiger said between giggles.

Just then Baxter looked up and uttered a loud, uninhibited belch. Jamie and Tiger were hysterical at this point and I couldn't suppress my own giggles. And just as my two angels began to lift my tired spirits, Jamie said, "Oh, Mom, Dad called and said to tell you he's going to be really late tonight."

Tiger was snuggled up next to me in Dr. Susan Chartwell's office and we were looking at waiting room magazines. She was in a cheerful mood, mostly because she was missing a day of school, but also because I had bought her an egg and sausage sandwich on our way to Baltimore. Having had my own greasy sandwich, I was feeling the need to wash my face and wondering self consciously if I smelled more like a bowling alley than the perfume I had sprayed on early this morning. But I was happy to be with Tiger. It was a luxury to have her all to myself.

"Okay, Tig," I said. I was flipping through the pages of an *Architectural Digest*. (There was a noticeable absence of *People*). "What are they trying to sell me here?" It was a picture of the back of a nude woman, the lower half of her draped in a large, Oriental rug. Tiger looked at the picture thoughtfully.

"Strange clothes?" she asked in an amused voice. "I don't have any idea."

"Neither do I. But, hey, maybe if I buy this rug, I'll look like her. What do you think?"

"I don't think so, Mom. But I don't want you to look like her, anyway. I want you to look like my mom, you know, with messy hair and stuff."

I laughed loudly and squeezed her closer to me. "Thanks for the compliment, kiddo. At least I think it was a compliment."

Eventually Tiger became comfortable enough with our surroundings to explore a basket of toys in the corner of the waiting room. I had explained to her that we were going to see someone who might be able to help make school less difficult for her, and in order to do that, she would be asked to do some reading and writing and answer a lot of questions. The reading and writing had concerned her, Tiger avoiding them at all costs, but she was a cooperative child and seemed to trust I wouldn't take her some place unpleasant.

I scanned the room, taking in the large, gilt-framed impressionistic prints on the walls and the polished wood-framed chairs that were upholstered in a beautiful rose and teal green fabric. An expensive, silk rug dominated the small room, the densely woven threads dyed in subtle, coordinating shades, giving the room a warm, soothing effect. I began to form opinions about Susan Chartwell based on the appearance of her waiting room. For one, she had good taste, or perhaps a talented decorator. She was also either independently wealthy or had a successful practice. I hoped it was the latter and that I was placing my child in the hands of someone competent. I didn't like being on the other side of the equation, it went against my nature to turn over control to someone completely unknown to me. Of course this must be how the families I treat must feel -- powerless and afraid. I inhaled deeply and looked nervously around the room. What do they say on the unit -- let go and let God? Okay. I can do that. I uncrossed my legs and smoothed my skirt. I glanced at Tiger and felt a surge of panic. Dr. Susan Chartwell, a professional who was about to judge my child and, in turn, me, was late, leaving me acutely aware of the growing anxiety I seemed powerless to curb.

Tiger startled when the door opened and quickly returned to my side. Dr. Chartwell entered the room with a large smile. "You must be Patricia," she said, with a little too much enthusiasm, and extended her hand to Tiger. Tiger hesitated, and then placed a limp hand in Dr. Chartwell's.

Tiger avoided her eyes but managed to say, "My name is Tiger."

"What did you say, dear?" Dr. Chartwell asked, leaning in closer while continuing to hold Tiger's small hand. I studied this stranger who was attempting to engage my reluctant child. She was most likely in her early fifties, at least ten years older than me. I think I liked that, I was relieved she wasn't younger, but of course there was the risk she wasn't up to date in her field. She was dressed in a black wool suit, accented by a black and maroon scarf that was fastened with a stunning gold brooch. The reds in her scarf were the same shade as her expertly applied lipstick. I wondered if her expensive clothing had been selected for the slimming effect it had on her slightly large frame.

Dr. Chartwell knelt before Tiger. The lining of her skirt made a swishing sound as it rubbed against her stockings. "I'm sorry, dear, I didn't quite hear you. What did you say?"

Tiger looked up at me and I mustered a smile, encouraging her to answer Dr. Chartwell. She crinkled her nose at me, she had hoped I would rescue her, and looked back towered the looming psychologist. "My name is Tiger."

"Tiger," she exclaimed, noticeably louder than Tiger's delicate voice. She articulated her words so that every vowel and consonant were discernible. "Now that's an unusual name. But I like it. I like it very much. Shall I call you Tiger?" she asked as she continued to kneel before Tiger.

"Yes, please," Tiger answered softly. Dr. Chartwell's close proximity made it difficult for Tiger to avoid her insistent gaze. I could smell her expensive perfume and the increasing intimacy unnerved me. I hadn't been acknowledged yet.

"I love cats. Do you like all cats or just tigers?"

"Tiger loves all animals," I interjected, immediately regretting it. Dr. Chartwell looked over at me and pushed herself up so that she stood before me.

"Excuse me, Tiger, but I would like to introduce myself to your mother. Hello, Mrs. Cunningham," she said warmly as she reached out for my hand. I stood quickly, disliking having to look up to her, and shook her hand firmly.

"It's a pleasure to meet you, Doctor Chartwell. I appreciate you seeing us on such short notice."

"We certainly got lucky, didn't we?" She smiled and then turned back to Tiger. "And it's nice to meet you too, Tiger. I'm looking forward to our time together. We have lots to cover. We'll be playing a lot of fun games and I'll be asking you a lot of questions, so if you get too tired, just let me know. We'll break for a snack and you'll be able to have lunch with your mom, too. Mrs. Cunningham..."

"Please, call me Kate."

"All right, Kate, and you may call me Susan. As I said on the phone, the testing will take approximately two days."

"Testing?" Tiger said in alarm. "You didn't tell me I was going to take a test, Mommy!"

I hugged Tiger and looked back at Dr. Chartwell. "I never used that word."

"Oh." She reddened at her mistake. "It's not the kind of test you take in school, Patri--, I mean, Tiger. I think you'll find my tests are a lot more fun," she said slightly flustered. "But let's get started. Let me show you my office. Your mom will be right here when we've finished. Oh, and by the way, you may call me Doctor Susan." She held out her hand to Tiger who placed her small hand in hers obediently and walked into the awaiting office without looking back. The solid wood door closed quietly behind them.

After thirteen magazines, a short nap and three calls to the hospital from my cellular phone, Tiger finally emerged with Susan Chartwell. She smiled and ran over to my side. "How did it go?" I asked.

"Just fine," Susan said brightly. "Tiger is a delightful child and I am enjoying her immensely." Tiger grinned with pride and I felt an absurd pang of jealousy. I put my arm around her protectively.

Susan gave us directions to the nearest restaurant and Tiger and I found our way to a diner that glowed in an abundance of chrome. We sat across from each other in a vinyl booth and munched on our grilled sandwiches. "So, how do you like Doctor Chartwell?" I asked, trying not to sound overly interested.

"I'm supposed to call her Doctor Susan," she reminded me. Classic Baltimore, I thought to myself. Dr. Susan.

"Right, I forgot. How do you like Doctor Susan?"

"Is she a real doctor? Like Doctor Greenbaum?" she asked. Dr. Greenbaum was her pediatrician.

"No, she's not a medical doctor. She studied in school for a long time and earned her Ph.D. That means she can be called 'doctor.'" Tiger looked at me as if in a trance. It was clear she didn't understand my explanation, but something else was wrong. She hadn't eaten her grilled cheese sandwich and it seemed that everything confused her. She had even gotten lost in the hallway on her way to the restroom.

"My head hurts, Mommy," she said and rested her forehead on the shiny table.

"Tiger, honey, please, we're in a restaurant. Come on, we only have a few minutes. Here, eat your sandwich."

Tiger's head remained on the table. "I'm too tired."

"Tiger," I said shaking her, "please get your head off the table."

"I can't help it," she said, "I'm just too pooped to move."

I wasn't sure what to do and looked around the room. I signaled the waitress, ordered a cup of coffee "to go" and tried to pick Tiger's head up as we waited for the check. "Trisha," I whispered sternly, "get up, now!"

Tiger slowly lifted her head and looked at me with disdain. I held her up as I paid for our lunch and then escorted her swiftly out of the restaurant. More than once Tiger drifted off the sidewalk and dangerously close to the rushing lanes of traffic. I felt more like a sheep herder than a mother with a ambulatory child as we made our way back to Susan's office building. And although I had desperately wanted Susan to notice how close Tiger and I were, by the time we entered the familiar waiting room, we were unmistakably annoyed with one another.

"Tiger is a little disoriented," I said when Susan emerged from her office. "And she didn't eat much."

"Well, that happens sometimes," she said cheerfully and motioned for Tiger to follow her.

"It would have been helpful to know that," I said before she closed the door.

Susan stopped and looked at me. "Every child is different, Kate. I assumed you already knew Tiger tires easily when she does this type of work. Surely it's not the first time you've seen her disoriented. But you and I will have a chance to discuss these things after next week. Right now I would like to finish up with Tiger," she said crisply. "I won't keep her much longer."

"Of course," I said and sat down. I watched them disappear again and immediately regretted losing patience with Tiger. Would she tell Susan? Would Susan label us dysfunctional and diagnose Tiger with an emotional problem? Did Tiger have an emotional problem? The green and pink windowless room was making me feel claustrophobic. I grabbed my coffee and walked quickly outside. After pacing up and down the sidewalk I perched on the brick wall at the bottom of the steps leading to her office. I called Max, but his formal secretary informed me importantly that he was in a deposition and couldn't be disturbed. Then I tried Leslie, but Betty said she was in a session and I declined her offer to leave a message. I put my phone back in my bag. I watched a man of around thirty-five smoking on a bench across the street and longed for a cigarette. I hadn't smoked a cigarette for almost twenty years but the thought of the ritual of smoking was compelling. It would be something to occupy me. I sipped the coffee but hated the way the Styrofoam cup seemed to change the flavor. I put it down and went back to pacing. I don't know how long I was out there, but it was long enough for Susan and Tiger to not be able to find me.

"Mommy!" Tiger squealed. She and Susan were standing in the doorway. "You promised you wouldn't leave."

"Oh, baby, I'm right here. I just needed some fresh air." I ran up the steps and hugged her. She looked even more tired than before, so I suggested she wait on the steps while I finished with Susan.

Susan and I walked back into the waiting room, leaving the door ajar so that I could keep an eye on a disoriented Tiger, and scheduled the next session of testing for the following Wednesday. I sighed when she informed me it would take another full day. Warner's bald spot flashed before my eyes. "Is it too soon to know what the problem is?" I asked as I clasped my date book.

"I won't know until I've had a chance to analyze her scores."

"Do you at least have an idea of what might be wrong?" I pushed.

"It would be careless to give you a diagnosis this early." Susan glanced around the room and then bent down and picked up a book from her polished wood end table. "But maybe this would be helpful in the mean time." I looked down at the small white book resting in her manicured hands. It was a thin, children's chapter book entitled *Josh, A Boy With Dyslexia*.

I stared at the title. "Susan, is this what you think Tiger has?"

Realizing she'd made another, but much worse mistake, she looked at me, flustered. "Why, Kate, I thought you must know it was something like this."

I couldn't find my breath and the tears were forming in my eyes. "I had no idea, Doctor Chartwell. No idea." I took the book from her hands and turned to leave. "I appreciate what you're doing for Tiger, but this was a lousy way to tell me she might be dyslexic." A large tear escaped from my eyes and I brushed it away as it rolled down my cheek. "I need to go. We'll see you on Wednesday." I shut the door quickly and shooed Tiger into the van. I was grateful when she immediately laid her down on the seat and fell asleep because I was unable to control the tears as we drove silently home.

The Colonel had arrived for his morning session an hour early again. We had scheduled a standing appointment for the next five Mondays at nine o'clock. Leslie and I entered the hospital through the side door in order to avoid him. "I'm impressed with how well you're handling the Colonel, Katie," Leslie said as we walked toward the elevator.

"Oh, so you're impressed with the way I'm ducking him?"

"No, seriously. He's an intimidating man. He really gave me a hard time in the family education group last week. He kept challenging the facts I presented about alcoholism, saying it wasn't a disease, that sort of thing."

"Rob's antennae have been going haywire ever since he arrived on the unit. He can sniff out a drinker a mile a way."

"That's it! He's an alcoholic. Now why didn't I think of that? No wonder he was in so much denial about his son's alcoholism. It's a good thing you're on the chemical dependency unit and not me," Leslie exclaimed.

"And it's a damn good thing I'm not over on the psych unit. I'd be clinically depressed by Tuesday. You underestimate yourself. You're very good at what you do. Besides, you're gorgeous." I pushed the elevator button and smiled at her.

"Oh, and you're so homely. Look at you -- you have such a unique style. I love how you dress in those cute skirts and tights. And that pin is outstanding. Where did you get it?"

I smiled. "Tiger made it for me in art class."

"No way! I love it. Tell her I want one too."

"It would make her day. And by the way, thanks for the compliment. I always feel so disheveled in the morning. One of these days I'll show up for work without my hose or something."

"Hose? Katie, you are so from the Midwest. The correct term is 'stockings.'"

"Hose, pop, I refuse to change."

"Well, from what I see, you don't need to. I see the way Max still looks at you. The man is totally in love, and after how many years of marriage? I envy that more than you realize," Leslie said wistfully.

I studied her. "Are you okay? I know I've been wrapped up in myself this past week, and you've bailed me out more than once, but you seem bugged. How are things with David?"

"You're sweet to ask. I know how you disapprove of our relationship."

"Leslie! Far be it from me to judge anyone. I just wish the guy wasn't married. Or that he was at least married to the woman he's boinking."

"Don't be crude."

"I just think you deserve better, not what you settle for. David has no idea how special you are."

"And uptight, perfectionistic, anal..."

"Hello? Is there a self esteem at home?"

"I'm not so sure anymore."

I turned to look at her. "Listen, toots, you are one of the kindest people I know. If you think you're avoiding intimacy, maybe it's because of the man you're trying to be intimate with. I have no doubt you have an endless capacity for love and closeness. Maybe you're afraid to break it off with David because of the insecurity of not having someone in your life." I paused. "Will you listen to me? I sound like one of the docs. So what do they say next? Oh, I know, that will be one hundred fifty dollars, please, for the elevator ride analysis."

Leslie leaned down and hugged me. "Unlike most of the docs, I think your analysis was right on target." The elevator stopped gently and the door opened to the second floor.

"Alcoholics, drug addicts and overworked staff, second floor. Next stop, maniacs and psychotics."

"Katie!" Leslie laughed. "Keep your voice down," she called form inside the elevator. "And hey, thanks for your help. You've given me something to think about. Good luck with the Colonel!"

"The Colonel I can handle. It's everything else that's shaky. Which reminds me," I said, walking back toward the elevator. "Any interest in going out with Warner, Our Georgia boy? I think he likes you and I could really stand to be on his good side, especially since I need to ask for more time off."

"I think I would do just about anything for you, Katie," she said as she let the elevator doors close, "but that! I may by insecure, but I'm not desperate. Good-bye darling," she called and left me alone in the hall, fishing for my keys in my oversized bag.

The Colonel sat rigidly in his chair, his pants perfectly creased, his starched hat on his lap. His hair stood at attention due to his cropped, military cut. Danny was in direct contrast to his father's crispness. His pants hung down below his boxers and his tee-shirt and flannel overshirt were both wrinkled and untucked. Four beaded, hemp necklaces were entangled around his neck and his hair, shaved underneath, hung in a blunt cut over his eyes. There were two gold earrings in one ear and a tattoo encircling his wrist. He was small for his age, but looked even slighter next to his father's erect posture.

"Perhaps you could enlighten me as to why you need to know so much about my family, Mrs. Cunningham."

"And Danny's mother, too, Colonel Boles. It's part of Danny's treatment. Alcoholism is a family disease -- it effects every family member and most often occurred in earlier generations. I write a social history for each patient on the unit. It helps us develop a program for Danny and to understand, and hopefully disrupt, any destructive family patterns. If you'll just bear with me this morning, I think you'll find it quite fascinating. Let's start with you telling us a little about your childhood. Were you an only child, sir?"

Despite his initial resistance, the Colonel seemed to appreciate the chance to talk about himself. And Danny, despite his veneer of indifference, was riveted to his words. According to his father, there have been "Colonels" in Danny's family for three generations.

As the Colonel talked, the more apparent it became that he had been raised by a militaristic father who routinely physically abused him. As if in a trance, he described how he had been beaten and berated. Unlike the colonel, Danny had never been touched by his father and was visibly shocked by his father's story. And despite the horror of his words, I suspected the Colonel was minimizing these experiences and had no interest in receiving our sympathy, or worse, our pity. We both listened intently and when he finished, I realized I hadn't moved in over forty-five minutes.

"I didn't know Grandpa was such a bastard," Danny said after a respectful silence.

To the Colonel's credit, he overlooked his son's profanity and looked directly into his pale, green eyes. "Daniel, your grandfather was the worst bastard you'd ever care to meet." They looked hard at one another and I felt a chill rush up my spine. The Colonel, with his childhood feelings brought to the surface again, was able to have more understanding and even respect for his son's rebellion. Danny, in turn, was seeing his father as a human being who had suffered greatly, as opposed to someone whose sole purpose in life was to make him miserable.

They were quiet as they stood to leave and walked together toward the door. I followed them and the Colonel turned to shake my hand. "Thank you, Mrs. Cunningham, thank you for listening. I hope I didn't dominate the session."

"On the contrary, Colonel, I would like to thank you for your honesty."

Lesson Three:
Extend The Family

In order to create an environment of support and love,
parents should allow the ideas and personalities of others
to enrich their children's experience
and knowledge of the world.
Remember to protect and beware of those with ill intentions,
but to also be charitable to others.
Encourage your children to share their love and generosity.
Grandparents, aunts and uncles, good friends
and neighbors enrich the family and widen
both a parent's and child's perspective of the world.

After declining Leslie's offer to go out to lunch, I sat at my desk, poking holes in my whole wheat bread with my finger. My other hand rested on the phone and after three false starts, I dialed my home in Ohio, praying my Aunt Matilda, and not my mother, would answer.

"Hello?"

Thank you, God. "Aunt Matty? It's me, Katie."

"Katie! What a pleasant surprise."

"It's so nice to hear your voice. I'm sorry it's been so long since I've called."

Other than my close friends at work, I hadn't told anyone about Tiger. Depending on my family members for support never seemed to be an option. I often felt as if I were the chassis holding my complicated family motor in place. Although the weight had been overwhelming at times, I had always kept it that way. Throughout my family's crises, and we've had more than our share, I have been the one they could count on to be okay, to listen without interruption, because, as my mother liked to say, I am the "normal" one. It has been my role in the family since the day I was born, the last of three girls, the one who was supposed to complete the family by being a boy. But since I was "all girl," much to my father's dismay, I had tried to save the family in my own way.

"Katherine Davis Cunningham, how dare you apologize for having a life of

51

your own," she exclaimed. My heart warmed at her words. "Tell me everything, I know it's the middle of the day and you're at work, what's up?"

"Oh, nothing much, well, maybe there is something..."

"Katie, what's got you so rattled? I know you and something is on your mind and you're holding back so you won't burden me. Well, listen up, we're cut from the same cloth, you and I, and we're at our best when we're helping others. I need to feel useful these days so please, spill it, I'm listening." I was surprised at how quickly she zeroed in on my reluctance. But I shouldn't be. Aunt Matty is a psychologist and had worked in the public school system for twenty years before she retired a few years ago. She had never married and after my father died of cancer when I was ten, she became my other parent. Not only because she was there for me, but because she supported my mother through her grief and subsequent depressions. When my mother was emotionally unavailable, my sisters and I knew we could call Aunt Matty and she would be there. Obviously today was no exception.

I took a deep breath and said more quickly than I had expected, "Tiger's teacher told me she thought Tiger had a learning problem and so I took her for testing last Friday and the psychologist gave me this little book about dyslexia and told me to read it and so she must think Tiger's dyslexic and -- dyslexic! Tiger! Can you believe it? In our family?"

Aunt Matty was quiet for several moments. "Well what do you know. I've always thought Tiger had a different outlook on the world. It's always seemed she could see things others missed, almost as if she was an old soul. This would certainly explain it."

"You're making it sound as if it's a good thing," I said quietly.

Aunt Matty broke her train of thought. "Oh, honey, I'm sorry. It's just that I know a few dyslexics and they are some of my favorite people. And don't think just because they don't succeed in a classroom, they aren't intelligent. In fact, I think dyslexics are so bright they often transcend us other folk. Did you know Albert Einstein was dyslexic and actually flunked out of school?"

"I guess I did know that, but in this day and age Tiger doesn't stand a chance if she can't read or write. I know she's bright, but she's no Einstein. I feel so lost. And I don't have a clue how to help her."

Aunt Matty was my mother's older sister by six years. Their parents died in a freak auto accident when my mother was in her senior year of high school. Their parents, still recovering from the depression, had had no room in the budget for life insurance. So Matty postponed marriage and committed herself to ensuring her sister received a college education. Although it wasn't her intention, she never married. Instead, she poured her energy into her work at Case Western Reserve as a researcher and professor of psychology.

But it ended the day my mother phoned her two weeks after my father's death to say that she hadn't left the bedroom since the funeral. When Matty arrived three hours later, finding my sisters and me in the living room watching television, looking hungry and terrified, she rolled up her sleeves and went to work. She always said she would return to Cleveland once she knew we were all right, but it never happened. Eventually she took a job in town as a school psychologist for very little pay and less prestige, and became my other parent. And while my mother was emotional and easily daunted, Aunt Matty was strong, supportive and adamant that my sisters and I would succeed.

"So what are you going to do? We used to send children with learning disabilities to special education in the public school system."

"Special Education?" I interrupted. "I remember the kids that were in special education. They wore hair nets and had to wipe the tables off in the cafeteria."

Aunt Matty hesitated. "Yes, some of them worked in the cafeteria. But I also think some of them did fine. I would do the initial testing and help set up the IEP's (Individual Education Plans), but I had five schools to cover and didn't have the opportunity to follow up on them. But so much has changed. Schools are required to do a lot more for these children than they used to."

"These children -- special education, this is Tiger we're talking about. My Tiger. A member of the Davis family, no less. Come on, Aunt Matty, Megan was valedictorian, Stephanie never got below an 'A-,' even through her doctoral program! I was in the top ten of my class, and Mom always said I would have had been number one if I didn't like boys so much. How could this be happening to one of my children?"

"Get it out while you can, Katie, but don't let Tiger hear you say these things," she said softly.

"No, I would never, I mean, I have no idea how to feel about this, it is just so completely off my radar screen. I know families, emotions, alcoholism, parenting, psychopathology, you name it, but I am clueless about learning disabilities. I couldn't wait to send my children to school so I could watch them excel. I'm one of those parents who's always pushing for advanced placement classes and gifted and talented programs."

"Life has a crazy way of shattering expectations, Katie. It's never how we expect it to be." Her words stopped my rapid stream of thoughts and I was reminded how her life had certainly gone down an unexpected path. I felt ashamed and self-indulgent. "You can handle this, Katie, dear, you just don't know it yet."

"Have you told your parents about Tiger?" I asked Max. We were sitting next to each other on the sofa in front of the fireplace, a chenille throw hand knit by my mother, was draped over us. It had been unseasonably cool that day and the girls had requested we have the first fire of the season. Max had been game and made it a production, enlisting the girls to bring in the wood, wad up the paper, and informed Jamie that this year he would teach her how to light a match. She had been nervous as a cat until Tiger came over and expertly lit the match on her first try. We were stunned as we watched her ignite the crumpled newspaper. We knew she loved camping and the outdoors, but were shocked to see that she had mastered this potentially dangerous skill. Jamie had watched her sister in awe and later allowed Tiger, and not her father, to teach her the secret to not burning her fingers.

They were both asleep, yet again in Jamie's bed, and Max and I had decided to take advantage of the fire and his being home and uncorked a bottle of Merlot. We sat in the darkened room, the firelight dancing on the shadowy walls, with Baxter stretched out on the rug in front of us. It should have been a perfect evening, but I was filled with anxiety.

"No, I haven't told them. I thought I would wait until we receive Doctor Chartwell's report." Max was relaxed and seemingly content with his feet stretched out on the ottoman, his rugged face glowing handsomely.

"Why wait for the report? She'll probably just announce her findings in the waiting room again," I said.

"Jesus, Katie, if you don't like this woman, why are we paying her fifteen hundred dollars?"

"I'm just venting, okay? I'm sure she is perfectly competent. She came highly recommended, she just made some mistakes on Friday. And she acted as if I was supposed to already know what the problem is. That really unnerved me." I took a deep breath and exhaled slowly. "Just let me talk. Please don't start problem solving."

"Sorry. I just had to state the obvious."

I picked up my wine glass and looked at him out of the corner of my eye. "No, you didn't. Anyway, back to your parents. Don't you think it would be helpful if they knew? We could use all the support we can get. And I don't want to take them by surprise in case it is something serious."

"It's too early to start blabbing our problems to everyone. We don't even know what we're dealing with. Maybe Tiger just reverses her 'B's' and 'D's' because she's seven. It might not be anything. Hell, I still can't tell my right from my left and I have a law degree from Harvard."

"Nobody wants that to be true more than me. But, well, do you think maybe you haven't told your parents because you're embarrassed that one of our children might not be a straight 'A' student, you know, Ivy League material?"

"No, Kate, I don't," he said, growing frustrated. "You're just projecting your anxieties onto me."

"You are not licensed to use those terms. Besides, I told Aunt Matty."

"That doesn't count. You could have told her we'd had sex change operations and she would have taken it in stride."

"That may be true, but it was still hard."

"Katie, my parents are the least judgmental people I know. They will be very supportive if and when they are needed. I don't know what I would say right now. Once the testing is completed, providing there is something to tell, I will inform my mother and father about Tiger. Okay? Now, I'm having a very relaxing evening with my lovely wife and I'd like it to continue." He stretched out his arm and rested it on the back of the sofa behind me and began twisting his finger through hair.

"Oh, Max." I leaned forward and put my head in my hands. "I just can't stop thinking about Tiger. I feel so out of control, so in the dark. I don't understand how you can relax. Maybe you can relax because you know I'm worrying. Maybe I'm doing the worrying for both of us."

"Katie, I love you very much, but it is a real challenge living with you!" he said in exasperation.

I sighed, poured us more wine and nestled back under his arm. "You know what? I find it challenging to live with me too."

Max laughed heartily and stroked my face. Before long he began to unbutton my shirt and kiss my neck. Although I was a little annoyed that he'd had this agenda all evening and had been less than interested in my conversation, I needed desperately to relax and decided to put my energies into our lovemaking instead of my nagging anxieties. And so we touched and held one another, lingering in our play, not wanting the night to end and turn into another day of worries and uncertainty.

Wednesday's testing was shorter, but equally disorienting for Tiger. Despite this, she continued to be cooperative, never complaining. She seemed comfortable with Susan, and I suspected Dr. Chartwell's talents were in her work with children, as opposed to interacting with their parents. I had known teachers with the same dichotomy: awkward and nervous with adults but confident and effective with children. Considering this I had decided to work harder to get along with Susan, for Tiger's sake.

When Tiger and Susan emerged from her soundproof office for the last time, I smiled and stood to greet them. Tiger immediately went out to the steps again. It had gone against her nature to be indoors for such a long stretch of time. I sat back down to write Susan a check for fifteen hundred dollars. She waited expectantly and seemed comfortable asking for such a large amount of money for less than two days of her time. I began to wonder if the paintings on her walls were originals. Susan held the check in her hand and smiled. "The final step will be for me to meet with you and your husband without Tiger so that we can go over the results. You will have received my report in the mail prior to that meeting, so why don't we schedule it two weeks from today? I'll also need you to sign a release so that I can send a copy to her school, if that's all right with you," Susan said in her articulate manner.

"Of course it's all right. The sooner we all know what's going on, the better," I said, trying to be as compliant as possible.

"I'll mark it confidential and address it to Mrs. Larson. You can decide who sees it after that."

"I'm not particularly worried about who reads it. In fact, I would like all of Tiger's teachers to see it, art, music, phys. ed, I think it would be helpful if everyone knows what the problem is, don't you?" I asked.

"Not necessarily, Kate. Unless there is a learning specialist at the school."

"No. They don't have anything like that."

"Why don't I just address it to Mrs. Larson until we've had a chance to talk in two weeks." I was puzzled by this but decided, for once, not to press her further. Susan, noticing the change, looked at me suspiciously. "I will be able to explain a lot more in two weeks. Unless of course you have some immediate questions."

"No. But could we possibly meet in the evening, Susan? It's very difficult to take so much time away from work."

"I'm sorry, Kate, I don't have evening hours. Besides, it will be easier for you to come while Tiger's in school. How about two weeks from today, say, ten o'clock? It shouldn't take more than two hours."

I got out my date-book, resisting the urge to argue this further. As Susan walked behind me toward the door she said, "Where is the dyslexia in your extended families?"

"What?" Having begun to subconsciously mimic Susan's articulate manner, I said, "First of all, I'm assuming by your statement that you have concluded Tiger is dyslexic. This, of course, follows your statement that we must wait for the report before discussing anything further. Secondly, no, there isn't any hint of learning disabilities on either side of our families. The closest we come is confusing left and right. So how do you make sense of that if you are already convinced Tiger is dyslexic?"

Tiger must have heard my raised voice because she pushed open the door and said, "Mommy, can we go to the park?" She looked back and forth between us with a worried expression.

"Of course we can," I said as I pulled her close to me and petted her silky, brown hair. "Thank you, Doctor Chartwell, we will see you in two weeks and I look forward to receiving your report. Say good-bye to Doctor Susan, Tiger."

"Bye," she called sweetly, and I closed the door behind us before Susan had a chance to say more.

We had ended earlier than expected, which afforded Tiger and me plenty of time to visit the park near our house before Jamie's school day ended. We stopped at a convenience store and paid a ridiculous sum of money for a bag of doughy, white bread to feed to the ducks, and when at last we arrived at the park, we slammed the van doors shut, held hands, and skipped down to the duck pond. The wind blew back our hair as we pranced down the path, turning our ears a bright pink.

Tiger's face came alive again at the chance to move and be outside. We selected the bench nearest the pond and huddled close together, occupying very little space in order to keep warm. We were both panting from our jaunt down the path and looked like a pair of steam engines as clouds of our breath puffed out before us in rapid succession. I squeezed Tiger next to me.

"That was great," I said as I tried to catch my breath. "I need to skip more often."

Eventually Tiger began to tear the bread into pieces and toss it into the water. A flock of mallards circling nearby became interested and swam closer. The ducks quacked enthusiastically at the presence of Tiger's croutons and I watched uncomfortably as the more aggressive ducks nipped at the others, asserting their authority.

But Tiger was oblivious to the building tension in the duck pond and instead, projected her own sense of fairness onto the flock. "Look, Mommy," she said happily, "I think that one's the mommy duck and those are her children. Look how cute they are. I think they're saying, 'look, Mommy, food!' Oh, and that one's saying, 'get out of the way, brother, that was my piece!" She continued to toss the bread into the water, being careful that each duck had an equal share. "Where's the daddy duck, Mommy?"

"He must be working late," I teased.

"Mom!" Tiger complained. "I mean it, which one is the daddy?"

"Maybe that's him." I pointed to a drake swimming nearby.

"Yes. That's him," she said, satisfied. "He's back there so he can protect his family. He's letting them eat first." That was Tiger, always thinking the best about everyone, even a male duck, who I, on the other hand, hated because of the way several males tended to pursue one, lone female, sometimes holding her head under the water in an attempt to mate with her. I refused to take the children to the pond during mating season and would complain to Max that I didn't want my daughters to witness "duck gang rape."

"Look at that one."

"Which one?" I asked, glad that Tiger had brought me back to her world.

"That one, swimming by itself. It looks different from the others. I'll bet it's the youngest. It's not as fast as the others. Look, it swims funny." She was right. The duck was swimming differently than the other ducks its size.

"Come here, sweetie," she called in a high pitched voice. "Come and have a piece too." Tiger stood up and tried to get closer to the lone duck. It shied away from her until she heaved a piece of bread close to it. Tiger smiled when it snatched the bread before the other ducks swam over. She squatted close to the ground, the bag of bread dangling between her legs, and looked thoughtfully at that duck.

"Look, Tiger," I called. "It has something wrong with its foot, I think that's why it swims that way."

"Of course it does," she replied matter-of-factly. "It's different from the others. That's why they aren't playing with it."

"I like the way it swims, Tiger," I said quickly. "And it's getting around okay, just a little slower."

Tiger stood and looked at me pensively, debating whether or not to continue this line of conversation. After a moment she brought the half-eaten bag of bread back to the bench. "I'm going to go swing for a while," she said, and walked over to the playground.

I sat alone, watching the disabled duck struggle through the opaque water. It was paddling twice as hard as the others who were swimming circles around it, searching for any missed morsels of bread. Eventually the ducks realized the source of their unexpected meal had gone and swam away, leaving the lone duck to struggle in their triangular wakes.

I was thankful it was Friday. Jamie had plans to spend the night at a friend's, but Tiger had decided to stay home and spend the evening playing all the imaginative games she hadn't had time for during the week. I had hoped she would have her own friend spend the night, and warned that she would be bored by six o'clock without her sister to play with, but she had declined.

When we arrived home, Jamie went to her room to pack and Tiger hopped on her bike. She was out of the garage and halfway down the street before I noticed she wasn't wearing a helmet, requiring me to chase after her. Eventually she saw me waving my arms and reluctantly put it on. She was like those motorcyclists who claimed mandatory helmet laws were a civil rights violation. But Tiger was a free spirit, fighting any constraints on her ability to move freely and feel the wind on her face. It was all I could do to keep her from hanging out the van window with Baxter.

After changing out of my work clothes, I sat in the safe haven of my kitchen, sipping fresh coffee and flipping through catalogs. I was shaking my head at some of the frivolous gifts they were peddling when Jamie walked in with her pillow, backpack and field hockey stick. "What's wrong, Mom?" she asked tentatively.

"Nothing, really. I'm just looking at these overpriced, useless trinkets that are the kind of thing you would shove in a drawer and never use and then sell in a yard sale a year later, that's all," I said.

"Geez, Mom, take a breath."

"Why thank you, dear, I will. For instance, here's a bronze turtle with diamond eyes for a mere three hundred forty-nine dollars! Now what would a person do with something like that? I'd probably lose it."

"Why can't you just look at a catalog like normal mothers, you know, and order things?" But Jamie was in a good mood and I could tell by her smile that she appreciated my questioning of things. "I mean, I'm the only girl in my class whose mother lectures her about self-esteem when I play with my Barbie Doll."

"Are you still playing with that doll?" I asked. "The next thing I know you'll be ordering a Bob Mackie ball gown for it. Look, here's one for four hundred dollars. What do you say, kiddo, should I put it on your Christmas list?"

"Uh, no." Jamie said in the sarcastic manner that had become the language of her fledgling generation. She stood at the open refrigerator for longer than I would have liked, but eventually grabbed a blueberry yogurt, slammed the door, and said, "I'm going to wait for Jessica's parents outside." She kissed my cheek and looked down at my stack of catalogs. She sifted through them and I watched her with amusement. "Here," she said, pulling a Wayside Gardens from the bottom of the pile. "Try this one," and walked out the door.

On Fridays I gave myself permission to order out, eat on paper plates and rent videos, and I was looking forward to the evening that lay ahead. Max would be picking up a movie and Chinese food on his way home from the office. This was not always the best plan, however, because by the time Max made it to the video store the selection was so sparse we usually ended up with one of the violent, shoot-em-ups that lined the walls of the store. But after the past few weeks, I was beginning to see the merits of sitting on the sofa watching buildings explode.

I chatted briefly with Jessica's mom, and after waving good-bye, came inside to find Tiger engrossed in a television show. I brought her a pear and some sliced cheese for a snack and realizing I had some rare time to myself, decided to work in the yard, my therapy.

"Mom," Tiger called. "Phone's for you, it's Grandma!"

"Be right there," I called. I dropped my rake and stiffened. "Grandma" was Max's mother, a very kind, but proper woman who I knew had not been informed about recent events. I pulled off my gloves as I walked toward the house, wondering what to say to her. Although she was well versed in social graces, she was also very intuitive, a "Miss Clavel" type who knows immediately when something isn't right.

"Hi, May."

"Hello, dear. I hope I'm not interrupting anything," the kind, but aging voice said on the other end of the line.

"Not at all. In fact, I was raking leaves and your call is providing me with a much-needed break. I'm afraid our lovely trees are too mature for me."

May chuckled. "Why don't you leave that for Max, you already do too much around there. I don't know what it is about my sons, but they seem to be lacking in the handiness department."

I laughed appreciatively. "Is everything all right, May? You haven't said why you were calling."

"Everything is just fine. I'm sorry to call on such late notice, but Max and I were hoping to go to the Annapolis Boat Show tomorrow, and I just had this need to see you. Do you have plans for tomorrow afternoon? I certainly don't want to intrude on your busy lives."

"Jamie has a field hockey game in the morning and then we're home for the rest of the day and would love a visit. You know you're always welcome. We don't see you enough as it is, particularly with you so nearby. Why don't you come for dinner -- Max will cook, because he loves to, and we'll make a night of it. The guest room is ready and you can relax, have some wine, and not worry about driving back to Potomac at night. What do you say?"

"I say I have grown more spontaneous in my old age and would love to. But only if you promise not to go to any trouble."

"It's a deal. By the way, have you talked to Max recently?" I asked tentatively.

"No, dear. But I hear he's been busy with a very important case. I know he's talked to his father about some of the details, but much to my chagrin, he hasn't requested to talk to his dear, old mother. Why, is something wrong?" I started to feel shaky from the genuine concern in her voice.

"Nothing unmanageable, May. You know Max and me, we can handle anything."

"I agree, and I believe the Lord won't give us more than we can handle, but that doesn't mean it isn't trying at times. Are you sure everything is all right?" she pushed gently.

"The only thing wrong is that we don't spend enough time together. I'm looking forward to catching up tomorrow."

"I'm serious about not going to any trouble. Don't worry about cleaning your house. I raised four sons and I know what it's like to have children underfoot. Give the girls my love and we'll see you tomorrow afternoon. Good-bye, dear."

I clicked off the phone and rolled my eyes at May's last comment. She may have had four boys, but she also had a cook, nanny and gardener. May's standards of cleanliness were very different from mine, and although I looked forward to a chance to talk with her about recent events, I found myself immediately looking around our "cozy" house with a critical eye.

Four sons: Max attended Harvard Law School, Justin, Johns Hopkins Medical School, Blake, University of Virginia Darden School of Business, and Dusty studied art in Italy for years and recently opened his own studio in Soho. But despite their privileged backgrounds, they were four of the kindest, funniest men I had ever known. May intimidated me all right. And I wondered how I would talk to her about Tiger. I was also growing angry with Max for not telling his parents, especially knowing he talked with his father more than once this week.

"Katie, the house looks fine! Will you please stop running around like a fool? My mother could care less how this house looks. She adores you. In fact, sometimes I think she likes you better than me." Max was chopping garlic at the center island and the aroma of onions sauteing in butter filled the house.

"Max, don't you see? This house could be a wreck and no one would think you're a poor housekeeper. Even if you were a bachelor! People don't hold men responsible for these things. But walk into a messy house and people immediately start forming opinions about the woman. Besides, I'm frustrated with you for not doing more around here. We both work full time but somehow cleaning this house is my second job, not yours." I was running from room to room with piles of shoes, toys, coats, and newspapers.

"Why can't you get Lois to do more around here?"

I stopped in the doorway and looked at him in frustration. "I've explained this to you before. Her job is to take care of our children which is enough. If we expected her to clean the house as well then that would inevitably become her first priority and the children would come second. Do you remember this conversation?"

"You know what, I think I'll just stay out of your way for a while." I turned around and walked back into the next room. "But I mean it about my mother," he called after me, "she really doesn't care what our house looks like." The garlic sizzled as he added it to the onions.

"Hello, May," I said warmly, kissing her on the cheek. She smelled faintly of Channel No. 5 and was dressed in a black boiled wool jacket and ivory wool pants that flattered her slender figure. Her hair was silvery white and pulled back into a

61

flawless chignon.

"Hello, Katie, dear," she said, returning my kiss. Having heard the sounds of someone new, Baxter ran into the room with a dirty pull-toy dangling from the sides of his mouth. His wagging tail thumped our legs and with an uncanny discrimination, jumped on the person in the room who least welcomed his greetings. "Hello, Baxter, aren't we excited today," May said stiffly.

"Max," I said through gritted teeth. "Get Baxter!" As Max dragged a resistant Baxter out the door, Max Senior engulfed me in one of his characteristic bear hugs. He was wearing a heavy, navy blue cotton sweater that smelled of the crisp outdoors. I loved his hugs and lingered in his arms an extra moment.

Max's father had always been special to me having lost mine so young. He was tall, like his sons, and had grown more loving and affectionate since his retirement. Max had often complained of his dad's distance and preoccupation with his work while he was growing up and was confused by the recent transformation. Although he was thrilled to finally have his father's attention and interest, part of him resented his father deeply for being unavailable during his childhood. Max and his next two brothers were also silently resentful of the youngest, just now turning thirty, for getting the majority of their father's attention. And yet they never blamed Dusty, they knew it was a matter of timing. In fact they seemed to admire Dusty's bravery for going down such an unconventional path. Max's intact, relatively healthy family had been one of the things that had drawn me to him. The energy created by the six of them was thrilling and contagious. It was a complex, high performance, yet smooth running motor, perhaps an expensive import. I'm sure Max would agree with me on this point. But I felt a part of something special when we were all together. They were the "normal" family I never had.

"Hi, Grandma." Jamie had come into the room. She kissed her Grandmother and hugged her Grandfather. Jamie and Tiger had a more formal relationship with Max's parents than with my mother and Aunt Matty. When my "mothers" visited, they were immediately in their arms, talking non-stop, competing with Baxter for their attention. But with May and Max they were more reserved. Jamie would talk with them politely about school and field hockey, but sooner rather than later, she and Tiger would return to their own activity. I knew Jamie loved her grandparents, it was just a different kind of love. And although Max and May loved and admired their grandchildren, it was clear they were more comfortable sitting with us sipping cocktails, than sitting on the floor playing Candyland.

Tiger wandered in after Jamie and I found myself wishing I had reminded her to change her shirt before her grandparents' arrival. Although she had on a cute pair of black leggings that showed off her thin, muscular legs, she was also wearing an oversized Naval Academy sweatshirt with cranberry juice and macaroni and cheese stains from lunch. "Hi, Grandma. Hi, Grandpa," she said softly.

"There's my Tiger!" Max Senior knelt down and hugged her. There had always been a closeness between them and I was grateful in light of recent events that Tiger had someone other than her parents to make her feel special. May hugged her after Max stood up, and, just as I had expected, Tiger and Jamie went back to their stuffed animal game.

We settled into the living room after Jamie and Tiger's quick exit. It was the smallest room in the house, but I loved the intimacy it necessitated. There was only room for a love seat and two wing chairs and despite the room's formal label, I kept the decor warm and comfortable. The love seat was upholstered in a soft, sage green velvet and the two adjacent chairs were slip-covered in a faded sage and terra cotta floral cotton. A small oriental rug warmed the wood floors and the windows were treated with pleated valances and painted white shutters. The walls were a flat, sage green with glossy white trim that reflected the firelight.

Max placed his latest creation on a small table and we sipped chilled wine and nibbled on warm crab dip and crackers. I had been surprised when Max Senior had refused his usual dry martini and wondered if his post retirement drinking habits had gotten the better of him.

Max and his father immediately launched into a discussion about the Chesapeake Bay Foundation case and, having little interest in competing with them in their conversation, May and I began our own, separate discussion. We covered several topics, May's new golf lessons, her work with the American Cancer Society, Jamie's joining the field hockey team, the remodeling of the kitchen, and, as usual, there were no questions about my job. Although she found it interesting at times, she never seemed to understand why I insisted on working full time and usually left the subject untouched.

Eventually May asked about Tiger. "How does she like second grade?" she asked innocently.

"Honestly, May? Not much," I said, deciding at that moment not to pretend things were fine, something I had always done in the past.

May seemed surprised at my abrupt response, but she was gracious and unflappable. "What doesn't she like? The other children? The schoolwork? The teacher is all right, isn't she? I remember Jamie enjoying second grade very much. And it's such a lovely school."

"Jamie and Tiger are very different children, it seems, and unfortunately Tiger hasn't warmed to Mary Peterson as Jamie did. Or vice versa. In fact, I think Mary Peterson would be happier if Tiger wasn't in her class at all."

"Now what makes you say a thing like that, Kate?"

Sensing the shift in our conversation Max stopped mid-sentence and turned to us. "What are you two gorgeous gals talking about?" He leaned forward with a cracker in his large hands for a scoop of crab dip.

63

"We're talking about Tiger, Max. I was telling your mother that she's having a rough time in school."

"Only because she has a teacher who should have retired years ago," Max said confidently. "It seems this teacher isn't used to free spirits like Tiger who prefer not to sit in a chair for six hours a day. Of course, I don't know many seven-year-olds who can. She's just too traditional and Tiger and Mary don't see eye to eye. But you should see Tiger on her bike these days, she's a whirlwind."

I decided to follow Max's lead and say no more about Tiger, but I didn't like it. He looked at me purposefully as if to say, "not now." I was beginning to see how strong his denial of Tiger's problem had become. I was also noticing how hard he worked to impress his parents.

May appeared relieved to talk about Tiger's successes and said she would request a bike-riding demonstration before dinner. Sensing the need to monitor me, Max decided to halt the work discussion with his father and asked his mother about her golf game.

Dinner was pleasant and delicious, and I willed myself to enjoy the evening and not think about Tiger's problems, at least for one night. After Jamie and Tiger went to bed, Max brewed fresh cappuccinos and brought us each an oversized mug-full. He dusted the mugs with cocoa and placed a chocolate dipped biscotti cookie on each saucer.

We lingered at the table as the candles melted down to stubs. Max poured more wine while he and his father battled to see who was funnier. They began telling stories, each one funnier than the last, and May and I laughed until we cried.

"Hey, Dad, thanks for your advice on my new case, but you should see these guys at the Bay Foundation," Max said as he emptied the wine bottle into our glasses.

"What do you mean?" Max Senior asked with a smile. His eyes danced with the anticipation of another story from his son. "I thought you said they had a strong case?"

"They do, no doubt about that. And it's a worthy case, they're absolutely right about the State's neglect of the law. But these guys are so left wing they make me look like Jesse Helms!"

"Then change, please!" I said, laughing.

"Seriously. For instance, I was over there yesterday and I threw my empty soda can in the trash on my way into our meeting, and do you know the receptionist followed me into the conference room and handed it back to me!"

"No!" Max Senior laughed.

"No shit!" Max's face glowed from the wine. "I wanted to crawl under the table. I mean, this was pretty embarrassing. So I looked around the table and said, 'should I tell her it's empty?' and do you know nobody laughed? They just left me flapping there in the breeze, holding that empty soda can!"

"Oh, Max, how embarrassing," I said.

"That sounds like something Dusty would do to me," May laughed. "He's always pulling my bottles and newspapers out of the trash."

"How's old Dusty doing, anyway? Last we heard he has a serious girlfriend," Max said.

"Yes, he does, but we haven't met her yet. He's very happy, though, and we had a wonderful visit with him in New York a few weeks ago," May said dreamily.

Max noticed and grew louder. "Do you remember the time we were in Aruba for spring break and we were all debating about who was the best swimmer, the best runner, all that crap, and Dusty blew past us with a surf board and sailed right into the water?"

"Do I ever!" May said.

"He was amazing -- the best natural athlete I've ever known."

"How old was Dusty?" I asked, feeling warm and content.

"Seven," Max and May said in unison, and then laughed. "We were so self-conscious about our chest hairs and muscles that we weren't willing to get in there and try something new," Max said in admiration of his youngest brother. "But he showed us all. Hey Mom, tell Katie about the time I tried to teach Blake how to ride a bike while you were in the house with Dusty."

And the stories continued, each one more outrageous than the next, and I was reminded of how much I loved this active, embracing family. The wine loosened our tongues and we sang each other's praises well into the night. I knew they loved me, Max Senior and May, despite the obvious difference in our backgrounds. They appreciated my mothering of their granddaughters and my love for their son, and I knew their love was unconditional. It was the kind of rare love from in-laws that told me that even if Max and I were no longer together, they would love me just the same.

"You don't look so good, girlfriend," I said to Leslie as we walked through the hospital lobby. I was feeling good and glad to be back at work after the weekend. It was my refuge, my self-esteem builder. "What's going on?" I asked as I put my arm around her taller shoulders affectionately.

"I can't talk about it in the elevator this time, Kate, do you have a minute?"

"I always have time for you and you know it. Come up to my office. My session with the Colonel doesn't start until nine, although he never seems to know that. Come on, I'll get Dolores to brew us some of her special coffee, guaranteed to heal the soul, and the nervous system." I pulled her into the elevator and didn't let go of her arm until we were safely inside my office.

65

Leslie sat down on the edge of my office couch and, after finding us each a cup of coffee, I sat next to her. "I don't know if your influence is good or bad, Katie. I thought a lot about what you said the other day about David and me, and so I confronted him Friday night. I told him he had a problem with intimacy and he could either, well, shit or get off the pot! I said that, I really did! He was a little surprised. But, of course, so was I. But I meant it, Kate, enough is enough. I said I wanted a real relationship, with the works, marriage, children, mortgage, he was shocked."

"So what did he do?"

"Three guesses, first two don't count," she said weakly, and I began to see the deep lines under her eyes, despite her attempt to hide them with her expensive make up. She was also underdressed for work by Leslie's standards and wore a loose, corduroy dress and flat shoes.

"He was incredibly calm and well mannered. I wanted to scream at him! He said he was sorry that I couldn't be more patient, that he loved me and wanted to be with me, blah, blah, blah. What he says every time I get impatient with our relationship. He said he desperately wanted to leave his wife, but he was worried about the children, same old crap. But this time, Kate, I had this rare sense of clarity, and I could see how ridiculous our relationship has been, and how he's used his wanting to leave his wife as a way to draw me in, keep me with him. It's really pretty sick when you look at it. And I told him that. I made him leave and he looked like a kicked puppy. And do you know the sickest part?" Leslie was crying pretty hard by now and I kept my arm tightly around her. "I felt sorry for him! I wanted to comfort him, I even found myself feeling attracted to him!"

"That's the social worker in you, honey, I guess it is a kind of sickness."

She laughed through her tears. "I do love him, Kate, and it hurts to know he won't do anything to keep us together. I guess he never did love me, the bastard."

"Oh, he loves you, Les, you know that in your heart. But he was stuck, afraid to make a change. It was safer to stay where he was, but deep in his heart he must know that. I guess I feel sorry for him too. See, we're both sick!"

"Very!" she moaned.

I squeezed her tightly. "Have you been eating? Why are you wearing this big dress?" I touched her arm could feel her bones through the bulky fabric.

"I try to eat, I just can't. I have zero appetite. I know it's not good, and I know it doesn't look good. I barely have breasts, I'm so damn skinny." She had stopped crying and was dabbing at her swollen eyes. "I've just felt unbelievably lonely lately. I used to love my independence, but now it feels like a black hole. I envy your family, you're surrounded by people who love you."

"But Leslie, you are a part of my family. Remember one of the advantages of adulthood is you can create your family, and I'm part of it, whether you want me or

66

not. Tell you what, I'll call Max and tell him he can work late tonight, which he was more than likely to do anyway, and you're coming over for dinner and spending the night. We'll play with the girls, who, by the way, will be thrilled to have you there, and then we'll pop popcorn and watch a movie, a good one, with some sexy, irresistible actor." A loud knock on my door caused us both to jump. "Come in," I called, puzzled.

Warner walked brazenly into the room and was surprised to see Leslie and I huddled on the couch. "Why hello, Leslie," he said lecherously. Although he was famous for crossing boundaries with most of the women in the hospital, I knew some of us could handle it better than others, and Leslie was in no shape to ward off Warner this morning.

"What is it, Warner?" I stood up to meet his gaze and positioned myself protectively in front of Leslie.

"Will you excuse us, Leslie?" He looked around me and smiled. "There's no need to involve you in this, and I'm sure you have plenty to do on your unit. But stop back any time, you know you're always welcome around here," he said in a slower than usual drawl.

Leslie stood up and squeezed my arm as she passed behind me, "You're on for tonight," she whispered, "I'll pick up the movie." Warner watched her closely as she walked out of the office and I was disgusted when he turned to watch her walk away.

"What is it, Warner?" I asked again and he turned back to me with a grin.

"Did Leslie marry that guy of hers yet?"

"Leslie's gay, Warner."

"Nice try, Katie, but see, that turns a guy like me on even more. But I know she's not, I'm just not so sure why you work so hard to keep me away from her. I'm not such a bad guy. But enough of that, you have bigger problems than trying to protect your friend. I see you need another day off next week and I think we have a serious problem."

"And what problem is that, Warner?" I crossed my arms defiantly. But my habit of subconsciously mimicking people had taken over again, and I realized too late that I had begun to speak with a trace of a southern accent.

"Whether you like me or not is irrelevant, Kate. You simply aren't putting in sufficient hours and I'm here to let you know that I've written you up, it's in your personal file. It only takes two write ups to lose your job. Consider yourself warned."

"Warner, I tried to explain to you, my daughter's having some problems. We only have one more appointment, then things should be back to normal. What if I talked to personnel and made some arrangements for taking leave? " Despite my efforts to remain self-composed, I realized I was pleading with him, my voice noticeably higher than usual.

"Katie," Betty's raspy voice called over the intercom on my phone, "your nine o'clock is here."

"The bottom line is you need to be here full time, like it or not," Warner said roughly. "There is no part time position available on this unit. Everyone puts in long hours, period. No exceptions. You will take leave without pay next Wednesday, and there will be a write up in your file today. It sounds as if it's time for you to get to work." Warner turned around briskly, causing the back of his suit coat to flip up, and walked away.

I tried to breathe, but my heart was racing. I buzzed Betty at the front desk and asked her to tell the Colonel I was running late. "Please tell him I'm sorry, Betty, I know he doesn't appreciate lateness." I stepped into the hall and saw Dolores and Rob in the staff lounge smoking cigarettes. I walked quickly down the hall and into the lounge. I shut the door and leaned against it. "I think I'm having a panic attack!"

"What's wrong, Katie?" Rob asked with concern.

"It's Warner, I swear he's out to fire me, I don't know what to do." I was breathing rapidly and began to feel dizzy. I leaned my head against the door.

Rob came over and put his arms around me gently. "Like hell he is," he said. His strong arms felt wonderful and I rested my head on his shoulders and began to cry. He held me until the tears slowed.

"Shit," I said into Rob's shoulder. "I can't believe I let him get to me this much. Please tell me he's not out there watching this."

Rob lifted my head with his finger and wiped away a tear. "He's nowhere to be seen, which is good, because I think I'd kill him."

"I'll pay you!"

Rob laughed and hugged me again. "Hang in there, Kate, you can handle this. We all know you can handle this."

I smiled weakly at Rob. "I don't know why he's giving me such a hard time. I'm just trying to help Tiger. She doesn't have anyone else to help her, it has to be me, it should be me. Why can't he understand that?"

Rob pulled back and brushed a loose strand of hair out of my eyes. "I don't know what his deal is, but I know you've got your priorities straight. Just get through this next meeting and then things will get back to normal. Ignore Warner. He needs a hobby."

I laughed through my tears. I was breathing normally again but I didn't want Rob to let go of me. I knew I was enjoying his comfort more than I should and we were startled when Dolores said, "Don't let Warner get to you, honey, he's just full of hot air." She patted my back as she walked past.

Rob stepped back and I smiled at him, "You're the best, I hope you know that."

68

"I try to be."

"I think I can face the Colonel now." I stepped forward to hug him good-bye but he took another step back.

"I don't think that's such a good idea." Rob surprised me with his comment, hugs were standard fare on the unit. I studied his face to try and understand. "I could comfort you all day, Katie." He looked at me with intensity, his blue eyes narrowed.

"Right," I said quietly. "I understand, I really do, more than you know." I felt a strong heat between us. I left the lounge quickly, feeling dizzy again from the range of emotions I had experienced in the last ten minutes. I buzzed Betty to summon the Colonel and was glad to have the next hour to focus on something other than my confusing feelings.

Lesson Four:
Fathering

Our society underestimates the importance of fathers,
good and bad.
Children need to love and trust both parents.
A father's presence, or absence, has an equal, yet different impact
on a child's development.
Boys and girls require a relationship with their fathers
in order to develop into healthy, trusting adults.
And fathers have the ability to enrich a child's life,
beyond their ability to protect and provide.

"Good morning, Colonel Boles," I said as I shook his hand. "I'm very sorry to keep you waiting. I had a small emergency up here on the unit, but the fire's out for now. Would you like some coffee?"

"No thank you, Mrs. Cunningham. I've had my one cup for the day." The Colonel entered my office and waited for me to sit down.

"I'll get Danny, I think they're in school already. I told him to go on with the other patients instead of waiting in the lounge for our session to begin."

"Mrs. Cunningham, could I speak with you privately for a few minutes? I mean, if that's all right. I don't want to break any hospital rules."

"That would be fine. Just let me shut the door." I retrieved my coffee from my desk and sat down across from him. It wasn't until I had tucked under my skirt and crossed my legs that the Colonel took his seat. "And let me remind you that whatever you say will be in confidence. If you would like to share with Danny what we've discussed, then you're welcome to tell him, it just won't come from me."

"I understand, Mrs. Cunningham, and I appreciate it." The Colonel smoothed his pants with both hands. "I'm not sure where to start. I've been doing a lot of thinking since our last session. Something happened to me here. I talked about things I've never told anyone before, not even my wife."

I waited for him to say more but he seemed to be at a loss for words. "Colonel Boles, are you feeling conflicted about telling Danny about your past?"

"Yes, ma'am," he said and paused, looking to me for help.

"Part of you is feeling --"

"Relief. It was like a purging, if you'll pardon the expression. I felt as if a weight has been taken off my shoulders," he said earnestly.

"I'm glad. Those things must have needed to be said." I waited for him to say more. After I sipped my coffee I said, "And another part of you is feeling--"

He hesitated. "Ashamed." He looked down at his polished shoes. "I shouldn't have told Daniel those things about my father. He's his grandfather, an adult, who should be respected, and what must he be thinking of me? I'm his father, his superior officer so to speak, and I sat here talking about my childhood like... like a child. What I said was disrespectful to my father. That is not good role-modeling for a son who is already displaying delinquent behavior. So although you may think it needed to be said, I think all I've done is give Danny permission to disrespect me."

"I imagine it was confusing for Danny, too, Colonel Boles, to experience you in such a different light. But I'm not sure any of this has to be detrimental." I was careful to pace myself with the Colonel. Although I knew he had opened a door with his son, I also knew it went against generations of father-son relationships to allow this to occur. I would have to tread lightly or he could close himself off permanently to Danny and the therapy.

"Well, that's where I'm confused. I know I'm failing Daniel or he wouldn't be here. His mother calls me every day, telling me what a lousy father I am. She's threatening to sue for custody and take him to the Midwest with her. She'll have to sue, though, because Daniel is old enough to decide for himself. And as far as I know, he doesn't want to leave his friends. But I wonder if it might be better for him with his mother." The Colonel was avoiding eye contact with me, I knew he was in agony about what to do. "I think I may be in over my head."

"What do you want, Colonel Boles?"

"Whatever is best for Daniel. You see, the Boles men are excellent officers, we can command an army better than anyone. But we're lousy at running families and if Daniel is better off with his mother, then so be it." He seemed to already be defeated and I knew I had to act quickly.

"But would you want Danny to stay with you, I mean, if it was best for him?"

"Yes ma'am. He's my son and I've missed having him at home these past few weeks, even if all we did was argue."

"What if I were to tell you that although if felt inappropriate to open up to Danny, I think it was very helpful to him and to his recovery." I tried to regain his eye contact, but he kept his head down. He was deep in thought.

I grew nervous waiting for him to respond. After several moments he lifted his head and looked at me. "I would be curious as to how that could be, Mrs.

71

Cunningham. I think I have added to his burden."

Good, I thought, I haven't lost him yet. "I'm sure you've heard us talk in family education about how important it is for the patients to 'get honest' with themselves. They spend a large part of their time here looking at their behavior and their drinking in an honest way. And in Danny's case I think he's always known something wasn't right with you and his grandfather. Kids can sense these things, particularly someone as sensitive and intuitive as Danny. Hearing you say what really happened must have confirmed what Danny already knew on some level. If anything, Colonel Boles, you have helped him feel more at peace with his family, things make more sense to him now, and your role-modeling was one of an honest testimony of a painful experience, which is exactly what we're encouraging him to do here."

"Did he say anything to you about last week?"

"I can't disclose what Danny has told me, but I would recommend you ask him yourself when he joins us. And I'll help you, Colonel Boles. I know this is unfamiliar territory."

"Yes, and very uncomfortable. But Daniel doesn't need a friend, he needs a father," he stated matter-of-factly.

"I agree! And if you two continue to work the way you have, I don't see any need for a custody battle or a move to the Midwest. Maybe what Danny needs is a 'friendly father,' someone who is honest and feeling, but also firm about rules and expectations. I have no doubt you are capable of being just that kind of father to Danny, you've already taken the hardest step by opening up to him. I've seen people in therapy for years before they could do what you did. Try to trust the timing. It happened now for a reason, even though you're not sure why."

"It all makes sense, Mrs. Cunningham, but I'm afraid everything will fall apart when Daniel returns home."

"Then we'll make sure we have the right supports in place. A family's support and understanding are crucial in relapse prevention. And one more thing, Colonel Boles, do you know how amazing it is that with your history of violence that you never physically abused your son? The odds were against you, and yet something enabled you to break your family's violent cycle. You and Danny may need to make some changes, but I have no doubt about your abilities as a father. Now, shall I retrieve Danny? He's probably wondering what we're doing. But, perhaps that's good," I added, smiling. "It keeps him on his toes to think his dad's talking to a therapist without him."

The Colonel reddened at my teasing. "Who would believe I would be in here with you is right. At least everything at the Pentagon is top secret. No one would ever believe 'stone-faced Boles' was talking to a counselor."

I smiled. "Whether he intended to or not, perhaps Danny's behavior has actually helped his family now that the two of you are talking honestly and openly."

"You sound like an optimist to me, Mrs. Cunningham. I guess you would have to be in this job."

"I'll get Danny, please excuse me." The Colonel rose stiffly and waited until I'd left the room before sitting down again.

By the time Leslie arrived, the bread maker was nearing the end of the baking cycle and a pot of minestrone simmered on the stove. The aroma of baking bread filled the house and she smiled as she walked through the door, "I think I feel an appetite coming on."

"Good," I said as I stirred the soup. "I intend to fatten you up."

Leslie slipped out of her coat and handed me a bottle of red wine. "Would you like some now, or now?" she asked.

"Now would be good, the corkscrew is in that drawer, you know, the messy one, next to the messy one."

"Got it," she said.

"Aunt Leslie!" Jamie and Tiger called in unison as they careened into the kitchen, Baxter galloping after them.

"How are my girls?" Leslie knelt down and hugged them, one in each arm.

Tiger wrapped herself around her neck and said, "Mm, you smell good."

Leslie smiled and gave her an extra squeeze, "And so does that bread! Do we have time to play before dinner, Mom?" she asked playfully as she stood between Jamie and Tiger, holding their hands.

"Please?" they whined in unison.

"All right," I said, feigning reluctance, "as long as you promise to come the first time I call you to dinner."

"Okay!" they called. They were already on the stairs.

I covered the table with a red-checked tablecloth and lit some candles. I dimmed the lights and smiled approvingly at the warmth generated by my favorite room. This should do the trick, I thought to myself. We were about to immerse Leslie in the warm and loving arms of our family and help to heal her depleted heart.

I added the pasta to the soup and poured the wine, reduced the heat on the burner and carried our wine up to Jamie's room.

They had dressed the American Girl dolls and Tiger's stuffed animals in matching outfits, each one expertly coordinated by Leslie. She was brushing one of the doll's hair and Jamie was admiring a French braid Leslie had completed on another doll. "Not to be a party pooper, but have you two done your homework?"

"Yup," they both said. "Now go away, Mommy," Tiger added.

73

"I'm going!" I handed Leslie her wine and she winked at me. She looked radiant nestled between Jamie and Tiger and I ached with the knowledge of how desperately she wanted children of her own.

I walked into Tiger's room, tripping over an elaborate Lego creation, in search of her backpack. Mary had instructed us at back-to-school night to let the children do their homework independently. But under the circumstances I thought it best to disregard Mary's advice and check Tiger's homework.

Her assignment had been to complete two workbook pages, which was the norm for Mary's class. Second grade was a colorless world consisting of number two pencils and workbooks in every subject. It amazed me that even science had been condensed into black and white words.

My heart sank when I looked at Tiger's strained efforts. The instructions were to write a sentence about her favorite food in the two lines allotted for the task. Despite the size of the wide-ruled lines, Tiger's writing covered the entire page. In an unsteady hand she had written: "i lk apls." Her "p" and "s" were backward, and her "l" extended the entire length of the page. I flipped through the previous pages only to find more of the same. "se wz a bk dawg," and "cts r saf." Her writing was barely legible and Mary had rewritten each sentence below Tiger's awkward ones: "She was a black dog" and "Cats are soft." And in a bold, red pen she had written Write five times before going out for recess. It was as if Mary's pen had bled all over the page.

I stared at the messy pages and grew weary with the realization that Tiger's problem was worse than I thought, that it was not only the result of an unimaginative classroom, and that she was being punished for it. School had never been easy for Tiger, but in the past when I saw her struggling I would arrange for more tutoring. How many hours of ineffectual tutoring had she agonized through? My hope that she was okay evaporated as I stared at her workbook. How long ago had Tiger lost hope? The bread maker beeped insistently and I slowly returned to the happy trio. "The bread is summoning us," I said softly. I thought it better that the bread be held responsible for stopping their game than me.

"Will we have time to play with Leslie after dinner, Mom?" Jamie asked hopefully.

"Only if you take a good bath, hair included."

"We will!" Tiger said jumping up and running out of the room. "Come on, Jamie, the sooner we eat, the sooner we can play!"

"Will you French braid my hair after my shower, Aunt Leslie?" Jamie asked.

"I would love to," she said enthusiastically. "You have great hair, girl!" Jamie beamed proudly.

"I wish they would warm up to you, Les," I said as I pulled her up off the floor.

"I know, they really hold back."

74

Max arrived home halfway through the movie. Leslie had selected the one most likely to elicit cathartic tears and a growing mound of wadded tissues lay on the coffee table before us. "Okay, chicks movie!" Max said as he leaned over us to turn on the light on the sofa table behind us. I had forewarned Max about Leslie's breakup, and appreciated the enthusiasm he put into his greeting.

Leslie and I squinted like moles at the sudden burst of light. "Go away!" we complained in unison.

"No way," he protested. I've got the two best looking women in town sitting right here on my sofa, and I'm not going anywhere." He sat between us and we reluctantly made room for him. "Any good male bashing tonight?" he asked.

"On the contrary, can't you see we're drooling here?" I said, pointing to Brad Pitt's image on the screen.

"I smell a double standard. If I confessed to drooling over an actress, you wouldn't sleep with me for a week!" Max said, rising to the occasion.

Leslie giggled. "Go pour yourself a glass of wine and stop yelling."

"I'll do that." He patted both our legs as he stood. When he returned he had taken off his coat and loosened his tie and wedged back down between us. "I like having you around, Les. I never had a sister," he said putting his arm around her. "How are you? Hanging in there? David is a fool for letting you go. And when you're ready to get back into the dating scene, we have a recently divorced, new recruit at the firm who is perfect for you."

"Speaking of double standards, Max, you forbade me to fix up our friends years ago. Now listen to you!" I protested.

"Totally different situation, you have no case, madam. You're not any good at it, anyway. Remember the Whitcombs? What a disaster! Where as I can spot a perfect match immediately. And I have, so, what do you say?" he said turning back to Leslie.

"I say, when? As long as he's really divorced. Katie tells me I need more intimacy," Leslie said, sipping her wine.

I watched them interact and noticed the change in Leslie now that Max was here. Although I knew my friendship was important to her, there was something about his attention that was stimulating her. Her cheeks were rosy and she fluttered her eyes demurely. And yet beneath her beautiful, glowing face there lurked a scared and vulnerable woman. I knew she believed she was incomplete without a man. And although I liked to believe I was more secure and independent, I suspected that was naive and most likely the result of our different situations.

I considered how my father's death had left me hungry for a relationship with a man. I studied Leslie, whose father was alive and well and still married to her kind, but passive, mother. She was clearly lost and confused without an intimate relationship. Her father, a reserved and dignified man, had expressed great dismay when his only child chose to study social work instead of following in his footsteps as a successful businessman. And he had grown increasingly distant after her marriage to the man of her father's dreams had failed. Now their relationship consisted of an occasional formal letter acknowledging an achievement or questioning a decision.

I knew in my heart that the presence of a father was not enough to determine well-being, but the quality of that relationship. How many of my peers had grown having perfunctory relationships with their fathers? It stands to reason that as long as men continue to play a secondary role in the nurturing of children, that we would continue to live in a unhealthy world of insecure men and vulnerable, dependent women. I thought about Jamie and Tiger...

"Earth to Katie!" Max bellowed.

I blinked and realized I had been staring at nothing. I leaned over Max to smile at Leslie. "He is yelling, isn't he!"

On Wednesday of the following week I was once again in a rose and teal green chair in Dr. Chartwell's office. I flipped through a magazine, grateful she had updated her selection, and glanced at my watch nervously. Max was already ten minutes late. I was willing to consider divorce if he missed this meeting.

"Good morning, Kate," Susan said tentatively. "Is your husband coming?"

"I certainly hope so. He is perpetually late, however, so we can either get started without him, or wait a little while longer. It's up to you."

"Why don't we wait. Then I'm not repeating myself. Would you like some coffee?"

"Love some!"

Susan went back into her office and I realized how curious I was to finally see her inner sanctum. I was peeking around the door when Max breezed into the room.

"Whoa, sorry I'm late!" he said breathlessly. "I just sprinted through the parking lot and almost got run over by a UPS truck!"

"If you had gotten here any later you would have been run over by a speeding van."

Max leaned over and kissed me on the cheek. "Nice to see you too, Katie."

Susan returned with a steaming mug of coffee that smelled of freshly ground beans. I took the oversized mug from her with both hands and she turned to Max, extending her hand. "Hello, I'm Doctor Susan Chartwell."

"Nice to meet you, Doctor Chartwell," Max said, shaking her hand vigorously. "I've heard a lot about you." Susan looked at me suspiciously. "From Tiger, that is," Max said quickly. "She thinks you're great."

I looked away sheepishly, picked up my coat and purse and said, "Shall we get

76

started?"

Susan looked at me as if I had spoken out of turn, and then back to Max. "Please, call me Susan, Mr. Cunningham."

"All right, Susan, I'm Max."

She offered him coffee but he refused, he was agitated enough, and bid us to follow her. Delicate games were scattered neatly around her office, a computer displaying a geometric screen saver sat on a petite desk with chairs on either side, and more expensive artwork covered the walls. I stopped to admire a framed picture of Susan with her husband and two grown children, a boy and a girl. Leslie teases that I can read more into a family portrait than she can learn after spending an hour with a family. I'm always the first to notice wedding bands, cheap shoes, or dirty fingernails. She said I would have been a great detective. Susan's children were attractive and sat comfortably between their parents, a sure sign of a child-focused family, I thought to myself.

Susan interrupted my analysis by directing us toward a pair of small love seats that were nestled in a corner of the room. "Please sit down and make your selves comfortable," she said. "I just need to gather a few things. Did you bring your copy of the testing results?"

"Yes," I said. "It didn't arrive until yesterday, however, did you get a chance to read it yet, Max?" I realized too late that my comment had come across as another criticism to Susan and she was already defending herself.

"I had to wait for my assistant to send out the copies. Sometimes that takes a little longer than it should. Have you read the report, Max?"

"I scanned it last night, but I'm looking forward to your clarification of a few things." The love seat was small and low to the ground and it made Max look oversized. He rested his large hands on his protruding knees. Susan appeared nervous around him and I was reminded what an intimidating man he was. It was never his intention, at least most of the time, but part of his presence. He was articulate and confident and strikingly handsome with his blue eyes and dark skin. He was wearing a tailored, chocolate brown suit with a starched, icy blue shirt that brought out the clear blue of his eyes. He caught me staring at him and put his arm around me affectionately.

"Of course, that's what we're here for." Susan sat in a small, swivel chair directly across from us and crossed her ankles daintily. "First I would like to go over the testing, the procedures I used, Tiger's reactions, that sort of thing. Then I'll discuss the findings with you, followed by my recommendations for intervention."

"That's easy, we'll fire her teacher," Max said.

"I'm afraid its a little more complicated than that," Susan replied flatly.

Susan described her methods in detail and Tiger's response to the two days of testing. I cringed when she alluded to Tiger's mental state after our disastrous lunch together. Susan suggested in her report that Tiger may be feeling her parents expect too much, and that it was affecting her self esteem. When she began describing her findings, Max requested clarification.

"The report states that Tiger is reading at below a first grade level. I've heard her read and I know it's not that bad."

"She may be able to read some things, but inconsistency is the only consistent thing with learning disabled children. When she was with me her reading was at a primer level." Max flinched at the term "learning disabled." "Tiger is unable to decode consonant sounds which is what put her below first grade. Although she was able to accurately decode some of the sounds some of the time, she consistently confused her 'B's' and 'D's,' and several other sounds as well. And she has very little, if any, phonological awareness when it comes to vowel sounds, short or long, which is a first grade skill. Tiger guesses at words and has more success when there are pictures to refer to. She has good comprehension and her guesses were more accurate when she knew the content of the story. But as you can see, when there were no pictures, she was unable to read an entire sentence without error, and these were very simple sentences. Shall we move on?"

When we came to the math section it was my turn to question her findings. "It says in your report that her math skills are at an early first grade level. Did Tiger use a number line when she was adding?"

"No," Susan replied. "I gave her a piece of paper and told her to use whatever method she needed to assist her in her calculations. She could have written a number line at the top of the page or made hash marks, but chose not to. In fact, she simply refused to complete most of the addition problems, stating she couldn't."

"But I know she can add with a number line. Doesn't that make this finding inaccurate?" I asked, trying desperately not to sound accusatory.

"I'm afraid not. She had the tools but was unable to complete the problems. That's significant and indicates a delay in her math skills as well. She was unable to count past twenty accurately, wrote twenty-seven for seventy-two and was unable to recognize the difference between the two numbers. She added when she should have subtracted. And, unfortunately, her disability exists in her encoding skills, meaning her writing ability, too. Tiger had difficulty writing the upper and lower case manuscript alphabet and struggled with re-visualizing the letters when they weren't in front of her."

"Jesus!" Max sighed. "Not to jump ahead, Susan, but do you think Tiger needs to go back to first grade? What are we talking about here?" Max asked.

"I'd rather not jump ahead, Max. I want to make certain you understand the problem before we discuss what can be done for Tiger."

"I understand the problem all right, Tiger's failing school. It sounds as if she never should have left kindergarten!"

"I'm sure this is hard for you to hear, but I don't think it would be helpful if I were to minimize the extent of her problem."

"Of course not, Susan," I jumped in, "that's the last thing we want you to do. This is all very new to us, we had no idea Tiger had learning disabilities."

Hearing me say it affected Max unexpectedly and his head dropped into his hands. Susan and I looked over at him. His back was quivering. He was crying. I couldn't remember the last time I'd seen him cry. Susan looked at me nervously. I put my arms around him. "It will be okay, Max. We'll help our Tiger." His body jerked with his sobs.

Max kept his head buried in his hands. "Katie, don't you hear what she's saying? Tiger can't read or write or add two numbers together! For Chrissakes, she can't even write the numbers! All this time I thought she was really okay, I didn't want to believe she had these problems." His voice cracked when he spoke, "What was I thinking? Why didn't I pay more attention?" he said, sniffing loudly. Susan and I sat silently, our eyes misting with tears of our own. "Poor, Tiger. Poor, poor, Tiger," Max moaned. He looked as if someone had folded him into a ball, with his knees practically touching his ears.

Unsure of what to do next, I asked Susan if she was ready to begin discussing her recommendations for Tiger.

"Of course," she said, clearing her throat. "As I said in my report, Tiger has dyslexia -- a reading disability; dysgraphia -- a writing disability; and discalcula -- a math disability."

"Jesus," Max moaned again.

I kept my arm tightly around him as Susan continued. "I think it's important at this point to remind you that Tiger's IQ scores were in the above average range, and are most likely even higher, because it's impossible to completely eliminate performance as a factor in these tests. In other words, Tiger's IQ is much higher than her performance, that's the definition of a learning disability. If she wasn't intelligent, then she would be a remedial student. It is the difference in these two scores, intelligence and performance, that is significant."

Max finally lifted his head and I was grateful for Susan's sense of timing, at last, we both needed to hear something positive. Max quickly took out his starched, monogrammed handkerchief and blew his nose. His handsome face was puffy and his eyes, red and swollen. "I apologize for my behavior," he said softly. "I just can't believe my baby girl has these problems." He started to tear up again as he spoke. "Susan," he pleaded, his voice cracking. "Are you going to be able to help her?"

"I will not personally be able to help Tiger, Max, but I can make recommendations."

"But what are we talking about here, will she ever learn to read? Will she ever be able to sit on her bed and read the Hardy Boys, or the, what's Jamie always reading, the Baby Sitters' Club?" Max asked.

"Hopefully. But with the extent of her disabilities, she may never enjoy reading as much as you would like. Reading for Tiger involves twice as many steps as it does for you or me. It is an enormous, laborious task and requires her brain to work in a way that is actually painful to her, at least until she can train it to operate in a different way. Is there any dyslexia in either of your families?" Here we go again, I thought. "Because these things do run in families."

"Nowhere, Susan," Max said adamantly. "Not my brothers or my parents. And Katie's got a bunch of eggheads in her family. All they do is read."

Susan looked puzzled. "Maybe you should ask your families. Maybe it's something that just never got talked about."

"It seems we're getting off the subject," I inserted. "Susan, tell us how to help Tiger. What happens next?" Max straightened, he was much more comfortable fixing a problem than becoming aware of one.

"Tiger needs to be taught in a VAKT approach," Susan began. "One that engages all of her senses -- visual, auditory, kinesthetic and tactile -- simultaneously. She should be in a small, structured classroom that can be altered to suit her learning style. And she will need a multi-sensory approach to teach her to read, write and spell, such as Orton-Gillingham."

"What is that, Susan?" I asked.

"Orton-Gillingham has been around for many years, but it is still the best method for teaching children with Tiger's profile to read. It's a systematic, sequential, multi-sensory, VAKT approach to reading. Any language arts program she uses must have all of these components. There are a lot of new methods out there, but most of them are missing at least one or more of these important components. They just aren't as good as a solid Orton program. What does the Chesapeake Day School use for language arts?"

Max looked at me, wondering if I knew. "Open Court," I said.

"Oh," Susan said uneasily.

"What?" Max asked. "What's with Open Court? No good, Susan?"

"Well, it's based on phonics which is better than 'whole word' for someone like Tiger. Is it the updated version, Kate?"

"I doubt it. They've been using it forever. I didn't know it had ever been revised."

"Are they still using those convoluted sound cards?" she asked.

"Yes."

"Oh. Well, it sounds as if you should either put Tiger in a school for children with learning disabilities, or get her classroom teacher to make some major changes

80

to accommodate her. There's a special school here in Baltimore, you might have a good chance of getting Tiger enrolled because she's a girl."

"Slow down, Susan," Max said. "We're not taking Tiger out of her school. Are we?" He looked at me with concern.

"This is all too new for me to even think about that. Who teaches Orton-Gillingham, Susan? Would there be a teacher at her school who might be trained in it?"

"Possibly, but I doubt it. But it would behoove you to get Tiger into a program immediately."

I was feeling completely enervated and Max looked as if he'd been crumpled into a ball like an overworked piece paper. Susan seemed to sense our states of mind and concluded the meeting. She rose to shake our hands. "Tiger has many strengths, don't forget that. There are some wonderful books written about dyslexia, and there are many famous and successful people who are dyslexic. You might want to do some reading."

"Yes, I'll stop at the book store on the way home. Thank you Susan, for everything. If we should need you to meet with Tiger's teachers, could you do that?"

"Yes. Just give me some notice. I charge eighty-five dollars per hour, plus travel time and expenses," she said.

"Right," I answered flatly. "Well, I think we'll probably be calling you for that soon. Have you ever diagnosed a child from Tiger's school?"

"No, I haven't. But good luck with Tiger. Please tell her hello for me." Susan waved good-bye and closed the door.

"Can we go to lunch or something?" Max asked. We were standing outside Susan's door. Although we both had jobs to return to, and Gary was docking my paycheck as we spoke, neither of us moved. We had a strong need to stay together.

"That would be wonderful," I said in a tired voice and put my arm through his.

"I just want to run to that school, scoop her up in my arms and hold her," Max said painfully as we walked slowly to his car. I was deeply touched by his reaction to Tiger's problem.

"You're a wonderful dad, you know that?"

"Oh no I'm not, Katie. A wonderful dad would not have let her suffer silently as long as she has. A wonderful dad would have been around to help her with her homework and notice that she didn't know the difference between twenty-seven and seventy-two. God, I'm no different from my father! I might as well have been living on Mars."

"Max, please don't blame yourself. It's no one's fault. I'm sitting here thinking it must have been that glass of wine I had on my birthday in my eighth month of pregnancy. It doesn't help to blame anyone, it is what it is."

81

"You forget, Katie, I'm a lawyer, there's always someone to blame." I was relieved to hear his humor returning.

"You're different from your father, Max Junior. Even if you do work hard. You spend time with them, quality time, if you'll pardon the phrase. You take them fishing and to baseball games. And more importantly, they trust you completely, with their problems, feelings, everything. Who do they call out for in the middle of the night?"

"That's only because you sleep so soundly they know it's fruitless to call you."

I chuckled. "Max, seriously, your daughters feel free to be themselves with you, and that's rare. How many people have grown up expected to be on their best behavior with their fathers? But not our children."

"I don't deserve you, Katie."

"Yes you do," I said softly. I hugged Max and nestled my face into the collar of his wool overcoat. We stood, motionless, holding each other, on that cool fall morning, not wanting to let go. Somehow we both knew that once we parted, returned to our cars and to our busy lives, Tiger's dyslexia would at last be real. No more hope that it was a misunderstanding. No more wishing that Susan's report would make it all go away. It was here to stay and our dreams about Tiger's future had been altered forever.

Lesson Five:
Advocacy

By definition, children are small,
unable to navigate this vast world on their own.
An effective parent
will often take the role of advocate,
molding a child's environment to be safe
and thereby more conducive
to growth, discovery and well-being.

Jamie entered the kitchen the next morning and was shocked to see her father sitting at the table reading the paper. "Is everything all right, Dad?" she asked.

"Is it that much of a surprise to see your father in the morning?"

"Well, yeah." She slipped into a chair next to him and fished for the comics in the newspaper. "Seriously, Dad, you didn't lose your job or anything, did you?" Jamie asked as she poured her cereal.

Max put the paper down. "So let me get this straight, I decide to go into the office a little later than usual in order to spend time with my wonderful family and you think I've lost my job."

"Sorry, Dad, but it is a little unusual. Mom is the one home in the morning."

Max was flustered. After yesterday's meeting with Susan, he had desperately needed to connect with Jamie and Tiger. "Well hold on to your cereal bowl, because I'm driving you to school this morning!"

"You are?" Jamie and I asked in unison. I put my coffee down on the counter and looked at him.

"Now put your bottom jaws back in place, ladies. I said, I'm driving my daughters to school this morning."

"Do you know the way?" Max was always quick to make a joke, but Jamie's last question had touched a nerve.

"Yes, I do! I happen to be on the board of trustees, and if you don't watch your mouth, I may recommend you be expelled."

Their eyes locked, but it was Max who broke the stare with a defeated smile.

83

"I'll probably have to face you in a courtroom some day and I have a sinking feeling I'll lose."

Jamie beamed. "Hey, Mom," she said. "Tiger's still asleep in my bed and Baxter's on top of her. She didn't move when the alarm went off."

"If you really want to feel a part of things, Max, waking Tiger up this morning would make you an honorary member of the morning dream team," I said.

"I'm on the job." Max hopped up and ran up the steps calling, "Where's that Tiger cub, I'm hungry for Tiger cubs!" The floorboards shuddered as he growled and stomped his way into Jamie's room.

By the time Tiger was dressed and eating her daily orange, Max was wearing his coat and pacing. He was edging into his work mode and growing impatient with the children's slower pace. "Eat up, Tiger, you don't want to be late," he said.

"School doesn't start for another fifteen minutes, Dad." Jamie said. She was also ready to go, but was accustomed to waiting for her sister.

"It doesn't hurt to be a little early, you know the saying, the early bird doesn't hit the traffic jams."

"That's not it, Dad," Tiger said while sucking on her last section of orange. "It's the early bird catches the worm. But that doesn't make sense either, because I always see robins eating worms in the afternoon, right out in the front yard, and they get a lot of them."

"I never thought about that before, Tig, but you're absolutely right." Max looked at me and smiled broadly. He was reassured to hear her insights and be reminded of her obvious intelligence. He tousled her hair affectionately.

"Way to go, Max," I said, coming around the edge of the counter with a brush. "Do you know what an effort it is to get this child to let me brush her hair every morning?" I brushed it quickly, happy that it was short. "While it's nice to have you here this morning, it isn't good to be disruptive."

"I'll show you disruptive." Max reached over, scooped me up in his arms and planted a warm, wet kiss on my mouth. I was startled and felt myself blush in front of the girls.

"Well, now you've disrupted my hair," I said as I tried to fluff it back into place.

"Geez, Dad!" Tiger giggled. They were tickled to see their parents openly displaying affection, and while Jamie smiled shyly, Tiger crawled down from her chair and wiggled her way in between us, wrapping herself around our legs.

"You better get going," I said as I released myself from their grips and smoothed my clothes. "By the way, Max, I'm going to call Frances Larson today in order to schedule that conference. I'd like to do it after school on Friday so I don't have to miss any more work. Can you make it then?"

"I hate to spoil this wonderful mood, but after this morning I'm out of

84

commission until the weekend. We have a preliminary hearing tomorrow with the Bay case, and I'll be preparing for it all week. Unfortunately it means a lot of late nights from here. I trust you to take handle the meeting, Katie, take notes, and we'll talk about it later."

"What are you meeting with Mrs. Larson about?" Jamie asked.

I had thought about how much we would tell the girls, and had decided it was best to be completely open with them. I had found a book at the bookstore yesterday written for children that explained dyslexia in simple terms and Tiger, Jamie and I had read it together. Jamie had asked a lot of questions and was interested in the details and causes of her sister's problem. Tiger had seemed relieved there was a name for what she had been desperately trying to hide all this time.

"We're going to meet with her in order to discuss Tiger's dyslexia and hopefully come up with some ways to help her in second grade. Apparently there are some simple things Mrs. Peterson can do that will help Tiger. Doctor Susan put a whole list of them in her report, it's really quite interesting. For instance, just circling the plus and minus signs in different colors will prevent her from confusing addition and subtraction."

"Cool," Jamie said.

"I wish I could take some bubble gum medicine for my dyslexia and it would just go away," Tiger said matter-of-factly.

Max and I looked at each other and tears welled in my eyes. I knelt down and hugged her. "I do too, sweetie, I do too."

Annie, Jessica's mother, had offered to take Jamie and Tiger home with her Friday afternoon so that I could attend the conference with Frances. Jamie and Jessica had been best friends since nursery school, and Jessica had a younger brother in first grade who played well with Tiger. Annie had predicted that Tiger and Ben would be occupied for hours on her large, unkempt property and reassured me to take my time. When I arrived at Frances' office, I was surprised to find not only Frances, but Mary Peterson and Joan Pierce, the head of the lower school.

"Hello, Kate, please come in," Frances said, greeting me at the door.

"Hello," I said. I was unnerved by the crowd in the room and tried desperately to conceal it. I wanted to be strong and rational and avoid a repeat performance of my meltdown with Mary. "Hello, Mary, Joan." I nodded at them each. Mary and Joan smiled stiffly. I stepped into the room and was frustrated to see the only vacant seat was a stuffed chair that sat lower than the wooden chairs in which everyone else was seated. I was already outnumbered, so I walked over to Frances' desk and brought her chair to the circle of educators. Family therapy had taught me about the importance of power and the positioning of the chairs in a room. "I think I'll be more comfortable in this chair, Frances, if you don't mind." I placed it nearest to Frances. She was the one with the power and the one with whom I would need to negotiate.

"Why don't we get started," Frances said briskly. She placed her glasses on her nose and looked down at the papers resting in her lap. "I received Trisha's testing and have distributed copies to everyone here. I also went over it with Will Glazer. You know Will, Katie, the psychologist? His children are in first and fourth grade. Has everyone read it?" Frances asked, looking around the room.

I knew Will, all right, and found him to be pompous and competitive, bordering on unethical. "Frances," I interrupted. I now knew what Susan had meant about confidentiality. "You need our permission to show the report to anyone, especially someone not employed by this school."

"Now, Kate," Frances said, "There's nothing to worry about, you know everyone here and I think Will's opinion is important. I can assure the contents of the report won't leave this room."

It was dawning on me how little this school used protocol. I had always enjoyed the laid-back atmosphere, the accessibility of the faculty and staff and their friendly manner. I now realized how it could work against me. This was a time for policies and procedures, not the discretion of Frances Larson.

"It says in the report that Trisha is dyslexic, Kate, as you well know. It looks as if Mary's suspicions were right. Doctor Chartwell has recommended she receive Orton-Gillingham instruction and I want you to know from the start that the Chesapeake Day School doesn't use that language arts curriculum, nor is anyone trained in teaching it."

How Frances had managed to define Tiger's diagnosis as Mary "being right" was the least of my problems. Something was wrong and I panicked that the results of this meeting had already been decided. "I'm aware of that, Frances, but..."

"If you follow the recommendations of this report," Frances interrupted, "then the only conclusion is that Trisha doesn't belong in this school."

Despite my preparation for the worst, her words took my breath away. It had only been three weeks and they were already kicking Tiger out of school. "What are you saying, Frances? Are you expelling Tiger?"

"I'm saying perhaps this school isn't right for Trisha anymore. I only want what's best for her."

"It sounds to me as if you want what's easiest for the Chesapeake Day School."

"There is nothing easy about this, but the bottom line is Trisha has a learning disability that we're not equipped to handle," Frances replied confidently. She was tough and undaunted by my accusations.

"How can you say that when you haven't even tried? You decided the outcome

86

of this meeting before I walked in the door!"

"Please, Kate, I don't think there are any other reasonable options."

"Actually, I see two choices, Frances," I began to feel the adrenaline giving me the strength and clarity I needed. "Either you allow Trisha to remain here with supportive Orton-Gillingham tutoring which we will pay for or you refund our money for the entire year and we withdraw her from the school."

"We can't give you a refund, you signed a contract."

"It seems to me, Frances, that the contract goes two ways, the Chesapeake Day School agreed to provide an adequate education for my daughter."

"Kate, Will was very clear that keeping Trisha in this school with the extent of her disability wasn't a good idea. He said she needs total immersion in special education."

"Will is not an educational psychologist and therefore not qualified to make such a recommendation. Besides, he doesn't even know Tiger, so can we please leave him out of this. Besides, Tiger isn't going anywhere, she is a part of this school. I suggest we keep her in second grade and I will find supportive Orton-Gillingham tutoring for her. It may require her missing some school, but that seems appropriate under these circumstances. Once the tutoring takes hold, Tiger will be able to catch up to the other students and remain a part of the class, her class."

Frances' brow wrinkled in puzzlement as to how the meeting had taken a different course. "I'll need to think about that."

"I don't think keeping Trisha in second grade is best for her," Mary said sounding annoyed that Frances might be changing her mind.

"No, you've made that very clear, Mary." I said stiffly. "Homogeneous classrooms must be a teacher's dream, but even this school has to realize that children learn differently."

"Learning differently and learning disabilities are two different things," Frances interjected.

"Really? You might want to check that, Frances. But just because Tiger has a label, it doesn't mean she's unable to learn, or even flourish at this school. All I ask is that you make a few adjustments, as you would for any child who needed them. For example, what if one of the students had a broken arm? I'm sure you would all be willing to go out of your way in order to help that child carry books, eat lunch, even excuse the child from gym class and for doctor's appointments. Tiger won't require more than that." I was thinking on my feet and I was terrified I would negotiate the wrong terms for Tiger. How could I have agreed to attend this meeting without Max or Susan Chartwell?

"Doctor Chartwell suggested Trisha use a tape recorder, that I copy her homework assignments down for her, that I put fewer math problems on a page, that I don't give her timed tests, and more!" Mary said. "These things take a

87

tremendous amount of time. There is only one of me and twenty children, all with needs. If I make these accommodations for Tiger, it isn't fair to the other children. Soon they will all be asking to not take timed tests, or to have fewer spelling words. They'll see that Trisha is getting special favors."

I was amazed at their unwillingness to help Tiger. They didn't want to have to change anything. Tiger leaving the school was the easiest solution for them, but I wasn't ready to let that happen. This was a school, Tiger's school.

"I would hate to see Trisha leave, Kate, but Mary makes a good point. If we start making accommodations for Trisha, other parents will be expecting the same, and the next thing you know, the parents are running the school, not the qualified staff," Frances said, apparently trying to appeal to my sensibilities. But her logic was misguided. If they were qualified, then teaching Tiger wouldn't be a problem.

"Okay, I understand that modifying the classroom is too much to ask of you, so here's my proposal, and I think it's a good one: If you are willing to make a few minor adjustments, such as putting Tiger in the front of the classroom, not asking her to read in front of her peers, and allowing her to leave the classroom for, say, five minutes if she's feeling overwhelmed, then I will take responsibility for the Orton-Gillingham tutoring and find someone who can work with her a few hours a week. Give it three months and we'll meet again and evaluate whether or not it's working, for everyone. What do you say? Don't forget, Tiger is a very intelligent child, she is an asset to this school when it comes to her creativity and knack for science."

Frances looked thoughtful. Joan, the head of the lower school and third grade teacher, looked between us nervously. "I don't know, Frances, I think we should think about setting a precedent for other families. And I've seen Tiger's marks, she's not doing so well in science. If she stays at all, she should repeat first grade."

"First grade is full, Joan, so that's not an option. And although I agree with you, there are other considerations. Our numbers are good, but we don't want to start asking families to leave too quickly. As long as Kate is willing to evaluate this plan in three months, and, I must add, Kate, that you accept our recommendations if we feel Trisha doesn't belong here, then I agree to your proposal."

Of course the way to appeal to Frances was through her business sense. She may have outdated ideas about education, but she had managed to keep this school afloat in lean times, it was one of her strengths, something Max admired in her. "Thank you, and I do agree to accept your recommendations. But let's agree to have this meeting at the end of the semester. That way, if you decide to kick Tiger out, we will be able to enroll her somewhere else without as much disruption. And if that occurs, we won't pay for the second half of the school year. Not a penny."

"That will be left up to the board and the school's attorney, but let's not get into that now. I think we have a plan in place. Do you agree to Kate's requests,

Mary, about modifications for Trisha?"

"Just where would you like her to be able to go if she's feeling overwhelmed? I have concerns about her leaving the classroom whenever she pleases," Mary said.

"The only reason I asked for that, Mary, is in order to address what you seem to think is a behavior problem. I think Tiger is standing in the coat room because she is worried about something, for instance, reading aloud to her friends in reading partners. She's not trying to defy you, she's just ashamed she isn't reading. All I ask is that you don't publicly humiliate her. She'll be reading soon, once I can find a qualified tutor." I wanted to say more, such as my amazement at Mary's narrow-minded view of things, her lack of compassion for Tiger, and how she seemed to feel threatened by her dyslexia.

"I think that sounds reasonable, Mary," Frances said, "at least until the end of the semester."

"And how do I explain this to the other children? They're going to want to know why Trisha can leave the classroom whenever she wants."

"Maybe you could say she has to go to the restroom," Frances said, trying to be helpful.

"Maybe we should tell the class that Tiger is dyslexic!" I was getting angry again. "This is not leprosy, or something to hide. It's a learning difference. Nothing more. And if you would like me to tell the children, Mary, I would be happy to. Children can handle differences, in fact, they will most likely, if properly encouraged, be very supportive of Tiger. They do quite well when they understand things. And you never know, perhaps some of the adjustments you make for Tiger will benefit the other children as well."

"I'll tell them, in my own way." Mary looked at me with loathing, and as much as the thought of her explaining Tiger's problems to the class concerned me, I realized I needed to show a willingness to compromise.

"I would like you to put this in writing, Frances," I added.

"Why, there's no need for that."

"I would feel much better. I'll expect it in a few days. Thank you for your time. I'll tell Tiger you will be informing the class about her dyslexia," I said to Mary. "And I will expect the other modifications to be in place on Monday. I will let you know when I have found a tutor. Good afternoon." I stood and walked quickly out of the room.

Frances, surprised by my abrupt departure, called, "Good-bye, Katie, have a good weekend."

"How was your meeting?" Annie asked as she opened her kitchen door to me. "How was 'Queen Frances?'"

I smiled at Annie's terminology. "Quite regal, I assure you. How are the kids? I can't tell you how much I appreciate you bringing them home."

"Oh, they've been quite a problem," Annie said sarcastically. "I haven't seen Jamie and Jessica since we got home. They've been up in Jessica's room whispering deep, dark secrets to one another. And having Tiger here is wonderful! Ben loves her, and she keeps him completely entertained. They've been setting up a bug zoo in the garage. Most of them are dead, I think they got them from the window sills, but they've caught a few live ones, too. It's quite a lovely assortment. Why don't you come in for a while? We could even have a beer, after all, it's Friday."

"Actually, that sounds wonderful, I'm still a little tense." I said coming up the steps to her kitchen. I took a deep breath, allowing Annie's warmth to penetrate my weariness.

Annie and her family lived in an old farm house on a sizable piece of property for this urban area. The kitchen was large, with tall, paint-chipped cabinets and an old black and white tile floor. Drying herbs hung from a rack and a long, antique table stood at one end of the room with mismatched, antique chairs surrounding it. It was a house with a lot of potential. Annie had obvious taste, but lacked either the time or energy to pull it all together. She removed a stack of papers from the table and motioned me to sit down. "It's five fifteen, happy hour!" she said cheerfully. "Besides, Ben's in New York on business and won't get in until late tonight. And I don't even have to ask about Max, when do you expect him tonight, ten, maybe eleven o'clock?"

"You're right, you don't have to ask. Are you sure I'm not intruding?"

"Not at all. Please, rest your weary bones." Annie took two Amstel Lights from her refrigerator. "Sit, sit! We haven't talked in ages."

Although Annie and I were very different, she was a staunch conservative and kept her children well regimented in lessons and sports activities every night of the week, we had always found common ground in which to build a friendship. The most important being our daughters' friendship, which was good and healthy and worthy of our support. But we also worked full time, unlike a lot of the mothers who sent their children to the Chesapeake Day School, and we could talk for hours about the stresses of working and raising a family.

"How are you, Annie? How's the consulting business?" I asked, enjoying my first sip from the frosty bottle.

"Unbelievably busy, which I guess is a good thing, but I feel like I'm losing my mind! I usually try to take Friday's off so I can be out at the school or get things done around here, but I had to work most of the day just returning phone calls. And as you can see by the looks of my house, I didn't get a damn thing done around here."

"It looks better than my place."

"I doubt that, but the good news is we really don't care. So, tell me about your meeting. What's going on with Tiger?"

"I told you we had her tested, didn't I? Well, she's dyslexic. That's why she's been so slow to read." I wondered if Annie noticed the quiver in my voice. It felt unsafe to disclose Tiger's new label, almost like a betrayal. I worried that people would begin to treat her differently once they learned of her diagnosis.

"Wow," Annie said seriously. "So what does that mean? Does she read backwards or something? Isn't dyslexia where you reverse your letters?"

"That's certainly a symptom, but dyslexia, from what I understand, means the whole brain works differently than non-dyslexics. Her brain confuses the messages it receives when she's reading, or, in Tiger's case, any other activity, such as writing or calculations. I think. It's all new to me. I've been reading as much as I can about it." I took another long sip.

"So what did Frances say?" she asked with genuine interest that I appreciated.

"Well, at first they wanted to kick her out of school. Can you believe it? Mary Peterson has no interest in having her for a student, but Frances agreed to try it for a few months if I can get some outside tutoring for her. Needless to say, Mary was furious when Frances changed her mind."

"That sounds like our Mary. But she really isn't qualified to teach special education. I guess we can't expect that from the teachers. I know I wanted Ben, Junior to get some extra attention in math. He's miles ahead of the other children, and I just don't think he's getting challenged enough. But when I asked the school to accommodate his giftedness, they said they're doing everything they can. And as much as I wish they could do more, there is only so much that can be done with one teacher and twenty students. They really can't tailor their teaching to each child, there just isn't time, and it takes away from the other students."

My heart sank as I listened to Annie. Somehow helping Tiger was threatening to everyone. And how could Annie talk about her supposedly gifted son when I'd just confessed my daughter has a learning disability? And yet, three weeks ago, I probably would have responded as Annie had. Learning problems happened in other families, not mine. Children with special needs took time and attention away from the other children.

"So, what do you think will happen? Can Tiger get what she needs there? Have you thought about taking her out? I've heard there are some excellent schools for the learning disabled in Baltimore." Annie asked, sipping her beer and munching on a chip from the basket she had placed on the table. She was oblivious to how her words affected me.

I wanted to run away. The effects of the meeting and Annie's lack of empathy were draining what little energy I had left. Why was Tiger leaving the school the

91

only answer? It was as if no one wanted to have to think about her dyslexia, they just wanted her to go away so life could go on as before. "I want Tiger to be okay," I said quietly. "But I want her to be able to stay at school, her school, I don't think that's too much to ask. Besides, separate but equal has never worked very well in this country."

Annie's silence indicated to me that she disagreed.

"Hey, Annie, thanks for the beer, but I really should be getting the kids out of here, we've imposed on your good hospitality enough for one day." I called to Jamie and Tiger and began to gather up their backpacks.

"Mom," Jessica had come into the room, "Can Jamie sleep over?"

"It's okay this time, Jessica, but remember what I told you about asking in front of your friends?" Annie said sternly. "Sometimes I need to say no and that is very uncomfortable when your friend is here to listen."

"Actually, isn't it our turn? Jessica is welcome to come to our house," I said quickly, uncomfortable with the tone she was using with Jessica.

"Really?" Jamie asked excitedly. "Do you want to, Jessica?"

"Yes! Duh!" They both laughed.

"Great, grab your stuff," I said, "I'll retrieve Tiger from the zoo."

I concentrated harder than usual as I drove home. The beer had gone to my head and I realized I hadn't eaten since breakfast. I regretted drinking it, and couldn't wait to get home to a pot of coffee and my leggings.

"Hey, Tiger," Jessica said. She was always kind to Tiger and included her in her play with Jamie. "Why didn't you go to Kristin's, today? Isn't she having a slumber party?"

"I wasn't invited," Tiger answered softly. My ears perked at this, although Tiger and Kristin weren't best friends, they were certainly friendly and had been in the same class since preschool. She had always gone to Kristin's parties in the past.

"That was rude!" Jamie said, protecting her sister. "Since when did Kristin stop inviting you to her parties?"

"I don't know. She doesn't really play with me anymore. She's been playing with Julie and Sally, they're in the same reading group, and they're really smart. They read American Girl books on the playground and bring their dolls to school. I was going to bring my doll one day, but I don't think they want me to play with them."

"Well, you can play with us, right, Jamie!" Jessica said, sitting up in her seat and putting her arm around Tiger. Jessica's mother could learn a few things from her daughter, I thought to myself.

"Right, Jessica!" Jamie put her arm around Tiger's other shoulder.

Tiger smiled halfheartedly. Although I knew she appreciated her sister's support, I could see she had been deeply hurt by Kristin's exclusion of her.

I wanted to call Kristin's mother and yell "how dare you leave out some of the girls in that small class."

I wanted to be on that playground every day and talk to Tiger, play with her, show the other kids how wonderful and interesting she is!

I wanted things to be easier for her.

I wanted her to fit in.

I wanted her to be normal.

I wanted desperately for it to all go away.

Leslie and I were standing at the reception desk eating M&M's and admiring pictures of Betty's new granddaughter, when the Colonel approached us. "I know I'm early, Mrs. Cunningham, but I wonder if I could have a word with you?"

Leslie looked up with interest. "Of course, Colonel Boles," I said. "Is everything all right?"

"Not really, could we talk privately?" he asked, looking nervously at Betty and Leslie.

"Let's go up to my office," I said and smiled at him.

The Colonel began talking before the elevator doors closed. "I'm sorry to bother you before my allotted time, but my wife, I mean my ex-wife, has really stirred things up."

I pushed the button for the second floor and looked at him with concern. "What's happened?"

"She wants him out of treatment and in Wisconsin with her. Her lawyer has already contacted my lawyer, and I believe he's spoken with the hospital as well."

"What does Danny say about all this? I thought he was beginning to like it here, well, maybe not like it, but he's been working his program."

"I know, I thought so too. But he was awfully distant yesterday afternoon when I visited. He was so uncommunicative I left before family visitation was over. He's been talking to his mother several times a day and I think it's getting to him. For all I know it may already be too late."

The elevator doors opened and we stepped into the hallway of the unit. I could see Dolores by the nurse's station. She was measuring out medications into little plastic cups and looked up when we stepped onto the unit. A smile of recognition spread over her face when she saw the Colonel with me. I let him into my office and opened the blinds. My message light was blinking rapidly, but I decided it could wait. "Just let me check in with the staff, Colonel Boles, I'll be right back." I closed the door behind me.

93

"How much can you tell me in three minutes?" I said to Dolores as I put my arm through hers and pulled her gently into the chart room. Rob was seated at the table, a cup of coffee steaming in front of him. He was reading a chart, catching up on the weekend's events. "Hey, Rob," I said warmly.

He looked up and smiled. "Good morning, Katie."

"Wow, you smell great this morning, doesn't he Dolores?"

"You can say that again! I keep coming back in here just to get a whiff of Rob," Dolores replied. "What a pleasant way to start a Monday."

"Can either of you tell me anything about Danny's weekend?" I asked as I poured a cup of coffee. I sat down across from Rob. "I know you just got here, too, but the Colonel is already in my office and I hear Danny's had a busy weekend."

"Sure, Katie," Dolores said. She was walking around the room but sat down temporarily in order to tell me what I needed to know. "I heard a lot during shift change. Apparently Danny's mom has been calling him all weekend. She's been messing with his mind, telling him things like she can't live without him, he belongs with her, and how much his two younger brothers miss and need him, you know the drill. Unfortunately, it seems to be working. She's gotten him pretty upset."

I sat back in my chair and pushed my hands through my hair. "This isn't good. How do you deal with such a powerful force when it's hundreds of miles away?"

"There's nothing like a mom, good or bad, and this one has Danny in her clutches," Dolores added.

"You can say that again," I agreed. "But we've still got a dad in our clutches. I'm not ready to give up yet."

Rob leaned back, putting his hands behind his head and smiled. "Let's hear it, Katie. What's your plan?"

"I'm not sure yet," I said. "Don't rush me!" Rob laughed. "Okay, here goes. Danny has four weeks into his program, right? And I think he's doing pretty well, don't you? I mean, he seems to be looking at his first step fairly honestly."

"As good as any sixteen year old can in four weeks," Rob said. "He's admitting he's powerless over alcohol. He was working well in group until this weekend, but Rick wrote in his chart that he was back into his denial, stopped sharing, that sort of crap."

"Something is going on with Mom. At first she sounded relieved to not have to deal with any of this and that the Colonel finally had to step up to the plate and be a parent. But what's changed?" I sipped my coffee and thought hard about Danny. We balanced each other beautifully, and I knew between the three of us we would be able to come up with a plan for Danny.

"Okay," I said, sitting forward in my chair. "Number one, we suspect the Colonel may have a drinking problem, although neither Danny, nor the Colonel, has admitted it. Two, Danny's working the program and building up a support group in AA. Three, the Colonel is actually stepping in as a father and opening up emotionally, making himself available to Danny for the first time in his life, and, Danny responds to this. And now, number four, Mom starts to sabotage everything. What happened? Was she somehow hoping the Colonel would blow it? Is she threatened by their closeness? And why is she denying Danny's alcoholism? Same reasons, I guess. What do you think?"

"I think you're right on target as usual, Katie," Rob said grinning. "Danny is caught smack dab in the middle between his parents and that's a bad place to be if you're trying to get sober. He needs to be worrying about his drinking, not his messed up parents."

"I agree. Okay, I know what to do." I stood and headed for the door.

Dolores looked up at me, puzzled. "Did I miss something? What did we decide?"

"I'm not really sure, but I have some direction. We'll have more to go on after I've met with Danny and his dad. Let me see what I can do. Thank's for dropping everything to talk with me."

Dolores shook her head. "You two move too fast for me."

Rob winked at me as I pushed the door open, "Go get 'em, Katie."

As I walk toward my office I thought about Rob. I was confused by the warmth that spread through my body every time I was in his vicinity. Although I knew we had a good friendship that I trusted -- we worked beautifully together and shared a genuine compassion for the people we helped -- I wondered if there was a part of me that was enjoying his company a little too much. It was crossing a boundary and my life was already complicated enough. And yet, with everything else that was wrong, I wasn't about to give up something that made me feel this good.

"Okay, Colonel Boles," I said walking into my office, "we have a lot to cover. I'd like to talk with you briefly before Danny joins us." I put my papers down on my desk and walked over to sit down across from the Colonel. He was standing, waiting for me to sit down.

"Please, sit down, sir."

"After you, Mrs. Cunningham."

"Right," I smiled. "Okay, I would like you to tell me as honestly as you can what you want to have happen. Something tells me your ex-wife's sudden interest in having Danny back has made you realize how much you don't want that to happen."

"Yes. I believe it has. At first I thought she must know what's best for him, but now I'm not so sure I trust her motivations. I think this is more about getting back at me, than it is about helping Daniel. She's the one who thought he had a drinking problem in the first place and now she says he's fine?"

"Colonel Boles, why is your wife so angry with you? Why do you think she's trying to sabotage your relationship with Danny?"

The Colonel held my gaze as he was weighed his words. "You ask good questions, Mrs. Cunningham." He looked down at his hands and nervously twisted his starched hat. "I've learned something about myself in these meetings." He paused and I let the silence work its magic. "You see, Mrs. Cunningham," the Colonel looked up, misery lined his face, "I've done some drinking myself. I don't know that I'm an alcoholic, but, well, I have a problem." Wow, I thought to myself. I didn't even have to ask. "My wife used to complain about my drinking. In fact, that's one of the reasons she left. Of course she'd been having an affair for years, but she said my drinking was the reason. Not that I blame her. I know it was hard on her, always moving, my being gone for months at a time. You see, she's a shy woman, and small, like Daniel. She raised the children on her own, without much help from me. When I got the Pentagon job I think she thought everything would finally be okay. But the stress was hard on me and I would come home in the evening and start drinking, and I didn't stop until I fell asleep in the Lazy Boy. I might as well have been in Saudi Arabia. I wasn't a mean drunk, not like my father. I never raised my voice to her or the boys. I just wasn't worth much after my third or fourth scotch. And I think she blames me for Daniel's drinking. I guess I blame me, too."

"Let me stop you right there. Danny is responsible for his drinking and only Danny. He doesn't need anyone to blame."

"But my wife is right, Daniel needed a father, not a drunk in a chair."

"I agree, and I appreciate your honesty. It must be very hard to admit this to me."

"Maybe she's right, maybe I don't deserve to have Daniel with me."

"Colonel Boles, I can help you with your son, but not if you're going to stop paddling mid-stream. Danny needs you to fight for him, not give up. He may have needed a dad before, but he needs one now, too, and for once he actually has one. Doesn't he?"

The Colonel looked at me steadily. "Yes, ma am."

When Danny joined us the change in his appearance was startling. By Friday he had begun to look healthier. He had put on weight and his color had returned. But this morning he was pale and hunched over. He avoided his father's gaze and agony spread over the Colonel's face as he measured the change in his son.

"Hello, Daniel," he said stiffly.

Danny didn't respond.

"Good morning..." I said, leaning forward in an attempt to meet his eyes. "Are you going to look at me, Danny, or am I going to have to fall on the floor?" I asked, sitting on the edge of my chair. Danny chuckled and glanced up at me briefly.

96

"Good morning," he said quietly.

"Thank you," I said as I leaned back into my chair and crossed my legs. "Why does everything happen around here on the weekends? I hear from Dolores that you've had a busy one, Danny. And your dad tells me your mom has been calling you, too. It sounds as if she misses you." Danny remained silent, but he was listening intently.

"Am I correct in assuming she wants you to move to Wisconsin?"

"I guess," Danny said, continuing to look at the floor.

The Colonel shifted in his seat but I looked at him purposely, conveying with my eyes that he should remain quiet and let me do the talking.

"It sounds as if you're not sure what she wants."

Danny lifted his head. "No, I know. She wants me with her. She really misses me. I never should have stayed here. She's not doing so well."

"She really depends on you, doesn't she, Danny?"

"What's wrong with that? At least I was there for her!" He looked accusingly at his father.

"You're right, son. You were there for her, not me," the Colonel said in defeat. Danny looked away in disgust.

"It must be hard for you to be so far away, Danny. But don't you think she understands you have things to accomplish here in Maryland? She misses you terribly, but she's a grown up. Can you trust that she'll be all right if you do what you have to do here?"

Danny seemed to know what I was speaking to, his worries and fears about his mom's well being. He had always been the one she turned to and he felt a responsibility to her. But now she was using that closeness to punish his father.

"I don't know. She says I don't need to be in here. She thinks if I just get away from my friends, and, well, my dad, that I'll be fine."

"And what do you think, Danny? Is that all you need or do you have an alcohol problem?" I asked him gently.

Danny hesitated, but the four weeks had taken hold. "I have a problem. All I can think about right now is how much I want a drink."

The Colonel winced at his words, but eventually collected himself. "I know that feeling, son."

Danny looked at his dad warily. "What are you talking about?"

"I mean that I also have a problem with alcohol." The Colonel took a deep breath and exhaled slowly. "I don't know that I'm an alcoholic, but I know I use alcohol to numb everything and keep people away. I've learned that here, in all these groups and meetings. I don't intend to start going to AA or anything, but I have decided that if you come home to my house, I won't drink. In fact, I haven't had a drink in two weeks."

Danny continued to look at his dad.

"Can I clarify something, Colonel Boles? Do you mean you won't drink if Danny returns home, but you will if he doesn't?"

"Oh no, Mrs. Cunningham. I won't be doing any drinking no matter what Daniel chooses. I'm sorry if that wasn't clear. This is about me. I just thought Daniel should know."

"Good. Because Danny might be feeling he has to choose between his parents right now, and that no matter what he decides, he'll be letting one of you down. If he lives with his mom, you'll be lonely and may start drinking again. But if he stays with you, his mom will feel hurt and abandoned. And since Danny's loyalties have always been with his mom, I think he must be feeling very conflicted."

Danny's face softened with relief as I put into words the agonizing feelings that had been torturing him for so long.

"Daniel needs to do what's best for Daniel," the Colonel said with confidence. "And I think that means whatever will keep him sober."

I wanted to cheer at his words -- he was getting it. "Would it help if I called your mom, Danny? I could help her find some support in Wisconsin so you wouldn't worry as much and be free to continue your program?"

"What kind of help? Because, well, she really needs it." Danny was quiet for a few minutes. "Promise me you won't do anything, Dad?"

"What, Daniel? What are you saying?"

"Well, I guess Stuart, that's my step-dad," he said to me, "he's drinking, a lot. Mom's pretty upset, that's why she keeps calling me."

"Oh," the Colonel said grimly. "Are your brothers okay?"

"Wait, if I could stop that line of questioning. I understand your concern, Colonel Boles, I really do, but let's try to get Danny out of the middle. I would like you to talk to Danny's mother about your sons, not through Danny."

"Right, of course, Mrs. Cunningham. It's just going to take some practice to do it that way."

"Danny will need your help with that. He needs to trust it's okay to tell his parents to talk to each other, not through him. And he'll need your support right now so he can continue to work his program without worrying about his mother. Once he has your help, he'll be able to be his own advocate, to tell you both when you're putting him in the middle. That will free him up to be his own person, and to love you both, without feeling disloyal."

Danny's face had transformed. His face was flushed and the deep lines were fading. He'd been given a glimpse of freedom from the burden he'd been carrying for years, a responsibility he was powerless to control -- his mother's happiness.

"I'll call your mother this morning, Danny. I'll help you with this too. It sounds as if she could use an adult to talk to."

Danny was watching his father intently. "Are you serious about not drinking, Dad?" he asked.

"Yes. In fact, the surprising part is I've never felt better. I committed to this and I'm committed to you, son. I don't want to blow it again."

I watched Danny's face closely and could see he was probably going to risk trusting his dad. I made a mental note to talk with Rob about helping Danny let go of his role with his parents and to learn to be a kid again in his counseling with him.

We stood simultaneously and an awkwardness hung in the air. I caught the Colonel's eye and nodded toward Danny. "Daniel," he said, nervously. "I love you." He walked toward his son cautiously and embraced him.

"I love you too, Dad," Danny said, his head buried in his shoulder. I shivered from the emotion in his voice. Twenty years in this business and I was still greatly moved by the change I was privileged to witness in families.

By noon Danny was back on track. He was sharing in group and laughing in the lounge with the other patients. I had talked at length with his mother, and although she was in denial about her role in the situation, she appreciated being listened to. I gave her a list of licensed social workers in her area, and gently suggested she attend an Al-Anon meeting in order to help Danny. I was careful not to break Danny's confidentiality by mentioning Stuart's drinking, but I knew a good Al-Anon group could do wonders for her self-esteem and powerlessness.

I was sitting in the staff room writing notes in the charts from my most recent meetings when I noticed Dolores at the nurse's station with a small girl of around fifteen, dressed in platform shoes, black fish-net stocking that were torn in several places, a tight satin mini skirt, a strapless halter top and a worn, leather jacket that looked as if it belonged to someone much larger. Her face was caked with aged makeup and her vacant, brown eyes were smeared with dark blue eye shadow and heavy black eye liner. She was a new intake, right off the streets, and Dolores was concentrating on her stethoscope as she pumped the band around her arm.

Rob sat down and began to watch Dolores along with me. "I see we have a new recruit," he said eventually.

We continued to watch her through the glass dividing the two rooms, years of experience enabling us to draw conclusions of what lay ahead in the next six weeks we would spend with her. "God, she's still a baby," I said quietly. "Do you know her story?"

"A little. Admissions called before they brought her up. Apparently she's a runaway and the judge said she could either come here or spend some quality time in 'Juvie.' Needless to say she's not one of our more 'motivated' clients," Rob said dryly. "You should have some fun with her parents, though, Katie. They're rich as

99

hell, part of the Baltimore elite, and are quite dismayed their only daughter has been using drugs and God knows what else on the streets of that fair city for the past three weeks."

"Dismayed?"

"Hard to believe when you look at her. What the hell did they think she was doing? She's on her way down now, though. Look at her, she's getting the shakes. She must have been on some hard shit. I sure hope one of the docs is on the way because she's starting to deteriorate."

Dolores leaned toward her, talking softly, her instinctive maternal affection working its magic. A lonely tear trickled down the girl's smeared face and Dolores enfolded her in her tender arms. Her sad face rested on Dolores' shoulder and despite her seductive clothing, her large, dark eyes revealed her youthful vulnerability. "It still gets to me, Rob. She's not much older than Jamie. What did her parents miss?" I said looking at him.

He smiled sympathetically. "I don't know, but I trust you to find out."

I laughed, appreciating the lighter conversation. "Have you had lunch? I just noticed I'm starving. Care to join me for some cafeteria gourmet?"

"Sounds lovely, my dear."

As Rob and I stood and began to clean up the clutter on the conference table, the phone rang at the nurse's station. I pushed through the glass door and said, "I'll get it, Dolores, you keep doing what you're doing." Dolores nodded. "Hello, CDU, nurse's station--"

"Mommy?" a soft voice said warily.

"Tiger? Is that you?" Rob walked over to me quickly. "What is it, sweetie? Are you crying? Where are you?" I asked urgently.

"I want to come home," she squeaked.

"Are you sick? Honey, please, where you are?"

"I'm at school, in the office. I'm not really sick, but -- please come and get me, Mommy."

"I'll be right there. Don't move!" I slammed down the phone. "I've got to go to her." Rob and Dolores were staring at me with concern.

"Katie, was that Tiger?" Rob asked.

"Yes, she wants me to come and get her. Shit! I've got two sessions this afternoon, and group tonight -- what am I going to do? I've got to go. Warner's going to kill me!"

I'll re-schedule your sessions, honey," Dolores said calmly. "You just go and take care of your little girl."

"I'll call Leslie about group," Rob said rubbing my back. "I'm sure she's okay, just drive carefully. You know she isn't hurt or bleeding. And she knows you're coming."

"Right," I said, trying to breathe. As I turned to leave I met the dark eyes of the new intake. "I'm sorry, I didn't mean to interrupt. I'm Katie Cunningham. I'll be your family therapist." I extended my hand. She stared back.

"Hi," she said, softly, "I'm Blair." We shook hands.

"Jesus, Katie, go!" Rob said kindly.

"I'm going, but I need to contact Blair's parents, quick, give me your phone number. I can call them from home and we can meet first thing tomorrow." I grabbed my keys while Blair slowly wrote down her number on a piece of paper. I hugged Rob and then Dolores. "Thank you, both, yet again, for helping me out. I really mean it!"

"You would do the same for us in a heart beat, and we know it," Dolores said, the stethoscope still hanging from her neck. "Now go take care of your baby girl."

I ran into my office, grabbed my coat and purse and made sure to take the back stairs in order to avoid Warner.

When I reached the school office I was out of breath. I searched the room for Tiger and was surprised to see only Shelly sitting at her desk, typing calmly.

"Shelly, where's Tiger?"

"Oh, hi, Katie," she said stiffly. It may have been my imagination, but it seemed that Shelly's manner toward me had changed since my meeting with Frances, et al. "Mary convinced her to go back to class. I tried to call, but you had already left work."

"Did you try my cell phone?" I asked, trying to take in all that was happening. "I know it's on the emergency form I filled out this summer."

"No, I guess I figured you were on your way. I didn't look on the form, Katie, sorry," she said, not sounding sorry at all.

I wasn't sure what to do next. I sat down slowly and stared at the floor.

"Katie," Shelly said softly after several minutes, the kindness I had always seen in her returning. "Maybe you should check on her. She's not sick or anything, but she was pretty upset. I shouldn't be saying this, Mary wanted me to tell you to go back to work, but I think you should check in with Tiger."

I looked up at her gratefully. "Thank you, I think I will." Shelly smiled and returned to her typing.

As I walked down the hallway to Tiger's classroom I could hear activity behind each closed door, teachers talking authoritatively, children shouting and laughing. I admired the pictures on the wall from the most recent art activity and detected the faint smell of empty milk cartons and half-eaten lunches. When I reached the second grade, I peeked in the small window at the top of the closed door. It took a while to find Tiger, but then I remembered she was to have been moved to the front of the room, and there she was, right under Mary's nose, looking miserable. Mary stood at the chalk board, writing crisply. The children appeared helplessly bored, predictably tired after lunch, some resting their heads on their arms.

I knocked softly and stepped inside. Mary was clearly not glad to see me. "Mommy!" Tiger squealed, jumping out of her seat and wrapping herself around my legs.

"Trisha," Mary said sternly, "please return to your seat." But Tiger didn't budge and I didn't make her. "Hello, Mrs. Cunningham. Shelly should have told you you weren't needed."

The children watched with interest, glad to have a reprieve from the lesson. "May I speak with you for a minute, Mrs. Peterson? I'm sorry to interrupt class, but it's important." I rubbed Tiger's back protectively.

Mary hesitated, she was a woman of routines and was flustered by this disruption in her schedule. "Just for a minute, Kate, I can't leave the children unattended, it's just me in here, you know. Trisha, you may return to your seat while I speak with your mother."

"Actually, Mrs. Peterson, I would like her to join us. We can talk outside your door and you can still keep an eye on the class, it will just be a moment." I walked toward the door with my arms around Tiger.

Mary, stubbornly refusing to accommodate my suggestion, handed her chalk to Kristin and instructed her to write the names of anyone who misbehaved on the blackboard while she was in the hall. I felt sickened this discipline method was being used at this supposedly progressive school. Putting one student in charge of the others divided a classroom. Instead of encouraging cooperation, Mary was creating a sense of competition between her students for their teacher's good favors.

Mary followed us and closed the door quietly behind her. She adjusted the trademark sweater that was draped over her shoulders and crossed her arms. "Trisha shouldn't have called you, Kate, there was no need for you to come."

"I'm not so sure I agree with you. She sounded pretty upset to me. But I'd like Tiger to tell us what was upsetting her," I said as calmly as possible.

Tiger looked nervously between her teacher and me. Mary ignored her. Sensing Tiger's reluctance to anger her teacher, I knelt down and turned her toward me. I held her arms and looked steadily into her the eyes. "Tiger, I want you to tell me what happened. No one will be angry with you," I looked pointedly at Mary, "but we can't help if we don't know what's bothering you." I realized at that moment how important it would be for Tiger to learn to be her own advocate, I wouldn't always be there to help.

Tiger fidgeted nervously. She looked down at her hands that were twisting her cotton shirt. I gently lifted her chin with my finger and smiled. She took a shallow breath and, keeping her eyes focused on me, said, "Well, um, I guess I got upset

102

when Mrs. Peterson told everyone about my dyslexia."

"I tried to tell you on Friday that it was inappropriate to tell the other students," Mary interrupted,.

"Excuse me, Mrs. Peterson." I was trying desperately to keep my anger at bay. "Why don't we let Tiger tell us her side of things. It's important for her to be able to do this, especially now."

Tiger glanced nervously at her teacher and began again. "Well, Mrs. Peterson told everyone that I couldn't read and that I was going to have to get special help. She said school was harder for me than everyone else. And she said I had to sit in the front because I don't understand a lot of things, and, well, now everyone thinks I'm stupid and..." Tiger began to weep and buried her head in my shoulder. I held her tightly, fighting back my own tears. I was determined not to disarm myself with Mary ever again.

Mary rolled her eyes, she appeared to be unmoved by Tiger's tears. I was amazed at her apparent callousness. How could a second grade teacher be so hardened to a child's tears? Children cry for a reason, there is always a reason, whether an adult thinks it is justifiable or not. "I have no idea why Trisha is so upset. I never said she was stupid, I only did what you demanded which was tell them she's dyslexic."

"You told her to say that?" Tiger pushed away from me. "How could you?"

"Tiger, honey, I wanted the class to know about your dyslexia so they wouldn't wonder where you were going when you had to leave for tutoring, or when you were feeling overwhelmed, or needed to move around," I said rapidly. "What I wanted Mrs. Peterson to say," I stood to look at Mary, "is that you learn differently, not because you're slow or stupid, but because your brain learns in a different way than Mrs. Peterson teaches."

Mary and I locked eyes. "The last thing I want to do is undermine you, Mrs. Peterson, but I'd like to speak to the children about Tiger's dyslexia, in fact, now would be a perfect time, don't you think?"

"Mommy, no, please! I'm too embarrassed!"

I knelt back down to engage Tiger. "I won't embarrass you, I promise." I ruffled her silky hair affectionately and straightened out the wrinkles in her shirt. "Let's go back to your classroom for a few minutes." I took her hand and walked toward the door. "This will just take a few minutes," I said to Mary. "Please join us." Tiger looked over her shoulder nervously as we returned to the classroom.

There were several names written on the board, all boys, and Kristin was still standing guard in front of the class. "Mrs. Peterson," Joe, a boy in the class called out. "Mrs. Peterson, Kristin wrote my name down, but I wasn't doing anything! Michael was talking to me, but I didn't answer him!"

"That will be all, Joe, sit down and be quiet. Boys and girls, Mrs. Cunningham has something to say to you. I would like you all to sit quietly and give her your attention."

"But, Mrs. Peterson, I didn't do anything!" Joe persisted. He was half out of his seat and craning his neck for his teacher's attention. Mary placed her index finger to her lips and ignored Joe. Eventually he gave up and crumpled into his seat.

Fighting back the urge to hear Joe's side of the story, I stepped in front of the class and winked at Tiger. I cleared my throat. "Thank you for letting me talk to all of you, and I promise, I'll only be a few minutes, I know you have a lot to cover with Mrs. Peterson this afternoon. Mrs. Peterson tells me that she told you about Tiger, excuse me, Trisha's dyslexia today. Does anyone have any questions about what she said?"

"I do," Carrie, a small, quiet girl I had always liked said. "Will Trisha ever get better?"

"Get better?" I asked. "Good question, Carrie. This is all new to Trisha and me, but if Trisha is taught in a way that she understands, she will learn as easily as the rest of you. We just have to find that way. You see, her brain is very smart, it just learns differently." I was thinking on my feet and began to feel a small, growing sense of panic. I turned around and looked at the chalk board and saw what seemed to be a list of spelling words. "I see you're studying spelling this afternoon." I remembered an article Susan had given me about spelling and tried to remember its contents. "What's the hardest word on this list?"

Joe called out "begin." Kristin looked at him smugly and announced that they were all easy. Joe rolled his eyes at her. Some of the other students called out "begin," as well, and so I asked them if they would all agree that begin was the hardest word. Everyone but Kristin nodded. She was annoyed with the turn of events in the classroom. Kristin looked to her teacher for affirmation but Mary was standing by her desk territorially, staring at me, the invader, with contempt.

I clapped my hands together and took a deep breath, "Okay, let's see if I can remember how to do this." I glanced back at the board. "Normally you would be given this word in a list and told to study it for a test on Friday. Most of you would then go home, maybe write it a few times, or, maybe not," some of the children chuckled and I was relieved to have their attention, "come to school on Friday morning and take the test. Some of you would score well with just that amount of studying. That's because you learn best by seeing. But some of you might not do as well. You learn in a different style. So, with that in mind, let's try something." I picked up a piece of chalk and wrote "begin" in large letters on the board. "Okay, let's learn to spell this troublesome word. First let's say it all together."

"Begin," they said in unison.

"Great! Now, take out a piece of paper and write the word begin and try to fill

104

up the entire page." The class hummed from their movements. "Use a crayon or marker if you'd like, any color, and write as big as you can, try to use your whole arm. Does anyone need help?" I looked down at Tiger's paper and my heart ached when I saw the awkward letters. I put my hand over hers and wrote the word in large letters on her paper while I continued to speak.

"Now, look at the word and listen as I say it: begin," I said slowly, articulating every sound. "Now, close your eyes and see if you can picture the word 'begin' in your mind." I watched as their small eyes crinkled shut. "Great! You are very cooperative!" They smiled at the words of praise. "Open your eyes and trace the letters on your paper as I say the word again. Excellent! Now, trace the letters again, this time saying it with me."

"B-e-g-i-n," they chorused.

"Now, everyone stand up, and using the biggest movements you can, sky write the word while we all say it together." Their small arms sailed through the air with their exaggerated movements, their faces dancing with delight at the chance to use their active little bodies. Tiger smiled at me. Her body told her this was right.

Finally, I drew rectangles around each letter, and then drew the same rectangles without the letters inside. "And just in case we haven't reached everyone, this is for you. Do you think you could fill in these blanks if I asked you to spell begin?"

The class was murmuring with interest and Mary's agitation increased. I glanced at her and decided it was time to wrap it up. "Is there anyone who doesn't think they can spell 'begin?'"

"No!" they shouted, including Tiger.

"Good for you! That's because we have studied the word in every way possible, we've seen the word, pictured the word, written the word, and moved the word. The only sense we didn't use was scent. Since everyone learns in different ways, using different senses, it's important to try and use every sense when you are presented with something new. Trisha learns best by moving and touching. That's because she's dyslexic. And that's why she'll be leaving the classroom some days, in order to work with a tutor who teaches through touch and movement. You may want to ask yourself which way helped you and try it for your next spelling test. And even better, try all the ways and you can't miss!"

Tiger looked up at me with relief. "Thanks, Mom," she whispered. I smiled at her with relief that I had been able to help her.

"Well, that was interesting, Mrs. Cunningham, but it's time for us to get back to work." Some of the children groaned. "That will be enough."

"Thanks for listening, everyone!" I called as I walked out the door.

I called Leslie from the car to let her know I would be back in time to conduct the education group.

"That's great, Katie, because T.C. is supposed to call tonight and I want to be home," Leslie said cheerfully.

"What, you're dating 'Top Cat' now? I knew you were feeling depressed, but isn't he a little old for you?"

"Ha, ha. T.C. is Tim Collins, that lawyer Max was telling us about. He gave him my number and we've been talking every night. It's going very well, by the way. We might try dinner soon."

"Why am I the last to know these things?" I asked, trying not to sound hurt.

"Katie! It's no big deal. I'm not even sure if Max knows we're talking," she said kindly, sensing my childish reaction.

"Thanks. The last thing I need is a sneaky husband. So, is he a nice guy? How divorced is he?"

"Totally, and no kids. He was married for ten years. I guess they both had high-powered careers, long hours, and according to T.C. he came home one night and realized they had become strangers. The divorce was mutual -- no contest. They divided their assets and went separate ways. He said they still care about each other, but make better friends than lovers."

"He wasn't having some tawdry affair?"

"Katie! You can be so crude. No, he wasn't. He didn't make time for his wife, let alone an affair."

"And that's all changed?"

"He wants it to. He said the older he gets the more he realizes he doesn't want to be alone."

"How old has he gotten?"

"He's my age, Katie, that old."

"Okay, so far I approve. I can't remember if I've met him. I wonder what he looks like. How's his voice?"

"Dreamy."

"Dreamy? Now you sound like Sandra Dee."

"Maybe. But don't spoil my fun, a girl can dream, can't she? He's probably five foot two with a pot belly and no hair. Why can't we have Max cloned?"

"The world would not be a safe place. But I don't think Max would have given your number to a loser. And besides, you had coiffed and handsome and that didn't turn out so well. It's time to go for the personality."

"Why can't I have both?"

"Maybe you can. Why don't I swing by Max's office and take a peek? I don't think I can stand the suspense."

"No way! I get to see him first. And I will when I'm good and ready."

106

"Well, all right. So that leaves the name. What's with the T.C.?"

"I think it's kind of cute. I guess he's been called that all his life. He's a junior and that's how his family distinguished him from his dad."

"I guess I don't have any room to talk, being married to a Maxwell."

"Excellent point."

"Are you eating?"

"Yes, Mom."

"Are you talking, or just listening?"

"I'm talking."

"A lot?" I pushed.

"Probably too much, but I'd rather he know me now before things get more involved."

"This is beginning to sound interesting. Can I start getting excited?"

"Not until I see him."

"Deal. But don't go get a life or anything. Who will cover for me, or distract Warner, the pain-in-the-butt Georgia Boy?"

"I guess you'll have to find another lackey. But seriously, I would have been happy to cover group tonight. How's Tiger?"

"Okay, for now, but it seems that can change at any time. I'll let you go, stop by my office later if you have time. Thanks again, Les."

I turned off the phone and instead of listening to my usual public radio station, I tuned into the local progressive rock station. I rolled down the window and let the wind stir my hair and the loose debris in the car and turned up the volume and sang what few lyrics I knew to a fast-paced song about the world ending as I knew it.

Lesson Six:
Trusting Your Instincts

Much of parenting is about instincts.
Listening to your inner self,
your heart, not society's pressures and influences.
Remember when your infant cried?
The pediatrician said "let her cry,"
but your heart said, "I can't."
What your heart knew is that babies cry for a reason,
it is their only way of communicating and
she needed you to be there for her, even if it was
only to have you near, to know you were out there, listening,
watching over, taking care, keeping her safe.

"How's Blair?" I asked Rob when I arrived back at the hospital.

"Having a very rough detox. If you ask me she's lucky to be alive. She hasn't eaten in days, and I don't think she's slept in as many. Apparently she was living on crack, speed, acid, you name it. I guess rich kids can get higher because they have the dough to buy it. Anyway, Dolores has been by her side all afternoon. Doctor Tripp has been in there more than once, believe it or not, just to make sure she doesn't go into cardiac arrest. Hey, how's Tiger?" he asked warmly.

"She's fine. Thanks for rescheduling my sessions. So what can I do for you? Things have been a little one-sided lately."

"Your smile is enough for me, Katie Cunningham. One of those can get me through the worst of days." He squeezed my arm and walked out into the unit.

I watched him go, but immediately stiffened when I saw Warner approaching. "Nice to see you made it back to work, Katie," he said roughly as he strode toward me, not stopping until he had entered my personal space.

"Hello, Warner," I said, taking a step back. "Yes, I'm here. I just stepped out for a short time."

"You've been gone for three hours. It's helpful when you work in a hospital to actually be in the hospital. It's a concept you might want to consider."

108

"Warner, despite how it looks to you, I am doing my job. I haven't missed a single mandatory session, my charts are up to date and my social histories have been early, and extremely well written, I might add," I said defensively.

"That means nothing if you aren't here. What does it take to get through to you? The least you could have done is check with me before you left today."

"I agree, I really do, and I'm sorry. But I was in a hurry, it was an emergency. Tiger was crying at school and I had to go to her." Somehow, what seemed to be a legitimate reason for leaving, sounded insignificant in its retelling. I took a deep breath and remembered that I had a reason to leave the hospital -- Tiger had needed me, I had no choice but to go. "Everything was covered, Warner. I'll be here for group tonight. I had a great session this morning. There's nothing to worry about."

"I'll decide when I need to worry. And being here for part of the day isn't good enough."

"What are you saying?"

"I've discussed this with the president of the hospital and he said it's vital that I follow company policy. What if a patient's parents needed to talk to you? What do we tell them? 'Oh, our family therapist stepped out for three hours, you'll have to call back.' I don't think so. We run a business here and customer satisfaction has got to be the priority. You are on probation, Kate, I've already warned you, and the next time you miss work without it being pre-authorized at least two weeks in advance, you're fired. It's the corporate policy, no special treatment for you just because you're cute and feisty. I'm watching you." Warner turned to leave.

"Warner," I called. He stopped, turned halfway around and looked at me impatiently. "When did this hospital stop caring about quality? Have you looked at my patient review forms? Have you seen the relapse rate of our patients? It's far below national average. We do good work. When did that stop mattering?" I asked heatedly.

Warner looked at me blankly. "I think we're finished," he said and walked deliberately back to his office and closed the door.

"Shit!" I said under my breath. What was happening? Was I really at risk of losing my job? I was the most reliable person I knew. I always got excellents on my annual reviews, I had always been offered a job after an interview, and I'd always received my full merit raise every year. I helped people. I sat down with realization of how desperately I did not want to lose my job. It was about more than money, it was my self-esteem, my separateness from my family, my social outlet, my way of helping human kind. Was I going to be forced to choose between my children and my job? Surely our society had progressed beyond this. And yet, as health care became privatised, the more rigid and bureaucratic it had become. I no longer had Warner, or even the chairperson of the board to deal with. The hospital was owned by a national Managed Care company with stock holders and

109

depersonalized policies. I was an overpaid social worker because of my license and years of experience. They could replace me with a master's level social worker for half my salary.

My thoughts were interrupted by Dolores as she scurried into the room, looking tired and frazzled. "Have you talked to Blair's parents yet?" she asked hastily. "I think they may want to get in here. She's in pretty bad shape."

I stood quickly, responding to Dolores' urgency. "I'm on the job."

By nine o'clock I was apologizing to Lois for my lateness. As usual, she was more than understanding and reassured me that Jamie and Tiger were sound asleep. I thanked her profusely and thought how lucky I was to be able to work late without prior notice and know my children were safe and well cared for.

"You're a peach, Lois, I don't know what I would do without you," I said tiredly. "I just have a few things to wrap up and I'm on my way. Any word from Max? Maybe he'll be home before me, and you can get home."

"He doesn't usually call. I'll most likely be waiting for you."

"Right. I'll do my best. I know how much you hate driving this late at night. Why don't you call Art and let him know you'll be on your way home in twenty minutes."

"Yes, I'll do that."

"Thanks again, Lois."

Mr. and Mrs. Tilghman had been extremely worried about Blair and had arrived at the hospital shortly after my call. Blair was an only child and they had been distraught when she ran away. Before her most recent run, she had been attending an exclusive, private school, but despite her parents' attempt to limit her access to "undesirables," they were beginning to realize she'd been heavily involved in drugs since her first day of middle school.

I stopped in the waiting room and let them know I was leaving. Their manicured faces were lined with worry. After scheduling my next session with the Tilghmans, I stopped in the chart room and bid good night to the evening shift.

"It looks as if the Tilghmans will be heading home soon, now that they know Blair's going to make it."

"Thanks for staying around, Katie, good night."

I noticed Danny alone in the lounge as I was walking by. He was writing in his journal. "What are you working on, buddy?" I asked softly.

"Oh, hey, Mrs. Cunningham. What are you still doing here?" he asked.

"New patient. Remember those first days? Well, she's coming down hard, but she'll be okay. She's going to need your support tomorrow. She needs an experienced guy like you to help her through these first few days."

110

Danny smiled. "I'd be happy to help."

"Good for you, old timer. What are you working on?"

"Rob wanted me to do some more work on my first step. He thinks I need to focus more on my drinking, and not so much on my parents. He said it's too easy for me to blame them since they've been acting out. He doesn't want me to use that as an excuse."

"Rob's a smart man. He can zero in on a program pretty quickly. I'm sure he knows what he's talking about."

"Yeah, he's cool. I think I've got some good stuff here."

"Good," I said sincerely. "Take care, Danny, good night. I'll see you tomorrow." My keys echoed as I let myself out of the otherwise quiet unit.

I was sitting in the dark, staring out at the starry night, when Max arrived home. "Katie? What are you doing in the dark?"

"Thinking," I said quietly.

"Can I join you?" he asked as he put down his briefcase on the kitchen counter and came into the family room. Before he sat down he went back into the kitchen and popped open two beers. He sat on the couch next to me, loosened his tie and put his arm around me. "Are you okay?"

Part of me wanted him to know everything that had happened that day, but the other part of me was just happy to be distracted by his presence. "I've had a very strange day," I said matter-of-factly and took a long sip from the beer he had handed me. "Just let me ask you one thing. What would happen to us if I got fired?"

"That is clearly a hypothetical question, my dear," Max said without hesitation, "because you never do anything wrong, and certainly never enough to warrant getting fired. So, to answer your question, we'd tighten our belts and get by. Why would you ask me a thing like that, Katie?"

"Well, I guess it's more of a reality than I want it to be. Just don't be surprised when it happens. And don't quit your day job," I added.

"How about my night job?" Max asked playfully.

"Same difference," I said sarcastically.

"No, Katie, I mean my night job," he said as he gently ran his finger up and down the side of my face, stopping at my earlobe.

I shivered at his gentle touch. "Right. Yes, you are still gainfully employed," and feeling the need to work through the emotions of the day, I put down my beer and climbed onto his lap. Max was startled by my advances. I unbuttoned his shirt, put my hands on his strong chest and kissed him deeply.

It was rare for me to be the aggressor, but I was feeling afraid and out of control of my life and needed to take charge. Max responded, and despite his

111

attempts to take over, I kept him underneath me. It was a powerful experience and neither of us spoke as we climbed the stairs to bed.

By the end of the week I had exhausted my search for an Orton-Gillingham tutor. I had spoken with many tutors, but despite their claims of competence, none of them had been trained in a pure Orton approach. They professed to use Orton techniques or portions of the philosophy, but none offered the solid VAKT approach that Susan had said was vital for Tiger. It seemed everyone thought they could improve the method with modern techniques, but according to Susan, there was no need for improvement, a solid Orton program was the foundation for Tiger learning to read, write and spell fluently and accurately.

I was sitting at my desk crossing off names and doodling distractedly when Betty's raspy voice announced I had a phone call. I froze with fear. Tiger. I reluctantly answered the phone.

"How would you like some extra house guests for Thanksgiving?" a cheerful voice asked.

"Aunt Matty?"

"The one and only. You sure sound happy to hear from me, are you all right?"

"I can't think of a single person I'd rather it be. You're like a breath of fresh air in this stuffy, old day," I said with a sigh.

"Stuffy old day? You're starting to sound like a southerner, honey. I need to get you out of Maryland."

"Aunt Matty, Maryland was part of the Union."

"You're below the Mason Dixon line and that's south enough for me."

"Well, you have a point. Everyone on this unit is from Virginia or Georgia or worse and you know I absorb accents like a sponge. Did I really sound that bad?" I said laughing.

"You scared me, honey!"

"Oh, it feels good to laugh! But what did you ask me a minute ago?"

"Your mom and I want to come for Thanksgiving. We've decided you need us around. So, what do you say?"

"I say come tomorrow! Spend the month, how about the year! Why don't you both move in?"

"A simple yes would have been enough," she said laughing.

"Oh, Aunt Matty, I would love to see you. You have amazing instincts because a visit from you and Mom is just what I need -- something to look forward to. But what will my oldest sister say? She's used to being the hostess on Thanksgiving. I think she likes to run the show."

"Yes, Megan does, and she's good at it, too, but I'm sure she'll understand.

She'll have her in-laws and neighbors. She'll be fine." It was wonderful to hear Aunt Matty's reassuring voice.

"Speaking of in-laws, you know Max's parents and two brothers are coming. They'd love to see you. It may be a little crowded, but it could be fun."

"That sounds wonderful. I always enjoy May and Max."

"They're from Maryland, you know."

"Oh, right. Well, I'll try to overlook that. So tell me, how are you? How's it going with Tiger and school?"

I updated Aunt Matty on the recent developments and my frustrations with being unable to find a tutor. "I feel as if I'm losing precious time. Tiger's two months into the school year and she's just treading water until I can find a tutor."

"Have you tried the IDS (International Dyslexia Society)? I've been doing my own research and they should be able to give you a list of tutors in your area. I found a woman here who can train me to tutor in Orton-Gillingham."

"Train you, Aunt Matty? You're going to get trained in Orton-Gillingham?" I asked.

"You can teach an old gal new tricks, you know. To tell you the truth, this is all fascinating to me. I've been reading everything I can get my hands on and I've learned a lot, but I've got to tell you, I'm horrified that I didn't know any of this when I was working in the school system. The last book I read said that the most recent studies are finding that twenty percent of the population is dyslexic. Twenty percent! I couldn't believe it. Our school system is not meeting the basic needs of at least one fifth of the children it serves."

"Wow. I didn't know it was that many. But where will you be getting trained?"

"I'll have to go to Cleveland, but that's okay by me. I start next week and then I go every day for two weeks. It's a lot of driving, but I don't mind. I'll get some books on tape and make the best of it."

"I know you will. Did you find this training through the IDS?"

"Yes. They're a little over worked but very helpful. You might want them to fax you the list of tutors. It took three weeks for mine to arrive in the mail, and some of the phone numbers are out of date." That was Aunt Matty, she had high expectations for the world to be as smart and as efficient as she was.

"I needed a break through. I've hit a lot of dead ends trying to find someone qualified."

"How's Jamie, honey? Getting lost in the shuffle?"

"Well, I don't think so, she seems fine. But to be honest with you I've just been counting on her to be fine. She's seems happy and she's doing well in school, as always. She's been very supportive of Tiger. I'm impressed with how she's handled everything so far, but you ask good questions. I'll have to pay more attention." Something tugged at me, but I put it aside, I had enough on my mind.

"Oh, Katie, I didn't call to add to your worries. I'm sure she's fine with a mother like you. Now you get back to work, I'll tell your mother the good news. Speaking of Joan, have you talked to your mother lately?"

"We talked last weekend. She was very caring, but I hate to worry her too much."

"You can't stop her from worrying, it's what she does best. And she can also tell when you're holding back. She may be a worrier, but she can handle anything you throw at her. What about Max's parents? Have they been helpful?"

"Another insightful question. You should study psychology. Oh, that's right, you did. I don't think Max has even told his parents about Tiger. I don't really understand why. But you know Max, as long as he's working, everything is fine. If I think about it too long I'll start to get really pissed." I could hear Aunt Matty's soft, understanding laughter on the other end of the line. "It should prove to be an interesting Thanksgiving, are you sure you want to come?"

"Wouldn't miss it for the world! Families are complex but they're worth the trouble," she said lovingly. "Take care, dear, I love you all."

"Thank you, Aunt Matty. I feel better already."

I thought about the magnitude of what Aunt Matty was about to undertake. After being retired for years she was going to learn a whole new way of teaching language arts to children. My eyes welled with tears when I thought about her love and endless energy for the people she cared about. I felt honored to be one of those people. I may have a dysfunctional motor for a family, but today I felt as if I'd just had an oil change.

And she was right about the IDS. They faxed me a list of tutors and tutor training programs and after several phone calls I found a woman in Baltimore who could tutor Tiger two evenings a week. It wasn't ideal, but it was a start. We would begin next Tuesday. She agreed to meet us halfway and after some negotiations we settled on meeting in a public library in Glen Burnie, a lot farther than I wanted to drive, but I was willing to do whatever it took to get Tiger started.

After another quiet weekend of Max working, I headed back to the hospital for my final session with the Colonel and Danny. The hospital prevented social workers from continuing on with patients once they left the hospital. Referring a patient to your private practice was grounds for dismissal. I agreed with the policy but found it to be extremely hypocritical because it was standard practice for the psychiatrists to continue seeing their patients, often for years, after they left the hospital. Although I didn't have a private practice, several of the social workers at the hospital did in order to supplement their meager salaries. And most often patients wanted to continue with their social workers in therapy, but it never happened. The Colonel and Danny were no exception. Colonel Boles was leery about transferring to another therapist. He had never opened up to anyone before and it had been terrifying for him. He had learned to trust me and didn't want to start over. But be that as it may, I would be saying good-bye to the Colonel and Danny this morning.

I stopped to say good morning to Betty, as I did every Monday morning, and was surprised when there was no sign of Leslie. Betty and I chatted briefly over M&M's and shared funny stories about our pets and families and then I headed up to the fourth floor in search of Leslie. I was surprised to find her office door locked. It was eight-thirty, she was already half an hour late. I stuck a note on her door and headed to my office.

Rob was in the chart room and, as usual, looking handsome and smelling wonderful. We discussed an aftercare plan for Danny, Blair's progress, several other patients, and sipped our coffee. When we ran out of patients to discuss we continued to sit quietly, comfortable with the silence and each other's company.

"I hear you've been invited to speak at the AA convention in Ocean City next summer," I said, breaking the silence.

"Yeah, lucky me."

"Think you'll do it?" I asked, surprised at his nonchalance at such an honor. It was an international convention with the most renowned names in the field speaking.

"More than likely. They want me to talk about longevity in the program with an emphasis on integrity. Who would have 'thunk,'" he said sarcastically.

"I think they made an excellent choice. Your years of sobriety have given you a great deal of wisdom." Rob looked up with an intense gaze. A heat passed through me but I forced myself to return his gaze.

"I've been questioning my integrity lately," he said after several uncomfortable minutes. He stood slowly as he continued to look at me. He dressed the same every day, faded but clean and pressed jeans, boots, a tee-shirt with a blazer of some sort. He had started running the day he quit drinking and never stopped. He refers to it as his new addiction and runs several miles every morning without fail, leaving him with a tan, athletic glow to his skin. His deep, blue eyes revealed a passion that unsettled me. "We better get to work or Warner will fire us both. Good luck with Danny." Rob turned away, his boots clicked crisply on the floor.

"Thanks, Rob," I said quietly.

He hesitated and turned toward me, worry spread across his face. "Katie--"

"Yes?"

"Don't let them fire you, I mean, if you miss another day, that's it."

Rob seemed to know the path before me that I was still unwilling to accept.

"I won't." I smiled reassuringly. "You know I love working here. And I won't let them force me to choose between my job and my daughter. This is the new millennium. Besides, I finally found a tutor for Tiger two evenings a week so hopefully I won't have to be away from the hospital any more."

"It doesn't even occur to you, does it?"

"What?" I asked warily.

"That Max should share in this responsibility. Hell, he's a partner in his own law firm, he can leave the office whenever he needs to without risking his job. Katie, one more time and you're history. You don't even ask him to share the load. Neither you nor the school ever calls him when there's a problem, you assume it's up to you."

"Well, you have a point," I said, flustered. "It doesn't occur to me anymore. It used to. I was bound and determined when Jamie was born that we would share the parenting equally." I sighed deeply. I was more comfortable not thinking about how out of proportion things had gotten in my marriage.

"Hey, I'm sorry, it's none of my business." Rob looked away and began to busy himself around the room. "I'm no expert on how to live a life. I've been married and divorced twice and have one kid who barely speaks to me. You don't need a drunk who can't stay married to tell you how to deal with your husband."

"Rob, please, stop with the self-deprecating crap." He put down the chart he was holding and looked at me. "You are one of my closest friends and I respect your opinion more than you know. Just hang in there with me. Ever since Tiger's diagnosis I feel like my head has been in a trash can. I can't see anything clearly. Everything I used to know and believe is now in question. I appreciate your honesty and I desperately need your support. Don't start holding back on me or you'll ruin a great relationship," I said adamantly. "So, shut up, okay?" I smiled playfully at him. Rob smiled but his eyes held his sadness.

"Maybe I just never realized how important you are to me." Rob stuffed his hands in his jeans pockets and shrugged. "I guess you know now, though, don't you." Rob hesitated and then stepped forward and hugged me. I held him tightly, his strong body felt wonderful against mine, too wonderful. I patted his back and gently pushed him away.

"Thanks for caring," I said softly.

"You're welcome. Promise me you'll watch out for yourself, Katie. You give it all away and then there's nothing left for you. And if you lose this job, I'll be pissed as hell."

"I hear you." I felt another tug, I knew he was right. It's what I tell my families, my clients, but I hadn't a clue what to do about the growing imbalance in my marriage or my feelings for Rob so I decided to think about it later.

116

When Danny entered my office for our final session I couldn't stop grinning. The difference in his appearance was astonishing. Although he remained faithful to his grungy style of dress, he looked healthy and peaceful. His face glowed from the nourishment to his body and soul over the past six weeks.

"Danny Boles, I must say, you look marvelous. Look at him, Colonel Boles, what a handsome young man."

The Colonel was standing, as usual, waiting for me to sit down. I had grown accustomed to his chivalrous ways and smiled at him. "You are absolutely right, Mrs. Cunningham. You look good, Daniel."

It was unusual for the Colonel to compliment his son and Danny reddened. "Could we get on with this please?" he said, trying to sound annoyed.

"My pleasure," I said. We each sat down in our designated chairs. Danny and the Colonel waited for me to begin. "Okay," I smiled at them both, "the purpose of this session is to finalize the aftercare plan. This is extremely important and I'm sure you've talked in group and with Rob about relapse prevention, Danny. Colonel Boles, Danny has been told to go to ninety AA meetings in the next ninety days. During that time he should find a sponsor with more than twelve months sobriety and find one or more AA groups that he likes. It will take some effort to get him there and he'll need your help and support. He doesn't, however, need you to nag or punish him if he doesn't go. He'll work on that with his aftercare group. He will have to get a signature at each group and bring it to the counselor as proof that he's attending meetings. This has to be Danny's program. He's begun to work his twelve steps in earnest and seems to understand their spiritual significance. But what he needs from you is a father. He needs your love and support and he also needs reasonable rules, expectations and consequences when he doesn't cooperate."

"I'm not so sure about that part," Danny said, half-jokingly.

"Well I am," I said to them both. From there we spent most of the session going over Danny's rules and expectations. We kept it simple, most of the rules centered around helping out around the house, homework, and curfew. This was all new to them. Since Colonel Boles had been asleep in a chair most evenings, Danny had very little supervision and his mother had treated him more like an adult than a child. Danny had been coming and going as he pleased and as long as he had been supportive of his mother's problems, she felt no need to restrict him. But in the long run, instead of feeling cared about by his mother's permissiveness, he had felt neglected and out of control. He was an adolescent with the freedom of an adult and that was terrifying for him. So, despite his resistance, the Colonel's decision to set down rules and expectations was a relief to Danny. And the consequences were the easy part, Danny wanted his driver's license and the use of the car would be used as a reward as well as a consequence.

We also discussed plans for the Colonel to continue in therapy, although he was not sure he would follow through.

"Danny needs a healthy dad, Colonel Boles. You have to keep on your path or your family will fall back into its unhealthy patterns. How do you intend to prevent that from happening?"

"Well, I intend to do what we've been discussing, be a better father to Danny."

"Right, I know, and that is very important. But what about you?"

"What about me, Mrs. Cunningham? I'll go to work and support the family, and come home and be a father to Danny. There isn't much time for anything else," the Colonel said defensively. Danny watched his father intently. His father's defensiveness was making him uneasy. Although the Colonel had never struck Danny, he had learned to be wary of his father's temper. He was used to avoiding it, not pushing him as I was doing. And the tension between them was increasing with the anticipation of Danny returning home.

"How are you going to ensure that you don't start drinking again? And this has nothing to do with Danny."

"I know you want me to go into counseling, Mrs. Cunningham, but I don't know. You've been very helpful to Danny and me, but I want to try out what we've learned here. I'll call that counselor if things get tough."

"How are you going to ensure that you don't start drinking again?" I asked him again. Danny squirmed in his chair and the Colonel reddened.

"What are you getting at, Mrs. Cunningham? Danny is the one in treatment, not me."

"I agree. But I want to know what you're going to do about your own problem. What's your plan?"

"I didn't think, Mrs. Cunningham, that when I disclosed my poor drinking habits that they would be thrown back in my face."

"So are you telling Danny and me that you don't have a problem with alcohol?" The Colonel was quiet. I knew his denial was back in full force and if I didn't confront it here, it was only a matter of time before he convinced himself that one little drink after work wouldn't hurt.

"I don't know," he said softly and looked down at the floor.

"I have a suggestion, if you'd like to hear it."

"I'm sure you do, Mrs. Cunningham, I'm sure you do," he said in resignation.

"I would like you to go to an AA meeting yourself."

"Oh no, no, no. I have a highly visible Pentagon job and I'm not going to blow it by going to AA."

"AA is strictly anonymous, hence the name Alcoholics Anonymous. I think you will find it stimulating and helpful. And I think you'll be surprised at the number of men your age with high-profile, high-powered jobs at these meetings. I can recommend some in your area that will have people you can relate to, and certainly not the same meetings that Danny is attending. That has to be separate. Besides, it's a place to go, something to do in the evenings other than sitting in a chair. You could use some social outlets now that you're divorced."

Danny looked up and hesitated, he was measuring his words carefully, "I think it could help you, Dad."

The Colonel stared at his son and, for a moment, I thought he was going to chastise him for speaking up to him, but after what seemed like an eternity, his face softened and he smiled in defeat, "You do, do you?"

Danny said in a shaky voice, "Yeah, I do."

The rest of the session went smoothly and by the end of the hour the Colonel had accepted the "where and when" list of AA meetings which I had highlighted with recommended meetings. "Has anyone ever told you, Mrs. Cunningham," Colonel Boles said as we all stood to end the session, "that you're like one of those little dogs that latch onto your ankle and don't let go, no matter how hard you try to shake them off?"

"Why, Colonel Boles," I said reddening. "Are you making a joke?"

"I guess I am, I do that sometimes."

"Hm, so much for 'stone-faced Boles,'" I said.

"I thought it was pretty funny, Dad!" Danny said, encouraging his father.

We all smiled and I ruffled Danny's hair, "You did, did you? Well, Colonel Boles, no one has ever told me that before, but I would imagine there are others who would agree with you."

"I would imagine so," he said quietly.

Danny and the Colonel thanked me for my help and I wished them well. As I watched them leave the unit, Danny hugging everyone good-bye, the Colonel shaking hands, I felt a tremendous sense of pride that our team had helped to prevent this valuable young man from heading down a path of self destruction.

I was sitting at my desk writing notes from the session, when I heard a light knock. I looked up to see Leslie's face in the door. "Hey!" I said, "I've been worried about you!" I walked over to meet her in the middle of my office, "I don't think I've ever known you to be late for anything, let alone your job. What's going on?"

Leslie giggled, "I know, isn't it wonderful!"

"Wonderful?" I asked suspiciously.

"Now don't get judgmental on me. You're always late, well, sometimes late, and one little day doesn't hurt anything, and, oh, who cares!" She whirled around and sprawled out on the sofa. "I have just had the most wonderful weekend! I now know why people are always talking about sex!"

"Oh, boy," I said as I walked over to close the door. "Okay, so why are people always talking about sex?" I sat down across from her. "Let's hear it, I want to know everything. It's T.C., isn't it? Maybe he is Top Cat."

"Maybe so. Oh, Katie!" she sat up and smiled. "He's wonderful! We went to the Eastern Shore and stayed at this adorable bed and breakfast. We barely left the room to eat. He is tender, and funny, and gorgeous! No double chin, beer gut or receding hair line for him! Where has Max been hiding him?"

"The last time I talked to you, you hadn't even seen this guy. Now you're having sex all weekend?"

"Well, we had lunch last week. And then we had lunch and dinner the next day. And the day after that. And then it was Friday, and we had lunch, and decided we would have to have sex, preferably more than once, and we drove to the Eastern Shore and the rest is history. What possessed me to stay with David for so long?"

"So when do I meet him? He hasn't gotten my seal of approval. No more sex until I meet him."

"Too late, I'm seeing him tonight. We can't keep our hands off each other, so I'm afraid I can't help you out there."

"Is he really a nice guy?" I asked sincerely.

"Yes. Definitely yes," she said, grinning.

I sat quietly for a few minutes and then looked at Leslie. A slow smile crept over my face. Leslie's eye danced in anticipation and then I screamed, "Ah!" We jumped up at the same time and hugged each other, laughing and squealing and jumping around the room. Then I was marching, singing a Sousa tune and Leslie was right behind me twirling an air baton, and we marched around the office several times. We hugged again and laughed and fell into our seats.

"Let's have dinner Friday night!" Leslie said excitedly. "You and Max can come to my house. I can't remember the last time I had you two over to my house. It's about time I play hostess."

"You can say that again." Leslie rolled her eyes. "We'll bring the wine and I'll find a babysitter. Oh, Leslie. This is wonderful. Top Cat to the rescue!"

Leslie giggled uncontrollably, "Please don't call him that in person. I mean, we know each other pretty well, but, well, you know."

"Maybe I'll test out that sense of humor of his."

"Katie Cunningham, I'm warning you!"

"Maybe I'll buy him a little top hat-- "

"Katie, please! Things are good but I'm not ready for any major tests yet. Just be your sweet, demure self and things will go fine."

"Right. I can do demure. How long do I have to be demure?"

"All evening."

"Hm. Max won't fall for it. You'll have to take your chances."

"If I must."

"You look positively rosy! Sex flush suits you."

"Katie!"

"And I won't ruin the moment by telling you to take it slow, or play hard to get, too late for that, or by telling you to enjoy this happiness for what it is, or --"

"Thank you for not doing that," she said facetiously. "I think I'll go back to work now. See you later, darling." She waved and walked airily out of the room.

Tuesday evening was rainy and cold and driving half way to Baltimore was the last thing I wanted to do. Lois was nervous about driving in the rain, so I bid her good-bye and urged Jamie to get ready to take Tiger to tutoring. I was rummaging through the refrigerator when Jamie marched into the kitchen.

"I'm not going with you to Tiger's tutoring. It's raining outside and I have phone calls to make," she announced.

I straightened up and closed the door. I was still wearing my raincoat and could feel the wetness beginning to soak through to my clothes. "I'm sorry, Jamie," I said tiredly, "but you don't have a choice." I walked over to the fruit bowl and picked up an apple. "And it is raining, you don't need to say outside, it doesn't rain inside," I added, immediately regretting it.

"I do so have a choice, and I'm not going! Why should I have to ride all the way up there when it's for Tiger? I have homework to do, and I need a shower, and I promised Jessica I would call her so we can do our math together."

She was starting to whine and I grew tense. "I asked Lois to stay but she can't on Tuesdays. And I'd let you stay here, but we'll be too far away for you to be home alone at night. I know it's inconvenient, honey, but it's just the way it is."

"Inconvenient? It's unfair! And I'm not going!" Jamie marched into the family room and flopped down on the sofa dramatically. She put her feet on the coffee table and crossed her arms.

I slipped off my coat and looked nervously at the clock. We had forty-five minutes before tutoring and it was at least a thirty minute drive, probably longer in this weather. I didn't want to indulge Jamie's demands, but I agreed in theory that she shouldn't have to disrupt her evening for Tiger. I called Max's office but heard his formal secretary's voice inform me of my options. I left a message, but knew it was a waste of time. When Max worked late he was usually in the law library or bent over his desk with his phone turned off. He loved the later hours without the hubbub of the office to distract him. I thought about how luxurious it would feel to be alone in a beautiful wood- paneled office, working uninterrupted, surrounded by beautiful books and leather chairs and knowing all the other details of my life were being taken care of for me. The thought left me feeling envious and acutely

121

aware of the differences in our lives. I shook my head and dialed his car phone. Another voice mail, this time in his familiar, confident voice. After leaving another futile message, I approached Jamie.

"I know this is the last thing you feel like doing, Jamie. I just tried to call your dad but I can't seem to track him down."

"Maybe he's on his way home and you can leave me here by myself."

"Honey, I'm pretty sure he hasn't left the office. I just can't risk it. You're going to have to come." I looked at her and smiled. "Let's make the best of this, sweetheart. You can do your homework in the library or maybe we can play on the Internet."

"This is totally unfair and I hate it! I'm not going to play on the Internet with you and I'm not going to have fun!" She marched into her room and slammed the door.

I found Tiger in her room putting a large puzzle together. She was deep in thought.

"We have to leave for tutoring in five minutes, Tig, better get your shoes on."

"Tonight?"

"Tiger," I said in exasperation. "We talked about it this morning. We have to go to the library to meet your new tutor. I asked Lois to remind you this afternoon."

"Well she didn't," Tiger whined. "I'm tired, Mommy. I've been in school all day and then I did my homework and now I need to play."

The fatigue was setting in quickly. "I'm sorry, Tiger, I'm tired too, but we have an appointment and she's expecting us, so as much as I would like to sit next to you and do that puzzle, we have to go, now." I walked out of her room and stood in the middle of the hallway. "Announcement, please. I am going to the van. I expect both of you there within the next two minutes, shoes and coats on. If you do not arrive at the van in two minutes you will have a consequence to be named later. No, on second thought, you will lose an hour of TV for every minute you delay. This is your last warning." I walked down the steps, grabbed another apple and a diet soda and opened the door to the garage. Baxter was there, sopping wet, I must have left him outside when I said good-bye to Lois. He ran in the house before I could stop him and I sighed when I saw the muddy tracks all over the floor. I slammed the door and went to wait in the van. As soon as I shut the door I began to feel awful. I had very little time with my children during the week and I had just spent all of it yelling and threatening. So much for quality time. Helping Tiger was beginning to feel like a punishment for all of us.

Despite my best efforts, we were ten minutes late. I apologized when I introduced myself to Tiger's tutor, a surprisingly young woman who was soft-

122

spoken and understanding about our tardiness. Susan had cautioned about selecting someone who was inexperienced as a teacher. But she was here and that was the best I'd managed so far. Besides, her quiet demeanor was perfect for Tiger. I smiled at her gratefully.

She guided Tiger to a table in the corner of the library and they began talking quietly. I picked up a magazine and sat in a multicolored sofa that looked as if it had been purchased in the sixties. I sank so far into it that I wondered if I was going to be able to climb out of it without my skirt hiking up to my waist. I was debating whether or not to stand up and take my coat off when I noticed Jamie heading off to her own table at the other end of the library. She hadn't said a word since we left the house. She unzipped her backpack and pulled out her headphones.

An hour later, Tiger was nudging me to wake up and I squinted up at her tutor. She was smiling down at me. "We're finished, Mrs. Cunningham. Do you think we could talk for a few minutes without Tiger?"

I thought Tiger would object, but she ran over to Jamie and they asked me for the keys to the van and skipped out of the library to listen to the radio.

"I like Tiger very much, Mrs. Cunningham. She's a sweet girl and very cooperative."

"But?" I asked warily. "You can't help her?"

"I could, if we met at another time of day, but she was exhausted. She said her head hurt and she couldn't focus. I tried everything I could to make it fun, but she's simply worn out. I'm sorry, as much as I could use the extra income, I don't think it's fair to Tiger. She learns best when she's fresh. I'm afraid we didn't get very far tonight because she's too tired to retain anything."

"Are you sure? What if I made sure she got to bed earlier?"

"Well, the problem is the dyslexia. She works so hard during the day that her brain is exhausted, not to mention the tension of worrying about school. I'm really sorry. I liked her very much."

"I'm sorry, too. Well, thanks for trying. If you know of anyone available during the day, would you have them call me, please?"

"Sure," she smiled sympathetically. I handed her a check and went out into the cold, dark night. It was raining harder than before and I felt depleted from the frustration of having hit another dead end.

I was sitting in the dark again. Jamie and Tiger were asleep, the dishes were in the dishwasher, the dog was walked, the house was neat, the backpacks were empty, all was well, at least so it seemed. I had started my own fire and made a cup of herbal tea in order to warm my chilled bones. Baxter was curled up on the sofa beside me and I had rested my arm on his soft fur, appreciating his company. I stared at the fire and tried to clear my head. The silence was comforting, I was glad to be alone.

I was jarred from my empty thoughts by the slam of the garage door. "Hey, Katie," Max called cheerfully. "Sorry I'm so late, this case is grinding me. How are you?" he asked. His expensive wingtip shoes clicked on the floor as he moved around the kitchen. When I didn't answer him the clicking stopped and his head appeared around the corner. "Katie, you there?"

"Yes, I'm here. If I wasn't here then you would have to be, and since that's never the case, then why ask?"

"Well, that's certainly more of an answer than I was looking for. A simple, 'hi, dear, come join me by the fire' would have been enough."

I stood up. "The fire is all yours, I'm going to bed." My anger with Max was surfacing rapidly.

"What's wrong with you? I said I was sorry I'm late."

"If you want to know how your family is, then come home or call or do something that would make me realize that I am not a single parent." I tried to walk past him, but he grabbed my shoulders.

"What's going on? Do we need to talk?"

"The resident therapist is all talked out," I said pushing his hands away.

"Nice, Kate, very nice answer," Max said sarcastically. "Now, do you want to tell me what's bothering you or do I have to guess, because I'm damn tired too."

"Max, I'm off duty. I happen to think it's pretty obvious what's bugging me and so the answer to your question is no, I don't want to tell you what the problem is because I haven't the patience or the energy to explain it to you." I started up the stairs and this time, he let me go.

I crawled into bed and felt miserable. The social worker in me wanted to go back downstairs and fix everything. I assumed Max was waiting for me to come back, knowing my incessant need to talk things out, resolve things. But I wasn't sure what I would say. Why was I so annoyed? It was obvious that things were out of balance, but I had never let it bother me this much before. Max was always coming home late, in fact, what used to be considered late was now the norm. He rarely called with an expected time of arrival. An evening with him at home had become a special occasion.

I kept hearing Rob's voice, "whatever you do, Katie, don't get fired!" He had foreseen what my denial had blinded me to. I was going to lose my job. My career, my love for my work, my friends and colleagues, my self-esteem from doing my job well, I was about to lose it all. And yet what was most surprising is the pain of that loss and the anger that the responsibility to accommodate was only mine, was overshadowed by my love and deep concern for Tiger. She was in pain and needed someone to notice. I felt a wave of love wash over me, the kind of love I had never experienced until I had children. It took my breath away. And when I realized that my instincts to protect and care for my child were so strong, I felt an overwhelming sense of pride.

And so I made a choice. I could fight Warner and Max to make things right, more equitable. I could argue and negotiate and remind. But Tiger was out of time. And so I would set everything else aside in order to help her.

I curled up in a ball and clung to my side of the bed, allowing my sadness to surface. Everything was about to be compromised: my beliefs in shared parenting, my beliefs in job equity, my passion for my work. I cried, grieving the sense of self I was about to lose.

Max walked softly into the bedroom. He inched his way over and put his arms around me. I could smell the toothpaste on his breath. "Are you awake?" he whispered.

"Sort of."

"Katie, are you crying?" he asked, surprised.

"Sort of."

He squeezed me tighter, "I'm sorry, babe. I know you've been carrying all the weight around here. And I should have called. I'm sorry."

Whenever Max was empathic it would inevitably make me cry harder, something that always took him by surprise.

"Hey, Katie!" he said with concern. "I'm really sorry. Why are you so upset?"

"I'm not sure, otherwise I would tell you. Yeah, I'm pissed you weren't around tonight, and I'm pissed that you aren't more involved in what's been going on lately, but I guess I'm upset about other things, too, things that don't have to do with you."

"Like what?"

It must be the oldest child in Max, but it was hard for him to believe that there were things in my life that didn't revolve around him. I have friends who say it's a "guy thing" and that all men are egocentric. I have a little more hope for fifty percent of the human race. But Max certainly had those tendencies, and at times I found it infuriating, but tonight I felt more like surrendering than fighting the injustices of the world. I patted his hands that were still around my waist and said, "Please, don't worry, I'm just doing a lot of thinking. A lot has happened these past few weeks. Maybe we can talk tomorrow night."

"Okay," he said, tentatively. I could hear the relief in his voice that I wasn't angry with him. He kissed me on the cheek and rolled over. "Oh, did you get a sitter? Aren't we supposed to go over to Leslie's?"

"You know that I did."

"I guess I do. Thanks. Is it Corrinne? Do you want me to pick her up on my way home from work?"

"Sure. Good night, Max."

"Good night, Katie. I love you."

"Me too."

"Mom, I haven't seen the eagles in weeks," Tiger said on our way to school the next morning. "I think something has happened to them."

"Maybe they're on vacation," Jamie said nonchalantly. She was speaking to me again, now that she knew Tiger's tutoring hadn't worked out.

"I don't know," Tiger said with concern. "I thought eagles kept the same nest year after year. Don't they just keep adding to the one they have? I think something has happened."

Tiger was worrying about everything lately. She was always shooing Baxter in the house for fear he would get hit by a car, even when there were none in sight, and she had been getting up in the middle of the night to ensure all the doors were securely locked. It seemed that ever since her diagnosis and the realization that bad things could happen, she'd been more and more fearful of what the world had to offer. It saddened me to see this. I missed the fearless, trusting Tiger.

"Maybe they're out pestering the ospreys."

"I guess that's possible. We should look up in the sky more to see if they're flying around." She scooted over in her seat so that she could look out the oversized, tinted window. I glanced back at her beautiful face, her long, graceful neck, craning to find her lost eagles. Her dark-complected skin was shiny and clear and her large eyes that were the color of fertile earth were filled with a depth of thought and concern that touched my heart.

When I stopped in front of the school I noticed Frances was away from her post by the pillars and was startled when she slid open the door. She stuck her head in and said cheerfully, "Good morning, Kate, what's the news on tutoring?" Jamie and Tiger squeezed by her in order to climb out of the van. "I haven't heard from you and I know Mary is wondering if Trisha will be missing class."

I leaned over the seatback to look at her. "I still don't know, Frances. I'm hitting a lot of dead ends. We tried a tutor last night but Tiger was too tired to retain anything. I'll let you know as soon as I find something."

Frances furrowed her brow in what looked to be a poor simulation of concern. "Do you think this is good for her, Kate?"

I looked over her small frame to ensure that Tiger and Jamie were out of ear shot. "What exactly do you mean, Frances?"

She leaned closer into the van. "Well, I don't know, her performance isn't improving with the modifications Mary has made. I'm just not sure what good a couple hours of tutoring will do. Maybe you should look at some other schools, just to be on the safe side. I think it's best for Tiger."

I studied Frances, trying to read her concealed intentions. Why was she saying this now? "I'm doing the best I can, Frances. I appreciate your concern. You and Mary will be the first to know when I find something. But Frances, I thought we had an agreement about how to handle this. Isn't it a little premature to evaluate the plan? Particularly in the school driveway?"

"Now, Kate, I'm just talking to you, don't be so defensive! I was just wondering about the tutoring, that's all. And I'm concerned for Trisha. Well, they're piling up behind you. Have a good day, Kate. TGIF!" It took her several tries to close the van door. After one last heave, the door lumbered shut, and I instantly drove away. I was driving faster than normal and realized I should slow down. I looked up at the eagles nest and felt a pit in my stomach at its emptiness.

Frances' words haunted me that morning and although I wasn't ready to give up the fight, I decided it was time to explore our options. I called the public elementary school and scheduled a meeting with the principal during my lunch hour. I stopped by Warner's office on my way out to let him know I would be going out for lunch and he simply nodded his head. I felt like a school girl asking permission to use the restroom.

The secretary at the Bay Front Elementary School informed me that the principal was in a meeting and suggested I observe the two second grade classrooms while I waited. Although I was nervous about time, I agreed it was a good idea. The first class was watching a film strip so I moved on to the second and accepted the teacher's invitation to sit in one of the vacant desks. Once I found an empty seat, I squeezed into the miniature desk and tried to be as unobtrusive as possible. I smiled at the diversity of the group. The racial homogeneity of the Chesapeake Day School was something that nagged at me often. But I was uncomfortable with the class sizes in both rooms, with more than thirty students per class.

Some of the children stared at me curiously, but the teacher snapped her fingers and called their attention to the front of the room. They were studying addition and the she had written a problem on the chalkboard. They were adding two digit numbers and she was solving the problem on the board as an example. I looked around the room expecting to find cusinare rods or beads or something three-dimensional to help the children understand addition, but the room was neat and orderly and consisted primarily of piles of papers. My reading had taught me about the importance of concrete tools to help children learn the abstracts of math and I began to wonder if I was the only person reading the current research.

I could see some of the children fidgeting and the teacher had a difficult time keeping them focused on her lesson. She had to stop several times during her demonstration in order to reprimand the more disruptive students. I began feeling a little sleepy and wondered how these active children must feel. She invited a pretty, young girl to come up to the board to solve a problem and I could see the other children watching her closely. She solved the problem with ease and some of them rolled their eyes at each other. At last the teacher passed out a sheet of problems and the students bent over their desks to solve them. I used the lull in her teaching as my opportunity to leave. I waved to the teacher silently and mouthed a "thank you." I closed the door quietly behind me and was relieved to be out of in the hall.

The principal of the Bay Front Elementary School was an attractive, African American woman with a no-nonsense manner. She stood when I walked into her office and greeted me warmly.

"Nice to see you again, Mrs. Cunningham."

"Why, Mrs. Thompson, I'm flattered that you remember me. And please, call me Kate."

"It's my job to remember you, Kate, and you may call me Louise. So, what brings you back to our school?" she asked as we both sat down.

I began to feel apologetic for withdrawing Jamie from her school. Despite our frustrations with Jamie's kindergarten experience, Max and I had liked Louise Thompson. She had worked hard to convince us to keep Jamie in the school. Her reasoning had been simple and straightforward: she wanted involved parents due to budget cuts and she wanted students like Jamie who would perform and receive high test scores. Maryland public schools received funding according to the students' achievement scores and Louise knew Jamie would be a strong asset to her averages.

"As you know, Louise, we enrolled Jamie and her sister in the Chesapeake Day School, but not because we weren't impressed with this school. On the contrary, you run a beautiful school. If you recall our reasons had more to do with circumstances out of your control, such as class size."

"You still haven't answered my question, Kate, what brings you here today? Have you changed your mind?"

"Well, no, I think it's more the case of the school having changed its mind."

"Oh, I see. I know those tuitions have gone up every year. Public school is the best bargain in town. Do you know that in many of the third world countries people have to pay to send their children to any school?"

"I guess I did know that, but it's not about finances, Louise, although it is a stretch on the budget. The problem is that our youngest, Trisha, has been diagnosed with dyslexia, and the Chesapeake Day School doesn't seem to be equipped to help her."

"Ah," she said with growing interest. "Dyslexia. And you would like to enroll her here instead?"

"I'm certainly considering it. At first I thought we'd try private tutoring, but it seems to wear her down after school, and I want to know what options we have. If we were to enroll Trisha here, what would the school do to help her learn?"

"We have many children with learning disabilities here, so she certainly wouldn't be alone. Once our school psychologist had a chance to review her testing, then we would schedule a meeting with her teacher, the psychologist, myself, and you in order to develop an IEP for Trisha. The IEP stipulates what special intervention the school would need to take in order to help Trisha. Most likely she would get pulled out of the class several times a week for remedial reading with a small group of children. They would meet with the special education teacher to work on their reading skills. It's a nice group of children and we have an excellent teacher."

"Is she trained in Orton-Gillingham?"

"Orton, what?" Louise asked, confused.

"Orton-Gillingham, it's a method of teaching language arts to dyslexics."

"I'm not certain, Kate, but if she is, she doesn't use it in the class. I know she has a master's in special education and she's very well liked by the students. But she uses the same language arts program as the classroom teacher, so they can be consistent and not confuse the children. She just slows things down and gives them more individual attention. But not all the children in that group are dyslexic. We have a wide range of disabilities here. The public school takes everyone, you know. We can't be choosy. We are required to do our best with every student and I think our testing scores show that we do a very good job."

"I'm certain you do, Louise. The teacher I observed seemed very dedicated. But what happens if a child doesn't learn to read, even with special education?"

"Oh, most of them do, eventually. These things take time."

"How much time, Louise? And would she remain in second grade until she learned or would you advance her?"

"That all depends on Trisha. But some parents don't like to wait, and as I'm sure you know, it's those parents who end up suing the county."

"Actually, I don't know. What do you mean they sue the county?"

"Of course you know, Kate. Isn't that why you're here today, so that you can say in court that you've gone through the proper channels?"

I reddened. "I'm feeling very in the dark, here. This is all new to me. Honestly, I would really like to keep Trisha right where she is, and I haven't given up on that, I won't try and mislead you. But I have no intention of suing this county. What good would it do?"

Louise appeared genuinely surprised that I was unaware of this apparently common practice. "Most parents with any savvy usually sue the county for failure to educate their children. The law says that every child has a right to an optimum education in the least restrictive setting. So families take the county to court and say the public school isn't educating their children, and they almost always win. There are lawyers who do nothing but take on these cases and they have very lucrative practices. The county even has to pay their fees if it loses, and, like I said, it usually does. The county then pays to send that child to a private school for children with learning disabilities. Those tuitions usually run around $25,000 a year, some go as high as $35,000. And that doesn't include testing, buses, court costs."

"My goodness, Louise, just how many students is the county funding right now?"

"I don't know all the figures, but I know that there are two students from this school who are attending other schools on the county's dollar."

"That's over $50,000! Why, you could hire a teacher trained in Orton-Gillingham for that price and probably educate five times as many children. I had no idea. I really didn't."

"There are a lot of loopholes in the law, and, as usual, the lawyers find them. No offense to your husband, Kate. If those schools can help those students better than we can, then it must be the right thing to do, but I don't believe they can. And it's a shame the poorer students with parents lacking the skills necessary to pull this off don't get to go to the special schools, although I'm proud of what we do here. And I would much rather see that extra money right here where it belongs. I heard about a family who sent their child to a boarding school in Vermont and the county was paying the air fare for their visits. I think that's going a little far."

"I have no intention of sending Trisha to Vermont, let alone a special school. Although it has been recommended to us. I'm still getting used to the fact that she needs special intervention at all, let alone a special school." Something nagged at me, this principal had never heard of Orton- Gillingham and this was, by most standards, a good school, with master's level special education teachers. No one wanted their children to go to a "special" school. Something wasn't right if parents were willing to go to the expense of suing a school system to get what their child needed. Considering our experience with the Chesapeake Day School, however, it didn't seem quite so hard to believe. I was beginning to understand the breadth of the problem. "From what I know, the nearest school for the learning disabled is in Baltimore. That's an hour away. She would be riding in a car two hours a day. She has a hard time staying in her seat belt for ten minutes, let alone two hours. How do these families do it?"

"For one thing, the county is responsible for transportation so she would ride a school bus. I've seen a full size school bus from Anne Arundel County with one child on its way to a school in D.C. But Kate, if you decide to sue, you should know that the county is taking a stronger stand on this issue. We want to keep county money where it belongs -- in the public schools -- and lately, the county has been winning the court cases."

"Louise, you have shared a lot of useful information with me. I'm glad you could take the time to meet with me on such short notice."

"It's my pleasure, Kate, we like involved parents such as yourself here and if you decide to enroll Jamie and Trisha, we would be happy to have them."

"Thank you, Louise. That means a lot to me. Especially since we withdrew Jamie after kindergarten." I didn't see the need to tell her we would only be enrolling Tiger. "I can see where some administrators might feel angry about that. I appreciate that you don't. I'll get back to you on our decision." We shook hands and she escorted me to the door.

"Here's some information on our language arts program. We're using a brand new, state of the art program. It combines the best of phonics and whole language, and it has some lovely readers to accompany the program. Why don't you take it home with you?"

"Thank you, I will. Good-bye, Louise, have a good afternoon."

"Thank you, Kate."

I glanced at my watch and realized I needed to hurry in order to get back to the hospital within the allotted lunch hour. I began to regret alerting Warner to my departure, knowing he would be watching the clock until I returned. As I walked quickly down the hall I recognized the second grade class lining up in the hall. They were in single file and the teacher had her hand raised in a "V" signaling the class to be quiet. She snapped her fingers sharply at two children who were whispering and looked at them sternly. The pretty, little girl who had solved the addition problem was in the front of the line standing quietly. I had a fleeting thought that what these children were learning was not how to tap into their creativity and inner strengths, but how to stand in line and how to conform. I knew Jamie was like the little girl in the front of the line, that sort of school behavior came easily to her. But what I hoped she would learn in school was not more of the same, but how to take risks and find her voice, how to speak confidently and trust her thoughts and ideas, not stand quietly in order to please an overworked teacher.

I winked at the two children who had just been snapped at and they began to giggle. I quickened my pace for fear that I had gotten them into trouble. When I pushed open the heavy, institutional doors, I was glad to breathe in the fresh, cool air. I grabbed onto my purse and sprinted the rest of the way to the van.

When I arrived home that evening, I made popcorn for Jamie and Tiger and they settled into a movie. I used their immersion in the television as an opportunity to soak in a hot bath full of all the wonderful smelling gels and lotions that I never had time to use. By the time Max arrived with the sitter, I was relaxed and ready for a night out.

"Wow, you look great!" he said enthusiastically. "Is that a new dress?"

"Thank you, and, no, it was new three years ago. It's just your basic, little black dress."

"I like the little part." He leaned down and kissed me lightly on the cheek. "Mm, you smell good, too. Give me five minutes to change and we're out of here." He looked at his watch. "Tiger, Jamie, time me, if I'm not down in five minutes, I'll double your allowance this week!" and he sprinted up the stairs.

"Jamie," Tiger whispered, "will you tell me when five minutes are up? I can't tell time very well."

"Sure," Jamie said kindly. "Look at the microwave. What does the clock say?"

"Um, four, sixty-five."

"No, Tiger, you turned it around. It's six, forty-five. When it reads six, fifty, we win."

"Will you tell me anyway, Jamie?"

"N.P.'s. That means no problem."

"Okay. N.P.'s, Jamie," Tiger said confidently, looking up at her sister with complete trust. I was thankful that Jamie was patient with Tiger's dyslexia, I knew how it could easily be a source of sibling ridicule.

I greeted Corrinne, our sixteen-year-old babysitter. She put her books on the counter in order to pet Baxter and then showed Jamie and Tiger the Outburst Junior game she had brought.

"That looks like fun," I said. "That was thoughtful of you, Corrinne. Here's a number where we'll be and money for the pizza. It should be here any minute."

"We ordered anchovies just for you, Corrinne," Tiger said cheerfully.

"Yuck!" Corrinne groaned.

"Just teasing," Tiger said proudly. "We know you hate them. We got you double pepperoni and a big bottle of diet soda."

"That sounds much better." Tiger grabbed her hand and pulled her into the family room.

Max appeared in his khakis and a handsome sweater. It was six, fifty-two. "I owe you two some money," he said, feigning disappointment. "I figured it was worth it to your mom if it meant I had time to brush my teeth." He walked over to Jamie and Tiger and gave them each a loud, sloppy kiss. "Aren't you glad I brushed my teeth?"

"Ew, Dad, that is totally gross," Jamie said, wiping her face.

"Love you!" I called from the kitchen. "Thanks again, Corrinne. Don't hesitate to call."

"Don't worry -- we'll be fine," she called back.

Max drove a shiny, black Saab, with smooth, black leather interior. I sank into the warm, soft seat and breathed in the scent of his after-shave mixed with a faint smell of office air conditioning and leather. Unlike the van, his car was spotless. He slipped the sporty car into third gear and put his hand on my knee.

"Max," I said, "was there any talk at the last board meeting about enrollment?"

"Sure. Frances always gives an update in her head's report. Why?"

"Is there a waiting list for second grade?"

"Let me think a minute. I know there's always a waiting list for kindergarten and first, and sixth grade usually has one because the local middle schools are so crowded and full of drugs. Come to think of it, there is someone waiting to get into second grade. I remember because Frances said the family was pushing her to let their daughter in and put the class over the cap of twenty students. Her father is a new doctor in the area and they have a son in preschool. Frances doesn't want to lose this family, so she asked the board to consider making second grade twenty-one."

"What happened?" I asked.

"It's in the mission statement, we can't go past twenty, it really isn't debatable, although Frances would rather it be at her discretion." Max took his hand from my knee and downshifted, expertly driving around a corner, smoothly accelerating through the turn. "What's on your mind? I can hear the wheels turning in your head."

"Tiger mentioned that there was a new girl visiting the class today. You know how prospective students are required to spend a day at the school before they can be admitted. Tiger mentioned it because she said the girl was sort of snobby. I guess she said something rude to Tiger about reading baby books. She bragged about how many books she's read. But what I couldn't figure out is why she would be visiting when the class is full. Now I see why Frances was questioning me about Tiger's tutoring. Jesus, Max, they've already decided, they're going to kick her out! She's going to put this new girl in her place."

"I wouldn't be surprised," Max said thoughtfully. "Did Frances ever put your agreement in writing?"

"Believe it or not she did. But Tiger doesn't stand a chance until I find her some tutoring. I can't believe it's been this hard."

"We'll find something. I'll ask around the office, see if I can get some leads. In the meantime, Katie, you could use a night out. I'll be designated driver, you just relax and have fun," he said as he gently massaged my shoulder.

I turned and smiled at him. "Thanks, I appreciate it." I sighed deeply. "While we're on the subject of tonight, tell me about T.C. Why haven't I met him?"

"I don't know him all that well. He's only been with the firm a few months, but he seems to be a good guy. He works his butt off. He's already brought in a lot of money, I'm sure he'll be made partner before too long. What does Leslie say?"

"She's nuts about him!" I pulled the sun visor down and flipped open the mirror. "It worries me a little, but she deserves to have some fun," I said as I put on some lipstick. "Does he seem serious about her?"

"He doesn't say much, but he's been smiling a lot lately. You know the grin," he looked at me out of the corner of his eye and squeezed my leg.

I rolled my eyes and snuggled into the seat. "Why don't we switch cars for a week? I could get used to this one."

Max looked at me nervously. "You know the kids don't like to ride in this car. They said there are too many rules and they can't see out the back windows."

"I don't know, I think we should consider it. Besides, there is nothing Jamie enjoys more than riding around with you in this car. I guess it's that Oedipal thing, wanting to marry Daddy."

Max put his hand back on the padded steering wheel. "Is this something I should be worried about?"

"No, just be aware that she needs your attention more than ever. She's probably feeling a little uncomfortable around you now that she's maturing. It's an adolescent girl's biggest fear -- that becoming a woman means losing her father."

I felt a wave of nostalgia wash over me. That is what happened to me. I lost my father just as I was about to become a young woman. Although thirty years had numbed the pain, it still surfaced unexpectedly. The grief and fear were like an endless abyss that I kept safely covered with a thin layer of protective scar tissue, but every so often a feeling would seep out.

My sisters had both cried and cried when my father died. They sobbed to those who would listen and talked about how much they loved and missed him. But not me. I was the youngest. I worried. People whispered that I hadn't cried, but I didn't have the luxury. The backbone of my family was gone and the rest of them were incapacitated with grief. Who would take care of us? Even after Aunt Matty's arrival, I continued to worry. I was always on the lookout for the unwelcome and the unexpected. It made me strong and deliberate and determined. It wasn't until I had two healthy children and Max and I were on solid ground financially that I finally began to relax and trust that my life was on course. The worst was over. My life was controllable and predictable at last.

But that security was gone once again. Tiger's dyslexia and my inability to save her were disrupting the scar tissue. I had promised myself that my children would never experience the fear and uncertainty that I had as a child, that I would protect them from that. How naive I had been. It was, and always had been, totally out of my control. I shuddered involuntarily.

I looked over at Max and could see he was deep in thought about Jamie. I closed my small handbag and placed it in my lap. I took a deep breath and pulled my arms close, hugging myself, containing the shudder and pushing my dark thoughts back down.

"Adolescent girls. I can't think of anything more foreign to me. I didn't even have a sister to practice on," he said. "I am totally in the dark here, Katie. You're going to have to help me with this one."

"Don't worry, Max. You'll do fine. Just love her as you always have, hug her with those big bear hugs of yours, spend time with her, just reassure her that she'll always be your girl," I said quietly.

Max looked over at me and smiled. "I can do that. That part is a piece of cake. I guess I'll just follow her lead. Don't you think she'll let me know when she wants me to back off?"

"Yes. She's very good at that. But you may have to take the initiative with her. Respect her privacy, but don't stop knocking on her door."

"That makes sense. I hadn't thought much about it before. I suppose I probably would have distanced from her without even thinking about it. Shit! I'm not ready for this."

"She's lucky to have you."

Max pulled the car into Leslie's driveway, pulled up the emergency brake and leaned over and kissed me. I reached out and pulled him to me. I held him close and clung to his strong arms and breathed in his familiar scent. I had often referred to Max's cologne as my aromatherapy and I allowed it to comfort me now. Eventually he gently pulled away. "That was a nice start to the evening! Are you ready to have some fun?"

"Sure," I said softly.

The evening went smoothly and I eventually relaxed and enjoyed having an evening out. Max, Leslie, and I had been close for a long time and it must have been intimidating for T.C. But we had worked extra hard to make the evening a success and I could see that Leslie appreciated our efforts.

"Her name is Linda Goldman. I have her number if you want to call her." It was Max, calling me from the office on Monday. He had found a lead in the tutor search.

"How did you find her?"

"I put out an E mail to everyone this morning and one of the legal secretaries came to me this afternoon with this name. She has a dyslexic niece who attends her program every morning for a few hours. She's in Columbia. It's a little far, but it's a lead."

"That's great, Max. Please tell her thank you." I called the number as soon as we hung up.

"Linkages," a cheerful voice said.

"Hi, I'm looking for Linda Goldman."

"You've found her. Who's calling, please?"

I liked this woman as soon as I heard her voice and the more we talked the more impressed I was with her knowledge and competency. Her tutors were trained in Orton-Gillingham and she appreciated my awareness of this approach. When I described Tiger she said she would be perfect for her program.

"Linkages was designed for children like Tiger," she said, "the kids who fall between the cracks. Is she reading?"

"Very inconsistently. She'll read a word on one line and stumble over the same word on the next. It's very frustrating."

"Well, if you think you're frustrated, think how she feels. The only consistent thing about learning disabilities is the inconsistency." Linda described her program at length. Tiger would attend two hours every morning and then return to her regular classroom. "Do you think you can get the school to cooperate? We've had trouble with public and private schools. Even though we're saving them time and money, there's a real resistance to removing children from the classroom and putting them in a program outside the school. It seems to threaten them some how. But if these children don't come here, they fall so far behind sometimes there's no catching up. Why don't you send me copies of Tiger's testing and we can set up an appointment. Better yet, let's not waste time, why don't you fax me the testing today, mark it confidential, and then bring her by Wednesday morning. I'll look it over and develop a brief educational plan, and then spend time with her Wednesday. I can let you know that afternoon if I think we can help her. And if we can, which I think is more than likely, we'll start Thursday morning. Can you arrange things with the school by then?"

"Absolutely," I said enthusiastically. "I like your style, Linda. You don't waste time. I've been hitting a lot of dead ends, but something tells me you don't know what a dead end is."

"They are a waste of time. There's always a way," she said cheerfully. "Fax me those testing results and I will see you Wednesday morning. I'll fax you directions to our offices. I look forward to meeting Tiger."

When I hung up the phone I whirled around in my chair with delight. At last! I called the school and let Frances know that Tiger would be out of school Wednesday morning until eleven-thirty. And if all went well, she would be out of school every morning for some time to come. Frances was caught off guard. She

136

complained that it was more than the agreed upon two days a week, but I interrupted her and said we would have to give it a try and evaluate things later. That seemed to appease her and I ended the call before she had a chance to change her mind.

I jumped up to go tell someone the good news. Rob was in the hall talking with a patient. I smiled and waited for him in the chart room. I poured some coffee and sat down. He came in shortly. "You look like you just swallowed Tweety Bird. What's up?" he asked as he sat down next to me.

"I found a tutor for Tiger!"

"Finally! That's great, Katie."

"It really is."

"When does she start?"

"Wednesday morning. This woman is unbelievably competent and positive and I think for the first time that there is light at the end of the tunnel."

"Wednesday morning? What did Warner say?"

I hesitated, I hadn't thought it through, but I couldn't let Rob see that. "I'm not sure yet. But the important thing is Tiger will finally get what she needs."

"I agree, that's what counts, Tiger," he said distractedly. We both seemed to know what it meant. I would be forced to leave the hospital. The unspoken words hung in the air like a thick smog.

"Well, I have group in a few minutes. I just couldn't wait to tell you." I realized at that moment why I told him, it was the beginning of an ending. I was preparing us both for what was about to happen. I stood to leave and Rob stared at the table.

"I hate change," he said with an understanding smile on his face.

I felt a strong shifting of emotions inside me. "I do too. I resist it at all cost, but sometimes it's unavoidable."

"Yeah, it's like a damn pot hole in the road." He continued looking into his coffee mug.

"I'll talk to you later, Rob, don't leave today without saying good-bye." I left the room without looking back at him.

Late that afternoon I knocked on Warner's office door. He beckoned me and I entered stiffly, feeling detached, disassociated, almost as if I was observing myself from some remote place in the room.

"Well, Kate, I see you've managed to last the whole day. That's something new." Warner remained seated. It was noticeably rude for someone who prides himself on being a southern gentleman.

I decided to stand and cleared my throat. "Well, Warner, it looks as if you're going to get your way. I'm resigning from my position."

Warner's startled expression revealed his surprise. He was quiet for a moment but then broke into a wide grin. "Actually, Kate, I was hoping I'd get to fire you," he said, chuckling at his own wit.

"Jesus, Warner, could you please not be an asshole right now, this is hard enough as it is."

"I wouldn't want to disappoint you, Kate. So, why are you quitting? Can't cut the mustard around here?"

Feeling defeated, I sat down. "It looks as if I won't be able to put in the hours I used to. I have personal circumstances that will make it impossible."

"You make it sound as if you were here all the time."

"I am doing my best not to stoop to your level, Warner, but don't push me. I don't want to leave this job, you know that. I think I could do it justice with fewer hours. It's a temporary situation with my daughter, I just need a little more flexibility."

"And you already know that's impossible. Health care ain't what it used to be. It's forty hours plus or nothing."

"I'm sorry you see it that way, Warner. I don't think you're doing the hospital any favors. But if this is how it has to be, then I'll give you two choices, either I give you two weeks notice or tomorrow is my last day. If it's two weeks, I will not be here on Wednesday, Thursday or Friday mornings this week, or any mornings next week."

Warner was quiet and looked at me with squinting eyes. After a few moments he said, "You will work this week, minus the mornings, and Friday will be your last day. You can work out the rest with human resources."

I stood. "Fine. It's a deal. Good-bye, Warner." Warner said nothing and I slammed the door behind me.

"Good riddance, asshole!" I muttered through gritted teeth. I was looking down at the floor and almost ran into Rob. He was leaning against the wall opposite Warner's office with his arms folded.

"Is Warner going somewhere?" he asked seriously.

"No. I am, and you already know that," I said tiredly.

"When?"

"Friday is my last day."

"Oh."

I looked up at him and my eyes filled with tears. "Please don't make this any harder than it already is."

"I'm sorry, Katie, I'm not trying to make anything hard for you. In fact, I was selfishly thinking about me. About how miserable this place will be without you, that sort of thing."

"I'm sorry, I don't mean to make this just about me, I know how I would feel

138

if you were the one leaving." I tried to smile through my tears.

Rob put his arm through mine and walked me down the hall. "Let's get out of ear shot. Warner's fat ear is probably glued to the door."

We walked slowly, arm in arm, my head on his shoulder. "I love this place, Rob. I'll miss it desperately. I don't know what I'm going to do with myself."

"What about private practice?"

"I would get totally bored. I love the excitement of the hospital. I would go nuts in an office by myself all day. Besides, how many clients can come to therapy between the hours of twelve and three o'clock? I've got to be there for Tiger right now. I have a lot of thinking to do."

Rob rubbed my back affectionately. "You won't forget about me, you'll stay in touch?"

"Definitely. And don't you go fall in love with my replacement," I said in feigned protest.

"There isn't a chance in hell of that, I'm afraid."

Dolores walked out of the chart room and saw us. "What's going on?"

"Katie's leaving us, Friday is her last day," Rob said sadly.

"Oh no! This is terrible!" Dolores grabbed me dramatically, which was her way, and made me feel special and wanted.

We hugged each other tightly. "Thanks, Dolores, I will miss you terribly. Mm, I have always loved your hugs."

Dolores ended the hug first and looked over at Rob. "We have to have a going away party. Friday afternoon! We need to start making preparations. I'll call Leslie over at adult psych, she'll want to help."

"Good idea. I hadn't thought of that. I was too busy feeling sorry for myself," Rob said.

"This one is going to miss you most of all," Dolores said, patting Rob on the back. I felt like Dorothy saying good-bye to the Tin Man. Rob smiled weakly and I said good-bye to them both for the day, feeling a need to get out of the hospital. My emotions were coming in waves and I began to feel a little dizzy. I turned out the lights in my office and looked back at that special place I had created, where all my creative energies, all my love and compassion for the people I had helped, and all my studies and talents were nurtured. I quickly closed the door and decided to take the back steps and the long way home.

Lesson Seven:
Sacrifice

From the day a child is born
parents begin to learn the true meaning of sacrifice.
No longer is a parent self determining,
but instead has to learn selflessness, compromise, and the hardest,
sacrifice:
sacrificing personal goals and pleasures
for the well being of the child.
Some learn this as early as pregnancy,
unfortunately, others never learn it at all.

"I can't believe Tiger doesn't have to go to school today," Jamie said as we turned down the lane to school.

"She is going to school, it's just a different school, and for part of the day. She'll be back before lunch."

"I don't want to go to a different school," Tiger said quietly.

This surprised me. No matter how Tiger struggled, she was adamant that she liked her teacher and class. Mary was punitive at times about Tiger's differences, and yet Tiger remained loyal to her school.

"What's worrying you, honey?" I asked her.

"Well, I might miss art, and I'll miss recess and the other kids will ask where I am. And Mrs. Peterson might be mad at me for being late."

I felt myself stiffen, but I was careful not to let Tiger know how I felt, it would only leave her in a loyalty conflict. The survivor in her knew she had to make peace with Mary Peterson. It was the only way. "I told you I've talked with her, and remember when I talked to the class? Everyone should understand where you've been. But if Mrs. Peterson gives you a hard time, I want to know about it."

"She won't say anything, Mom. It's how she looks at me. I wish I could be like everyone else. I don't want to learn differently. I just don't like it," Tiger said resignedly. The discussion was over. There was no reassuring her or making it better. This was the new Tiger, the one that accepted her fate, like it or not.

140

"This is weird," Jamie said as she got out of the van. "I feel like I'm forgetting something."

I smiled at her sensitivity. "I guess we'll get used to it. I love you, and don't forget, Lois picks you up today, I have to work late since this is my last week."

"Bye, Mom, I love you. Bye, Tiger, see you this afternoon," she called sweetly.

"What will you do, Mommy, if you aren't working?" Tiger asked as we drove away from her school.

I was careful not to leave the impression that Tiger was the reason I was leaving the hospital. She had enough on her shoulders without me adding to the burden. And this was the kind of thing she would notice instinctively. She often understood the true meaning of events before I did. "I'm not sure, Tiger. I think the first thing I'll do is get us organized at home, clean up, that sort of thing. I'm looking forward to having a little more time at home. And I'll have more time with you and Jamie. That's a very good thing."

"Who will take care of the families at the hospital?"

"Well, they'll need to hire a replacement. They need to interview some people and then pick the person they like best. And then that person will take care of the people at the hospital."

"I bet they'll miss you."

"And I'll miss them. But we'll still be friends."

"What about Lois, Mommy. What will she do?"

"That's sweet of you to think about Lois. But she's happy to work fewer hours. She's fifty-nine years old, you know. Which isn't so old, but she would like to have more time with her grandchildren, and she's getting so she doesn't like to drive at night. She'll still pick you up now and then. She's not going anywhere, she'll just be around less."

"What will she do for money?"

"She has enough money in the bank to live on, and don't forget about her husband, who still works and earns a good living."

"Will he share his money with her?"

"Of course, they're a family. Families share everything. It doesn't matter who earns the money, every one does their part to help out, whether it makes money or not."

Tiger's interest was leaving me with an uncomfortable feeling. Max had been more than understanding when I told him about the hospital. He knew it was the only way to help Tiger, and surely he knew it was either me or him. It just turned out to be me. But I had always worked in our marriage. I had always earned money. Tiger's questions were touching a nerve. "I don't share my money with Jamie. And she certainly doesn't share her money with me."

"No, she doesn't. But Daddy and I do, just like Lois and her husband."

"Mom?"

"Yes, Tiger?"

"If something happens to Daddy, what will you do for money now that you're quitting your job?"

Linda Goldman and Linkages were better than my greatest hopes. Linda was a wealth of energy and information and Tiger liked her immediately. By Wednesday at three o'clock I had received a fax listing all the things her program could offer Tiger. The list included an educational goal to correspond with each of Tiger's areas of difficulty. Linda would be expecting Tiger Thursday morning for her first Orton-Gillingham tutoring session. I let out a yelp as I read the fax. I was sitting in the chart room and looked around, embarrassed at my outburst.

Rob rushed in and slammed down a chart angrily. He was wearing a faded denim shirt and tan corduroys. His boots clicked on the floor and his sandy blonde hair was tousled. "That Blair is having a very negative impact on this group of patients. She is one powerful kid. Just when I think we're getting somewhere in group, she sabotages the process. She either undermines me or ridicules someone's sharing. She flirts with all the male patients and then slams them when they share an honest feeling. She has everyone so intimidated no one will share anything for fear Blair will disapprove. I've never seen anything like it."

Rob poured a cup of coffee and sat down across from me. "Have you looked at her chart? Doctor 'I'll take you on a Tripp' has her on all kinds of meds. He says she's either a borderline personality disorder or bipolar. He's talking about lithium! Shit, she's not manic depressive or borderline, or any of the above. She's a streetwise addict and she's even got him running scared."

I smiled at Rob. "What?" he said, annoyed.

"Nothing. Please continue."

"Excuse me, I'm getting pissed off here, don't interrupt. Anyway, I have set some very tight limits on her in group, and she doesn't like it one bit, but God only knows what damage she's doing out in the lounge when we're not around." Rob looked up at me and sighed. "You can talk now."

"You sure?"

"Yes, I'm sure." He took a sip of his coffee and his eyes smiled at me over the rim of his cup.

"I've got a session with her family this afternoon. I'll see if I can find out what makes her tick. I promise I'll have something by this evening. How's that?"

"I'll take anything you can give me. How is she with her parents?"

"At first she acted like a scared little girl, but once she detoxed she had her courage back in full force, as you well know. She's extremely manipulative and her parents don't know what to do so they just ignore her. Which of course only makes her act out more."

"I haven't heard you use that word in a long time, Kate," Rob said thoughtfully.

"What word?"

"Manipulative."

"Did I really say that?"

Rob smiled. "You did."

"I hate that word. People in our field are always labeling kids as being manipulative without taking the time to understand how they came to be that way."

"You've always said that if children are manipulating to get what they need, it's because they can't ask for it directly. I learned that from you, Kate, and I agree with it. So what is Blair asking for that she isn't getting? Attention? Love? Money -- not. Sex? Getting plenty of that. She's got half the patients out there drooling. It's really sad to see a kid that age so savvy."

"The last family session we had was a screaming match. Mom takes her on until she's outwitted, then she cries. Which is when Dad steps in and starts screaming at her for hurting her mother. It's a classic cycle. But we're missing something."

"I think it's old, Kate. I think it goes back before the drug use. She's an addict all right, and the drugs have become the problem. But there's a deep-seated pain that we're not reaching. Maybe it's in that family."

"Do you think she was sexually abused?"

"It's something like that. She says she wasn't, and I believe her. I think the sexual stuff came with the drugs, you know, turning tricks for dope. But she's pissed as hell at her parents about something." He offered me a sad wink. "But we'll find it, won't we Katie."

"Without a doubt."

"This isn't going to work," Leslie said as she walked through my half open door.

I looked up from my writing, "What isn't going to work?"

"You can't leave. I'm sorry, Katie, but you're needed here."

"I'm not thinking about it, Leslie. I'm in total denial, so don't remind me."

Leslie sprawled out on one of my sofas and I swiveled my desk chair around and put my feet up on my desk. I stroked my pen and we sat in silence. Leslie stared at the floor.

"I can't do this, Les," I said, putting my feet back on the floor. "I have a very

143

tough session coming up and I'm getting depressed thinking about Friday as my last day."

"Can't you file a grievance? Or maybe go complain higher up in the company? We all know Warner's an incompetent jerk. Why should he have the final say?"

"I think the company appreciates what Warner's doing. He's saving them money. Besides, technically I wasn't fired. I quit."

"You were forced to quit. That's like saying Richard Nixon wasn't impeached. It was a matter of time, Katie, Warner had you up against the wall."

"I'd rather quit than have it on my resume that I was fired. Or even that I filed a grievance. That scares future employers as much as a sexual harassment suit. It makes you look like a trouble maker, not a team player. And I definitely will be reentering the work force. Besides, appeals and grievances take time and Tiger started tutoring today. Lois picked her up, but she won't be able to do it very often. I need to focus on Tiger right now. Her dyslexia isn't going to go away, even if she learns to read. And as much as I don't want to leave, seeing her in a holding pattern while the rest of the world passes her by is worse."

"What's this world coming to? Managed Care calls all the shots and the schools can't educate the children. People work harder and harder and nobody has a life."

I looked over at Leslie, "Somehow I think the subject of our conversation has switched from me to you."

Leslie reddened, "Oops. I guess it did. I just need your secret on how you handle Max's working all the time. When T.C. and I are together, it's wonderful, but four weeks into the relationship and he's working late on Friday night! That's not a good sign."

"That firm really drives them, and T.C. is trying to make partner. I think they all compete with each other to see who can work the most hours. I doubt it's going to get much better, at least for a while."

"Thanks for the good news. I was hoping it was only temporary."

"Maybe it is, I don't know. I guess you get used to it, but that doesn't mean you'll like it any better. I'm sorry, Les. But you guys can work this out. Better you know the ropes now, than when you're more involved."

"Well, I'm feeling pretty involved already. Is it too soon to wrap myself in cellophane?"

"Definitely, besides, I heard that just makes you sweat."

Leslie laughed, "Don't make me laugh because I'm still depressed about you leaving."

I stood up. "We can't go there. Not now. I'm going back to my denial and you can't stop me. Go back to your unit, I've got a family in a few minutes and I need to come up with a strategy."

Leslie pushed herself off the couch and walked slowly to the door. "I hate this. I feel totally abandoned."

I sighed and walked her the rest of the way to the door. "We'll still have lunch and see each other a lot. We have to or I'll go crazy. And I need someone who's still out in the world to make sure I don't get loopy, you know, watching soaps and cleaning the house all the time."

"A little cleaning wouldn't be so bad."

"Get out of here!" I laughed and pushed her out the door.

The Tilghmans were late for their appointment so I checked in with Blair while we waited. She was sitting in the lounge smoking a cigarette. The adolescents were permitted to smoke as long as they had parental permission. It didn't surprise me that Blair's parents had allowed her to smoke. She had her feet up on the windowsill and was staring blankly out the window. She was wearing faded, hip-hugger jeans covered with peace signs and patches, and a midriff top that exposed her small, flat stomach and the shiny gold ring in her navel. Her hair was tousled, but clean, and although she tried to hide her youth with foundation and eye liner, I could see a very pretty fifteen year old beneath her well-planned facade.

I sat down next to her and looked out the window. "Your parents should have been here by now. But it's raining pretty hard, maybe they're stuck in traffic."

"No, they're late. It's their m.o. I think it makes them feel important. It's like they think they're Bill and Hillary Clinton, make people wait for hours until they find time to show up at the ball. I guess that makes me Chelsea, God help me."

"Well, Chelsea, this meeting is important, too, and I'm sure they know that. They'll be here soon."

"Don't delude yourself, Mrs. Cunningham. They don't give a shit about me. The only time they pay attention to me is when they can dress me up in some Donna Karan outfit and show me off to their friends. Shit, they have me tend bar at their parties. They think it's cute." Blair exhaled a long stream of smoke.

I waved away some of the smoke, "Isn't someone suing the tobacco companies for second hand smoke damage?"

Blair looked over at me, trying to muster the nastiest look she could. "Ha, Ha."

"Any idea what you'd like to talk about today?"

"Yeah! When do I get the hell out of here."

"Lucky for you your insurance covers the entire six weeks."

"Lucky my ass. I feel like a caged animal, locked in here all day."

"I think recreational therapy is taking you guys bowling today," I said teasingly.

"Oh, wow! Like I want to go throw some stupid ass ball around and look like

145

a total geek. I don't think so. I think I'll come down with the flu this afternoon, throw up a few times, that will scare them enough to let me stay."

"Well, in the mean time we have a session to get through," I said keeping us on the subject. Blair was good at throwing out all kinds of tempting issues, throwing up, tending bar, and although I made a mental note of everything she was saying, I had an agenda and had to stick to it. "I'm looking forward to this one, although it will be my last. Friday's my last day."

"What?" Blair sounded truly disturbed by my news. "But my parents dig you. You're the first one to get my father to come to therapy. Shit!"

"I like them too, but it wasn't me who got your parents to come to therapy."

"What, does this place kick me out or something if they don't come?"

"Well, families are strongly encouraged to participate in the program, at least one parent has to come to sessions and education group, but your dad chose to come on his own. You're the one who got him here, not me."

"You're on crack."

"Maybe, but back to you. You upped the ante with them, you finally got his attention."

"I don't need his attention," Blair said, trying to sound uninterested. "Besides, all my parents ever do is argue, that is, whenever they're actually in the same room together. It's like they each have their own wing of the house. I avoid them at all costs, which isn't hard to do in that house, the last thing I want is for them to focus on me." Blair took another long drag from her cigarette.

"And you're trying to help them with that."

Blair looked annoyed. "Nice technique, Mrs. Cunningham, being sarcastic with your patients. That was a put down."

"On the contrary, Blair," I said sincerely, "I mean it. You see, families are a system. You are very much interconnected with your parents. What you do affects them and what they do affects you and each other. It sounds to me as if your family has been in a very dysfunctional grid lock. Your running away and living on the streets has shaken up the system. And that's when change happens. You've even got your parents coming to therapy together -- in the same room. It's a kind of sacrifice, what you did, to help your family."

"This is totally rare! This is so comical! Tell my parents that my drug use is helping my family, I want to see this."

"I intend to, Blair."

Blair looked at me, her eyes narrowed. "Really?"

"Yes," I said, standing up. "I'm going to go check to see if they're here. I'll come back for you when they're on the unit."

"Whatever," she said, trying unsuccessfully to conceal the caring in her voice.

"And put a shirt on over that top, hospital rules," I said without turning around.

146

The Tilghmans were thirty minutes late and it surprised me how composed they were when they arrived. Mrs. Tilghman gave me a perfunctory apology, but Blair was right about this characteristic of her parents -- it did not appear to be unusual for them to keep people waiting.

Mrs. Tilghman sat immediately. She was wearing a tasteful wool suit with a scarf around her shoulders. Her husband was impeccably dressed with a tailored suit and beautiful woven silk tie. It was obvious that the money in their family went back generations. There was a time, with my meek, working class roots, when old, eastern money was intimidating to me. I would become less outspoken, and almost clumsy around people who were more sophisticated. But working in chemical dependency had taught me that alcohol and drugs were the great equalizers. Money, power, fame, had no impact on the devastation chemical dependency could cause. And Blair was a perfect example. The Tilghmans' only daughter had been prostituting herself in downtown Baltimore.

When Blair came into the office her parents stayed seated on the couch and she chose the seat farthest from them. There were no greetings, no acknowledgement of each other. She kept her eyes to the floor. To my surprise she had changed her clothes. She had on a plain pair of jeans and a beautiful, blue chenille sweater. She had washed off some of her makeup, tamed her hair and put on a petite pair of gold earrings.

"Hi, Blair, you look nice," I whispered.

Being careful to look only at me, she said, "Thanks."

It took some time to cover the fact that I was leaving and who would be their therapist the last weeks of Blair's treatment. Not long after that, Mrs. Tilghman announced to Blair that she would be going to boarding school after she left the hospital. Blair and I were both caught off guard.

"I'm not going to any fucking boarding school, and you can't make me!" she screamed.

"Watch your language, young lady," Mr. Tilghman retorted.

"I'm not going, Daddy! I don't want to! I want to be with my friends."

"You certainly have chosen a fine group of friends, Blair." Mrs. Tilghman said sarcastically. "They all look like they crawled out of the gutter, and they all use drugs,"

"Well in case you haven't noticed, Mommy dearest, so do I! And my friends don't put the drugs up my nose or stick the needles in my arm, I do! All by my little self!"

Mrs. Tilghman shuddered at Blair's words. I knew we would lose the whole session if we stayed on this topic, and I had a lot to cover that afternoon. "I know you want to argue this, Blair, but we have other things to discuss. You threw her a juicy bone, Mr. and Mrs. Tilghman, but Blair's aftercare can be decided later."

147

"It's not a bone, Mrs. Cunningham, it's reality. Blair is not returning home. We can't control her anymore."

Blair jumped up to leave and I quickly stood and rested my hand on her arm. "Wait, Blair. Hang in there with me. Please, Mr. and Mrs. Tilghman, drop the boarding school issue. You are way ahead of me. I don't want to hear about it right now, got it?"

Mr. Tilghman put his hand on his wife's arm. "Please, Dianne, do as she says."

"I must admit," I said, once Blair and I had returned to our seats, "Blair has given me the impression that the two of you argue a lot, and yet I haven't seen that here."

"That was inappropriate, Blair, it's no one's business how your mother and I get along and you--"

I interrupted him, "Mr. Tilghman, we expect Blair to be totally honest with us. And although Blair is in treatment for her drug use, it's clear that your relationship has been upsetting to her in the past. I was just commenting on how impressed I am that you have been able to come together for Blair's sake. Somehow her running away has brought you two closer together."

Mr. Tilghman shifted uncomfortably. "We have busy lives."

"But Randolph, you must admit," Mrs. Tilghman said, "you've been around more since Blair ran away. And we haven't argued as much. We've been too worried and upset to think about anything but Blair."

"You may not see it now, but I think somehow Blair knew your family was in crisis and needed help. I'm not condoning her drug use, in fact she has sacrificed herself enough for one lifetime, it's time she took hold of her life and started working a program, but it's important for you to see that her sole motive was not to make you miserable. It was quite the opposite."

"But Blair has been out of control since sixth grade, when she started her new school. This has been going on for years, Mrs. Cunningham," Diane said.

"What was Blair like before that?"

"Oh, she was a wonderful child! She was sweet, kind, always trying to please us. She was very involved in her ballet and she was good at it. She had nice friends and was well liked."

"How did she do in school?"

"Average. Which was a sore spot. Blair's IQ is quite high, but she just never tried in school. Her teachers liked her because she was well behaved and helpful. But her scores have always been average or below. And once she reached sixth--"

"Whoa!" I said, "Before. Let's stick to before." Why is it that parents are often more comfortable talking about the negative? "Was Blair ever tested for learning disabilities?"

"Of course not!" Mr. Tilghman jumped in. "She's a very bright child, we have proof of that, she just didn't try."

"I've never been good enough for you, Randolph!" Blair interrupted. Why didn't you just have another child and leave me alone! You called me stupid, you said I was lazy! And you didn't listen to me when I said I didn't get stuff. All you wanted was for me to be quiet and good and to please you. It was always about you. Mom hated me because I disappointed you. That's all I am to you--one big, walking, fucking disappointment! Well fuck your disappointment! I don't give a shit anymore. The people on the streets were nicer to me than you two!"

The room fell silent and tears began to stream down Blair's face. I waited for a few moments, then spoke. "I know it's hard to get past the language, but I want you to try to hear the feelings behind Blair's words. This is the first time in the three weeks she's been here that she's let down her tough girl facade. She took a risk just now, and I appreciate you not jumping down her throat." Blair was tough but the kindness in my voice brought more tears. She couldn't stop them now. Her chest began to heave and she buried her face in her hands. I could tell she was getting ready to bolt from the room so I motioned to her parents to go to her. Their discomfort spread across their faces, but eventually Mr. Tilghman sat forward in his chair so that he could stroke her back. Blair flinched at his touch, but didn't stop him.

"I know it's hard to think of Blair's behavior as anything but dysfunctional, but I think her problems are more complicated than being a drug addict. Blair needs to take responsibility for that, there's no question, but unless you make some changes, she doesn't stand a chance of getting clean. You are caught in a destructive triangle. It appears the only time the two of you spend time together and communicate is when Blair's in trouble. Somehow, subconsciously, she knows that. She never seemed to be able to please you, so now she's going to scream loud enough so that you can get your act together. At this point in her life Blair is probably wondering if you're waiting until she leaves home so that you can get a divorce. No wonder she doesn't want to go to boarding school. Look what might happen if she's not around to distract you."

"You don't mince words, do you, Mrs. Cunningham?" Randolph said.

"I don't have time to mince words, Mr. Tilghman."

Blair's parents fidgeted, clearly uncomfortable with what I was saying. Blair had stopped sobbing and was looking up at them stealthily. Mrs. Tilghman tried to bring the focus back to Blair, but before Blair could take the bait and take the family back to its familiar, unhealthy patterns, I stopped them. "What are the two of you going to do about your marriage? You owe it to Blair to let her know."

After an awkward silence, Mrs. Tilghman finally spoke. "I don't know why I'm telling you this, but you're right. Randolph and I are considering a trial separation." Blair stared hard at her mother, trying not to react. "And I guess I agree with you, it isn't Blair's fault. We haven't been close in years. We live separate lives."

"Have you considered marital therapy?" I asked.

"Not really, I think we're beyond that," she said matter-of-factly.

"Do you want a divorce, Daddy?" Blair asked in despair.

Mr. Tilghman cleared his throat, "I'm not sure, Blair. I don't know. Something has to give, and Mrs. Cunningham is right, you being in such trouble has made us aware of how bad it's gotten."

Blair turned to her mother. "Mommy? Is this your idea?"

"Blair, it isn't anyone's idea, or anyone's fault, it just is."

"Great! This is just peachy. Ship me off to fucking boarding school, get a divorce, and then say, 'we hope you get better dear.' Well fuck that! I'm out of here, Mrs. Cunningham, I know you've tried, but they're hopeless! Totally hopeless! Nice family, don't you think?" she said, standing up. "Really warms a kid's heart!" She started for the door but I stood and blocked her exit.

"We're not finished, Blair."

"Oh yes we are," she said, getting in my face and trying desperately to hang onto her anger so she wouldn't cry. "I have to get out of here. I don't have a fucking family so what the fuck are we having family therapy for?"

I gently put my hands on her shoulders and looked in her eye. "I have one more thing to discuss with your parents and I really want you to hear. Please?"

Blair was torn, she wanted to flee, to escape the pain, and it killed me to see her parents watch this passively. No wonder she was so dramatic, her pain had no visible effect on them. I gently turned her around and guided her back to her seat. I handed her a box of tissues and looked over at the strained faces of her parents. "I don't know what you intend to do about your marriage, but I would strongly suggest you enter therapy. You owe it to yourselves and your marriage to try. Even if you still decide to separate, the therapy can help you do that amicably, and with Blair's best interests in mind. I also think you should think twice about sending Blair away right now. If she can get her program on track she will need the support of her aftercare group to stay clean. And if she went to boarding school the pain of worrying and not knowing about you will sabotage any efforts she would make at school. We have a lot of guidelines and suggestions for you on how to set limits for Blair when she returns home and how to support her program. But this brings me to my final issue. I know it is unthinkable for you to consider this, but I believe Blair has a learning disability."

"Mrs. Cunningham," Mr. Tilghman interrupted, "The child has an IQ of 135."

"I didn't say she wasn't intelligent, I can see that she is extremely bright and intuitive. I know how hard it is to hear this, but you've heard a lot worse lately. I think she has a learning disability and that's why she did so poorly in school. When did you learn to read, Blair?"

Blair looked embarrassed and had clearly hoped to be out of the conversation, "Um, I guess it was around third or fourth grade."

"That's only because you were always on the phone with your friends," Mrs. Tilghman added accusingly. Again, I had to stop Blair from reacting.

"Do you like to read, Blair?"

"No. I hate it," she said quickly.

"This doesn't mean anything, Mrs. Cunningham," Mr. Tilghman said, annoyed.

"I would like you to consent to have our psychologist here at the hospital do some educational testing. Your insurance will cover it and it could tell us some things about why Blair's problems began when they did. If there is a disability, then it's not too late to intervene and get her the help she needs. Did you know that twenty percent of the population is dyslexic? It's much more common than most people realize and Blair has all the symptoms. Please, just give it a try. We owe it to Blair to find out."

"Of course you have our consent," Mrs. Tilghman said, glancing at her husband. "You know, my father was dyslexic. He had a terrible time in school."

"He was?" Blair asked in surprise. "But Granddaddy was a heart surgeon!"

"I know. But he had a horrible time in grammar school."

"I'll have you sign the consent form before you leave. I will also give you the names of some excellent marital therapists. In the next two sessions you will have to work with my replacement on setting up some structure at home for Blair, and perhaps finding a different school, or at least some tutoring if there is a disability. You have a lot to cover. I'll get the testing going right away so that you have the results by next week."

The Tilghmans stood to leave and, to my relief, Mrs. Tilghman hugged Blair. They stood there for a long time and I could hear them both sniffing. "I love you, honey," Mrs. Tilghman said softly. Mr. Tilghman stood stiffly, uncomfortable with his wife and daughter's embrace. At last he reached over and rubbed Blair's back. "You keep working in here, Blair. You can do it, I know you can."

Blair looked up at her dad and smiled. We said goodbye and I suggested Blair take some time for herself before joining group. She thanked me in a brusque manner but I could see the gratitude in her eyes. I understood and didn't push. It was still unsafe for Blair to let her guard down completely. She went to the lounge to smoke a cigarette. I wanted to join her. I was exhausted.

The going away party was bittersweet. There was a large turnout in the beginning. Even the president of the hospital came, but he didn't stay long. He

151

shook my hand and wished me well, but he was so nervous he couldn't stop moving around and left as soon he finished his square of cake and had thrown away his party napkin.   Warner appeared at some point and mingled uncomfortably. Eventually he said good-bye and that he would miss looking at my legs. Refusing to stoop to his level, I wished him well and told him that I sincerely hoped the unit would thrive. Most of the doctors stopped in, which meant a lot to me, including Dr. Tripp who said he would sincerely miss me at team meetings. I smiled knowingly. Another doctor who I had always respected and admired offered me a position in his private practice and gave me his office manager's number. It helped to know I had other options.

By the end of the afternoon the party had dwindled down to my favorite people and we all seemed to relax once we realized who remained. Leslie announced it was time for gifts and I protested. Opening gifts had always made me feel self conscious, but my objections were overruled. Betty proudly gave me my own cut glass jar, filled to the brim with M&M's. Dolores presented me with a framed needlepoint of the serenity prayer:

> *"God, grant me the*
> *serenity to accept the things I cannot change,*
> *courage to change the things I can, and*
> *wisdom to know the difference."*

Leslie had insisted on going next and smiled broadly when she handed me a gift certificate for a full day of beauty at a local spa. I practically purred when I read what was included: a full body massage, pedicure, manicure and facial.

I started to thank everyone when I heard Rob clear his throat. I looked over at him and felt tears begin to well in my eyes when I saw his sad face. I was mortified that I might cry in front of everyone and stood quickly to retrieve the small gift in his hands. "Last but not least," I said in an unsteady voice. Inside the gift box was a pound of coffee and a mug that said:

> *Without friends, life would be nothing but decaf.*

I looked up at him and said, "Ain't that the truth."

We smiled at each other and then he pulled a single yellow rose out from behind his back. I caught my breath, "My favorite. How did you know?"

"You mentioned it once, I don't remember when."

After a tearful goodbye, Rob offered to help me carry my boxes to the van. On the way down the elevator he said, "You were right about Blair, did you see the testing? She is dyslexic. Good job. I think Blair is very relieved to know what's been making her life so difficult all this time. She's actually starting to calm down and do some work. Way to go."

"Thanks. You know, I don't think that would have occurred to me if it hadn't been for Tiger. How many learning disabilities have I missed over the years? It would have to be a lot. I wonder how many of our prisons and treatment centers are filled with people with undiagnosed learning disabilities."

"When you first mentioned you wanted to have Blair tested, I worried that you were going to start suspecting everyone of having a learning disability. Remember when the recovery movement was starting up and it seemed everyone had been sexually abused?"

"But sadly, most of them had."

"Exactly, you were right about Blair, and right to question it. I can't believe I ever doubted you."

"I can't either," I said jokingly.

"I won't let it happen again." We both laughed.

When the last box was loaded he reached up, grabbed the leather strap and pulled the back door shut. "That about does it," he said brushing his hands off on his pants.

"I guess it's time to wash this poor thing," I said, embarrassed at the dirt on his hands.

"You don't belong in this big, clunky thing, Katie. It just isn't you."

"Hey!" I said in mocked offense. "It's a top of the line eight-seater 1996 Dodge Caravan!"

"You, my dear, belong in a little red convertible with two seats and five speeds. With your passion for life, you should be riding off into the sunset in a shiny red Porsche. That would be more fitting."

I blushed at Rob's comments. "I guess driving this van is one of the sacrifices I make for my children. It's not much fun for me, but it's more comfortable for them, and they can fit their friends into it. When we bought it I told Max I would own only one van in my lifetime. I said the same thing when we got the dog. Kids need vans and dogs. It's what you do."

"It still isn't you, not the you I see."

"But I guess it's part of me, a good part of me."

"So what happens to that passion? That love of life and excitement?"

"Oh, Rob. This is why I get so confused! I love how I feel when I'm with you, but I also know they are dangerous feelings. It scares me." Somehow leaving the hospital was enabling me to speak the unspoken between us.

"Damn, Katie," he said, grabbing my arms. "I can't get you out of my head. I know it's wrong, I owe it to you to try, but I get crazy when I'm around you."

I felt a tremendous heat deep inside, combined with a terror of letting go of my resolve. It was exhilarating. Our faces were just inches apart and I could feel the warmth of his breath. It was all I could do to push him away. I felt dizzy and confused and yet desperately wanted to be in his arms. I turned around and leaned my hands on the van, "Shit, Rob. Shit."

Rob started pacing back and forth, "I'm sorry, Katie, I'm sorry. You don't need me to complicate your life any more than it already is." He turned toward me and put his hands in his pockets, "Can we stay friends, or is it safer if I just keep my distance?"

"No!" I said immediately, turning around. "Don't stay away! I mean, I want to stay friends. I really do. I don't know what I'd do if you weren't my friend. I'm really going to miss seeing you every day," I hesitated. "But that really isn't fair to you, is it? You make me feel great so I want to be around you, but that's somehow leading you on or something."

"Katie, nothing has happened. I make my own choices here. I'm a big boy. It's worth it to me to be your friend, even if part of me wants more."

I blushed at Rob's words. All along I had thought that my feelings were one-sided. But hearing Rob say he wanted more sent a rush of fear through me. I looked at him with longing and yet I knew it was all wrong.

"Don't worry, Katie. I won't make this hard on you. I adore you and I always have. Friends?" he said and extended his hand. He smiled a boyish smile and looked at me as if in penance.

"Definitely." I took his hand and squeezed it. Rob leaned forward and kissed me lightly on the cheek, and then he leaned forward again and kissed me quickly on the lips. I felt a small flutter of terror at leaving the hospital and at leaving Rob and I quickly pulled him toward me. I kissed him again, much slower, and he responded passionately. I was pressed against the van and could feel his hard body against mine. I didn't want to let go of that kiss.

This time he backed away. "Katie, I'm sorry," he said breathlessly. "I'm so sorry. I don't know what got into me."

"Oh my God. What just happened?" I brushed my hair out of my face and looked away, embarrassed. Rob began to pace again. I looked back at him and began to giggle.

"Katie, for Chrissakes, what is so damn funny?"

"I don't know," I said giggling harder. "That was just so much fun! It was so wonderful that I feel all tingly and yet I know it wasn't right and yet I don't care. This has been such a bittersweet day that I'm beginning to think that was a perfect ending and... and... Rob?" I looked at him tentatively.

He stopped pacing and looked at me. "You're crazy, you know that?" he said smiling in exasperation. "But you're right. It was what it was. No regrets. Okay?"

"Okay," I said, starting to feel sad again. "Thank you, Rob. For being my friend and for the beautiful rose and for helping me this afternoon." I reached out my hand and he took it gently.

"I'll miss you Katie, more than you'll know." He took a step back so that only our fingertips were touching. It was extremely sensual and I felt another wave of heat wash over me.

I shuddered. "Good-bye."

"Please don't forget to take care of you, Katie." Rob smiled and stepped back another step. My hand dropped to my side. "And think about that red car. I can picture you in it already."

I laughed softly, turned reluctantly away from him and climbed into my van. I slammed the door and looked around, noticing more than usual the dog hair, fruit snack wrappers, wadded tissues and scattered CD's. I sighed deeply and pulled out of the parking lot for the last time.

At eleven o'clock Monday morning I was waiting in the lobby of Linkages for Tiger to finish tutoring. Linkages was located in part of an office building that had recently been updated from its 1960's colors and cinder block style. The waiting room was obviously decorated on a budget, but it was comfortable and tasteful. I poured some tea from a hot pot and sat down to read a magazine. Linda Goldman was passing from one room to the next and saw me. "Hello, Katie!" she said enthusiastically, "Nice to see you."

I stood up and was surprised when Linda only came to my shoulders. I had always considered myself to be on the small side but here I was, looking down on Linda's head. She had thick, dark hair with a touch of gray. She wore little to no make-up and a simple hairstyle, and yet she was an attractive and charismatic woman. "Hello, Linda, how are you?"

"Terrific. We are so busy it's wonderful. I'm going to have to conduct another Orton training in a few weeks so that we can get some more tutors in here. You got Tiger enrolled just in time! We started a waiting list this morning." As soon as she spoke she no longer seemed small. She had a strong presence that commanded attention and eliminated any doubt that what she said was completely true.

"No kidding? Do you allow parents to attend your trainings?"

"Absolutely, in fact I recommend it. The more you know the more you can help Tiger at home. Would you like me to put you on the list? We start right after Thanksgiving, and it's filling up fast."

"Yes, definitely. I would love it. By the way, how's Tiger doing? Do you still think she's appropriate for the program after having her for a few days?"

"Well, Jean, her tutor, said she was cooperative and starting to open up with her more and more. It's too soon to see any noticeable progress, but I think she'll do fine. As a matter of fact," Linda looked at her watch and thought for a few moments, "I'll go check on them now. They'll just be finishing up and I can do a few things with Tiger that will give me a read on how she's adjusting."

"Okay," I said, surprised at her flexibility and ability to accommodate me. Her energy was infectious and I was feeling more enthusiastic and optimistic just being in her presence.

Linda knocked quietly on one of the closed doors and let herself in. After fifteen minutes she emerged with Tiger and Jean. "Mommy!" Tiger said running toward me. She jumped into my arms and hugged me.

"Hey, Tiger cub, how are you?"

"Good," she said matter-of-factly as she got up from my lap. She was holding several large sheets of newsprint with large, cursive letters finger-painted on them.

"Tiger," I asked, "are those cursive letters I see on that paper?"

"Yup," she said

"Cursive! That's great!" Tiger smiled at my words of praise.

"Hi, Jean." Tiger's tutor was standing behind her, smiling. "It's nice to see you. Tiger is really enjoying her time with you."

"And I'm enjoying Tiger." Jean was around fifty years old. She had been a teacher for years but had recently retired and decided to tutor part time. She was a down to earth, gentle woman and I could see that Tiger was at ease in her company.

"It's such a relief to see Tiger actually enjoying schoolwork."

"Katie," Linda called from her office. "Would you come here for a minute so I can share some things with you? Help yourself to something from the reward jar, Tiger, your mom will be right back." Tiger walked over to a large tub filled with key chains, mini pads of paper, small rubber animals, and other inexpensive treasures.

I followed Linda into her office and sat next to her in a chair, my coat folded over my arms. "Okay, quickly, our focus with Tiger right now is her phonemic awareness. She's not hearing the distinctions between the short vowel sounds. And sometimes she doesn't hear the short vowels at all, that's why you might notice she omits vowels in her writing, she's not hearing them. Jean is starting to work on this with and is introducing each phoneme in a VAKT approach. She's basically starting from scratch, but you'll find she progresses rapidly. Don't push her to read right now. Jean will send home appropriate reading material as she progresses, so, for now, I would strongly recommend books on tape. She can follow along with the book. She'll enjoy the stories and it keeps her up to speed on the content." The ideas flowed from Linda as she spoke. "You may even want to record the stories from her school reader and have her listen to them for homework. Ask the teacher if you can take one of the readers home over the weekend and you can tape several stories at once. That way Tiger will know the stories and be able to contribute to the class discussions."

Linda was talking rapidly and I marveled at how easily she could switch gears without hesitation or confusion. "Thank you, Linda, I'll let you go. Thanks for taking the time to check on Tiger. I really appreciate it. It's such a relief to have her here. I can't tell you what it means to me."

She smiled warmly and walked me to the door. "See you tomorrow, Tiger," she called into the lobby.

"Bye," Tiger said as she stood up, wobbling a little from her heavy backpack. She had a colorful rubber lizard in her hand. "This is Henry," she said to me as I walked over to her.

"Hello, Henry," I said, looking down at the lizard. "It's very nice to meet you."

When we arrived at the Chesapeake Day School I parked the van and walked Tiger into second grade. The classroom was empty except for one, young boy sitting in front of one of the two classroom computers. He was playing a game and a pair of crutches rested against the back of his chair. "I guess we're a little late because I talked to Mrs. Goldman for so long," I said to a worried Tiger.

"Everyone must be at gym." Tiger looked nervously around the room. "I hope Mrs. Peterson isn't mad at me."

"Well, it's my fault, so let Mrs. Peterson be mad at me. Do you think she'll write my name on the board?" I joked, trying to ease Tiger's worry.

"What should I do, Mom?" Tiger was near panic. "Should I go to gym? But then I'll be late for that and what if they've already started? I won't have time to change into my gym clothes and--"

"Please don't worry, honey," I interrupted. "Would you like me to stay with you until Mrs. Peterson comes back?" I asked, feeling thankful I had the time to do it.

"Yes, please."

"No problem. Why don't you put your things away and go play on the other computer, next to Travis."

"Well, I guess it's okay," she said tentatively. I walked her over to the computer and greeted Travis. I inquired about his leg and waited for Tiger to start playing a game of Math Blaster on the other computer.

Once Tiger settled into the game, I walked around the room with my hands behind my back, looking at the various projects displayed on the wall. I was reading an essay about Columbus when I heard Mary clear her throat. "Hello, Kate, I didn't know you were here."

"Hi, Mrs. Peterson," I said pleasantly. "I'm sorry we're a little late today. It looks as if Tiger missed gym class."

Mary noticed Tiger and said, "Trisha, I'm going to need that computer. I have spelling tests to grade. You're going to have to find something else to do."

I looked at Tiger, horrified. She jumped up and quickly walked over to me. She stood very still, not uttering a word. It was as if she was trying to disappear. Mary busied herself at her desk, ignoring Tiger, gathered up some papers and went over to the computer. I stared at her for several moments. She was oblivious to what she had just done. She quit Tiger's game and began typing while Travis sat comfortably next to her.

I rubbed Tiger's back and whispered to her that we should go over to her desk. I helped her find some paper and suggested she draw quietly until the rest of the class returned. She did so, obediently, but she had pulled into her protective shell. Her eyes were vacant. I hadn't realized how quickly and completely she could disassociate herself from her surroundings. I have had patients who did this. It was a defense mechanism usually acquired after a severe childhood trauma.

Part of me wanted to walk over and blast Mary with my words. Part of me was resisting the urge to do her physical harm. But the rest of me knew anything I said or did would only come back to hurt Tiger. And there was Travis, clicking away at the other computer. It had never occurred to Mary that Tiger and Travis could share a computer, or take turns. Somehow his broken leg was a legitimate excuse to miss gym class, but Tiger's dyslexia was a different story.

I hugged Tiger tightly. "I love you. Don't forget, I'll be picking you up today. Remember, no more working!"

"Okay, Mommy," she said quietly, diligently working on a complex picture of jungle animals. Henry was perched next to her protectively.

Mary never looked up from her work as I walked out of the room, and I struggled to fight back my rage and disbelief at her insensitivity and cruelty. As I walked down the hall I encountered Joan, the head of the lower school. "Hello, Joan," I said stiffly. I was feeling as if I was walking through enemy territory. I was beginning to realize how Tiger felt every day.

"Hello, Kate. Were you dropping off Tiger?"

"Yes. I'm afraid we're a little late today."

"So, is this program helping her any better than we can?" she asked pointedly.

"One can only hope," I said looking her in the eyes, my anger quickly resurfacing.

"Well, I guess that remains to be seen. We are experimenting with you but I must tell you, I don't like it. This is a precedent I don't want to set."

"Yes, you mentioned that before."

"What if every parent could decide they didn't like the way a teacher was teaching? What if someone wanted to bring in their own teacher to, say, teach

158

math? Mary would have kids coming and going all day just to please the parents. We all would."

"What are you talking about, Joan? This isn't about Mary. It's not about taste in teaching. Tiger is dyslexic. She needs to learn in a multisensory method. And there is nothing multisensory in that classroom, or in this entire lower school for that matter!"

Joan stiffened. "If you are so unhappy with this school, then why are you paying to send your children here?"

I was beginning to regret mouthing off to Joan, this wasn't the time or place. "Everything needs to be updated now and then. As a department head I would think you would know that. Sometimes it takes a little push. Maybe that's what this school needs. And I think what we're doing can help Tiger. But I also think there are things you and Mary could do to help out. It almost seems as if you're--"

"What, Kate, say it. You say what ever else pops into your mind."

"No, this isn't the time. I'm just worried about Tiger. Go easy on her, okay? If you're angry with me, don't take it out on her. She only wants to please you."

"No one is taking anything out on anyone, Kate. If Trisha is struggling it doesn't necessarily mean it's the teacher's fault. Mary is a fine teacher and she is above taking out her adult feelings on one of her students. You liked her just fine when she was Jamie's teacher."

"Yes, that's true. Jamie had a good year with Mary. I had hoped that Tiger would too. What on earth did you do with dyslexics before Tiger came along?"

"We've had children who struggled but they got tutoring after school, it never disrupted the entire class. And we've never accommodated a parent to this extent before. I know Frances agreed to give it a try, but I don't like it. It's not the way we do things here. We never have."

"Well, I guess we'll just have to see how it goes, then, won't we?" I could feel my energy rapidly depleting, this was an unwinnable fight. "But we'll all keep an open mind, right, Joan?"

"You know how I feel. And just between you and me, if Frances allows Trisha to continue, I will not allow this to continue in third grade. I simply won't tolerate that kind of disruption in my classroom. You should know that now."

"I see. Well, I guess that's about all we have to say to each other then, isn't it? Good-bye, Joan."

I walked through the pillars, feeling more and more uneasy about the emotional well being of my daughter, and wrapped my jacket tighter around me. I took a deep breath and tried to clear my head. The cool air was soothing and my thoughts began to clear as I walked toward the van. Out of the corner of my eye I noticed something was different. I turned back toward the school and saw the boxwoods. They had been pruned to within inches of the ground. What were once beautiful, majestic shrubs, sculpted by years of slow but reliable growth, reminders of the history of this century old farmhouse, were now small, perfectly rounded little balls.

By the end of the week I began to see a pattern in Tiger's moods and behavior. It was as if she were two children, a happy, confident child at Linkages, and a worried, withdrawn one at the end of her school day. Jean and Linda remained positive about her progress, but I worried more about the impact of this emotional pendulum.

By Thursday evening I was already bored with cooking. A casserole I had thrown together was warming in the oven and we were all busying ourselves, waiting for Max, hoping to have a family dinner. "I'm starving, Mom," Jamie said as she wandered into the kitchen. "When are we going to eat?"

"I was waiting for your father, but I haven't heard from him and, well, I guess I could go ahead and feed you. It's ready. Could you tell Tiger?"

"Tiger!" Jamie yelled. "Dinner!"

"Jamie, I could have yelled from here."

"Oh, sorry."

We sat down around the table. Max's chair was noticeably vacant. "Mom," Tiger said, "I know you tried to make a nice dinner and all, but I hate it when things are all mixed up together."

"What's in here, anyway?" Jamie asked.

"Well, it's spaghetti, white sauce, mushrooms, and some other stuff. It's good for you. Just try it."

Jamie picked up a fork full and ate it tentatively. "It's okay." She hesitated. "Are you going to cook all the time now that you're not working? Because you really don't have to go to all this trouble."

"Maybe not," I said exasperated, "At least not with this kind of reception." My mom used to make stuff like this all the time and I had to eat it. Sometimes she would put it on white toast with a can of fruit cocktail for dessert." I looked at their puzzled expressions and sighed. "Why don't you each make a list of your favorite dinners. I'm out of practice."

"Okay!" Tiger said. "That sounds like a good idea. And I wouldn't mind the fruit cocktail part."

"Me neither," Jamie chimed in, trying to be positive and not hurt my feelings.

"Why didn't we wait for Daddy?" Tiger asked as she repositioned the food on her plate. "I thought we were going to have family dinners now."

"We're trying. I guess it didn't work out tonight."

"It's not that big of a deal," Jamie said nonchalantly. "May I be excused?"

"Take your plate to the counter, please."

160

Tiger hopped up behind her, relieved to be able to leave the table. "You too, Tig. Plate to the counter." Baxter perked up at the sight of their full plates heading for the sink. They each gave him a quick pat and grabbed an apple as they went up to their rooms.

I looked down at Baxter and sighed. Four days into retirement and I was feeling very confused. Although I was busying myself reading about dyslexia and trying to organize the house, I found myself feeling guilty when I wasn't doing something productive. I was working harder than I did at the hospital, feeling the need to justify my time. But somehow it all left me unsatisfied and restless. Particularly with Tiger's apparent lack of progress. I now understood how easily a parent could fall into the trap of measuring her self-worth based on her child's achievements. It was a dangerous arrangement for both mother and child.

"Sorry I'm late," Max called, sheepishly. Jamie and Tiger were asleep and Baxter and I were curled up on the sofa. "This case is heating up. Depositions start next week." He walked into the family room and sat down. "Wow, Kate. This house has never looked so good. I think I like having you home."

"I know you mean that as a compliment, but it isn't," I said flatly.

"Oh." Max looked at me cautiously. "Um, let's see, I should know this, but, why not?"

"Because a clean house is something that has to get done, but my self esteem isn't wrapped up in it."

Max slowly pushed himself up. "I think I'm glad to hear that, but something tells me there's more to this. I'm going to grab some food and noodle it a little more," he said as he walked noisily into the kitchen. "Mm, mystery meal," he called as I heard him lift the aluminum foil from the casserole.

When he returned with a mounding plate of food he sat down across from me and said, "Feeling creative in the kitchen, Katie?"

"I'm really not in the mood to be teased about my cooking, Max. I don't exactly have time to cook up gourmet meals every night. Do you know how much time that would take?"

"Whoa, cowgirl! I don't expect gourmet meals. At least not from you."

"Max!"

"Anyway, that's my department. Actually," he said as he chewed a large mouthful, "it tastes pretty good."

I looked at him skeptically. "You should have called to tell me you were going to be late," not allowing myself to be charmed by him.

"Sorry. I thought about it and then got busy with something else."

"I have no way to reach you once the secretaries go home."

"You could E-mail me."

"E-mail you? What am I, one of your employees?"

"Uh, Katie, are you feeling a little sensitive about quitting your job? Are you sure this is going to work?"

"No, I'm not sure, but you're not helping. This isn't easy for me. And don't get used to me doing everything around here. I still expect you to do your share and the last thing I want you to do is start taking me for granted by not calling or telling me what's going on."

"Okay," he said slowly, trying to placate me. "But, Katie, if you need to go back to work, then why don't you?"

"Max! I didn't want to quit, I had to! For Tiger! Don't you realize that? Our child is in trouble. She needs us to pay attention right now. It's now or never. I've seen what happens to kids who don't get help. Her self-esteem is already at an all time low. Don't you see that? This isn't about my predilections, this is something I had to do, I was forced to do, in order to help my, I mean our daughter!"

"Katie, if you're going to be miserable, then maybe this isn't the best solution."

"What other choice do we have?"

"I don't know. But I don't think you should have to sacrifice your happiness to do this."

"You don't?" I asked, incredulous. "So you think I should put my happiness first and allow Tiger to fail in school? Is that what you think? Because if you do, then I didn't realize how different our values were."

"Jesus, Katie! I value our children's well being just as much as you do, don't accuse me of not caring. I'm just worried about you."

"I'm worried about me too. But she needs us, Max. She's in terrible pain and she hides it from us so we won't worry about her." I leaned forward and wove my hands through my hair. "Whenever I get frustrated about not working, all I have to do is picture her face the way I saw it in that classroom the other day and I know I'm doing the right thing. But Max," I said looking up at him, "I really need you to understand that. It will only work as long as you appreciate that I'm doing it and you don't have to. There's no law that says it had to be me that quit. It was economics, pure and simple. I really need you to see that."

"I do. I don't know that I could do it. I really don't. But I'm thankful you can. It's a tremendous sacrifice."

"I just hope I can. It's so damn hard. And I hope I can stay sane and not drive the people I love insane," I said, losing steam.

"You just have to let me know what you need from me."

"I will. But I want you to think about it, too. I don't want to have to tell you all the time. Then I'm a needy, pain-in-the-butt."

"I'll let you know when you're a needy pain-in-the-butt," Max said, smiling, obviously relieved that the discussion was winding down without an argument.

"Yes, dear, I'm sure you will. Can we have lunch tomorrow? I'm feeling the need to get dressed up a little. Somehow the leggings and t-shirts aren't cutting it anymore," I said, fluffing my hair and feeling self conscious about my appearance.

"I would be honored, Miss Katherine," Max said, bowing his head slowly, "Queen of the mystery meal."

I threw a pillow as hard as I could at his bowed head.

"Hey, watch it," he cried. "You might make a bald spot!" Max picked up the pillow and threw it back at me, hitting me square on the head. Then he dove on to the sofa, growling, and tackled me. I kicked and pushed him with all my strength as he pulled me to the floor, but his superior strength was obvious. We proceeded to toss pillows and wrestle until we were out of breath and sweating. Eventually, he grabbed my legs and effortlessly flipped me on to my back and I found myself lying next to Baxter who was happily licking up the remains of Max's dinner. Max straddled me, kissed me lightly and fell onto his back beside me. We stared up at the ceiling, panting. Baxter wagged his tail, interested in the bodies on the floor, licked his chops and proceeded to lay over both of us. "I needed that," Max said as he petted the dog. "I really needed that!"

The phone startled me out of a trance as I hurriedly emptied and folded the grocery bags. I wanted to have enough time to get ready for my lunch with Max and I still had to transport Tiger to school before noon. I looked up at the clock nervously and debated whether or not to let the answering machine screen the call. But I had been blessed at birth with more than my share of useless guilt and answered the phone.

"Why, Katie! I didn't expect to find you at home, I was just about to leave a message. I hate to interrupt your evenings. Did you decide to have lunch at home? The children aren't sick, are they?"

"No, May, everyone is fine. Actually, I don't know if Max told you or not, but I've left my job at the hospital."

"What?" May said in astonishment. "But why, dear? What's happened?" I could tell by her reaction that although she had taken little interest in my job, she was fully aware of how important is was to me. I was touched by her sensitivity.

"It's sort of a long story, worthy of more than a phone call, but suffice it to say that we are all healthy and I'm getting along fine, considering," I added, knowing my current state of mind. "And it's much better for Tiger and Jamie to have me at home."

"I'm sure you know what's best for your beautiful daughters, but they've always seemed perfectly well-adjusted to me. Perhaps I could I take you to lunch

163

sometime, dear. That is, if you have the time. I would love to hear more about everything. I had no idea I was so out of touch."

"I would love to." After I corner my husband, I thought to myself.

"Why don't I meet you in Annapolis and take you to the Yacht Club?" she asked. "How does Wednesday sound?"

"Great, I'm writing it on the calendar as we speak. But you haven't told me why you were calling. Is everything all right with you?"

"Couldn't be better. I was calling to let you know that Dusty will be in town over Thanksgiving and I wanted to make sure you would have room at your dinner table for one more. You know I would be happy to host it here this year, but I know your mother and Aunt Matilda will be coming."

"I would love to have Dusty here. Say no more! That means all four Cunningham brothers will be together. Oh, that's wonderful! I can't wait!"

"That's very kind of you to say, Katie. You're very gracious and I appreciate your flexibility. Well, I'll let you go, even though you're no longer employed by the hospital, I'm sure you have plenty to keep you busy."

"At least for now, I do. I'm looking forward to lunch. Good-bye, May."

"Good-bye, dear." I was reminded again of the depth of May's kindness and sensitivity. Not once during our conversation did she judge or question my decision. Instead, she was interested and supportive and yet respectful of my timing and hesitancy to tell her everything right away. I was in awe of her consistent graciousness, because at no time did she sacrifice her warmth and caring for good manners. It was a flawless blend and I said aloud that I wanted to be May Cunningham when I grew up. I looked over at Baxter who was looking at me with one eye. "Fat Chance? Is that what you're telling me?" I said to Baxter. I sighed and folded up the last grocery bag.

"You're right, Mr. Labrador. I'll never be able to tame this mouth well enough to equal May." I headed up the stairs. "God help me, I'm talking to the dog."

Max was fifteen minutes late for lunch and I watched him come in the door from our corner table. We were dining in an intimate Annapolis restaurant that was housed in an historic, colonial building. The soft lighting enabled privacy despite the close proximity of the tables. Max maneuvered through the restricted spaces and I tried to see him the way a stranger would. I noticed several well-dressed men and women give his good looks a second glance as he politely begged their pardons. He was beautifully dressed and carried himself with grace, despite his large size.

When he finally reached our table he leaned over and kissed me. "Hi, sorry I'm late." He stopped scooting in his chair and looked up at me. "You are probably asking yourself why I am always stringing those phrases together."

"What phrases?"

"'Hi,' and 'sorry I'm late.' I seem to be saying it a lot these days. Isn't that what you were just thinking?"

"On the contrary, I was just noticing how incredibly handsome you are."

"Yeah, right," he said, scooting his chair the rest of the way in and picking up his menu.

"I was. Why is that so hard to believe?"

He peeked over the top of his menu. "What? That I'm handsome or that you were thinking it?"

An attractive, young waitress approached our table. "Hello, Mr. Cunningham. Can I bring you and your guest a glass of wine?"

I looked at Max, thinking how naive I was to be surprised that this waitress knew him. This was his world, ninety percent of his life. "That would be nice, Jeannette," he said. She smiled and Max went back to his menu.

"Well?" I asked.

"Well, what?"

"Max! Why are you so surprised that I might pay you a compliment?"

"I'm not, Katie. Really. Now, what would you like?"

I was feeling very strange and was glad when "Jeannette" (spoken with a French sounding 'J') brought the wine. I took a sip while Max ordered for us. "Very good," she said, and smiled directly at Max. He smiled back, with those sexy blue eyes, and she flipped her short skirt as she walked away.

Max leaned forward on his elbows. "So, how's your day going?"

I was feeling very icky inside. My confidence was slipping away. Normally, Max and I would be chatting nonstop about our jobs, the children, grateful for a few moments alone together, and I wouldn't give a cute waitress another thought. But I was feeling strangely vulnerable and hated it.

The only other time I had felt this way with Max was when I had learned that he had been unfaithful. Although Max claims it is important that it was only once, it had been devastating to me and to the marriage. It happened shortly after he had graduated from law school and we had moved to Annapolis. After supporting us through his schooling, I had eagerly entered into my own graduate program. He had been recruited immediately out of school by a youthful and busy law firm and after winning his first big case, had caught the eye of a attractive, young law clerk. One Thursday night Max had called me from work to invite me to a celebration at a local bar for his big victory. But I was in the middle of a paper that was due the next day and declined. The law clerk pursued him that night and after too much gin and too much ego, they had slept together. It didn't take long for word to get around his firm. Although no one blamed Max, they knew she had been shamelessly pursuing him, I did. It had been the closest we had ever come to

165

divorce. Max is attractive and always will be, but I knew I couldn't live in fear throughout our marriage that he would succumb to the beautiful women who were bound to try and seduce him, so I told him he needed to make a choice, and he chose to stay married to me. He eventually started his own firm with some other lawyers he had admired and described it as a more "grown up" place to practice law. But it had been devastating for me and a humbling experience for Max. Although we told no one, I had always suspected that May knew. She became fiercely loyal to me after that.

"Busy," I said, pulling myself from my thoughts. I had sworn to myself that I would never let anything shake my self-confidence again.

"Doing what?"

"Well, I took the girls to their respective schools, stopped at Fresh Fields, came home, got ready to come here, picked up Tiger and dropped her off at school and, well, here I am. Doesn't sound like much, does it? But for some reason I felt rushed and now I'm exhausted." Somehow what had seemed like a hectic day sounded empty in its retelling.

"Guess you're still worn out from our wrestling match last night, eh?" he said, smiling.

"You really are very handsome, even though you may already know that."

"Katie? Is everything all right? You're not going loopy on me, are you?"

"No. At least I hope not. So tell me about your day so far. How's the Chesapeake Bay Foundation Case?" I took another long sip of my wine.

Max was immediately energized with the opportunity to talk about his work and launched into a detailed description of the case. He abruptly stopped talking, stood and turned toward a man who was approaching our table. "Hello, Governor Glendenning," he said, shaking the man's hand firmly.

"Hello, Max. Still planning on suing my state?"

"It's my state, too, Parris, just doing my job."

The two men stood eye to eye and I was impressed with Max's cool demeanor, he was not the least bit intimidated talking to the Governor of Maryland.

"Well, hopefully this will blow over and we can settle without a high profile trial, even though the publicity would be great for your law firm."

"It won't hurt our reputation, I'll grant you that, but this is a legitimate case that needs to be settled in the right way. Most of this started during Schaeffer's tenure, that will come out in the press, I'm sure."

"I wish that were true, but you and I both know better. If the trial happens during my term, then I'm the one responsible. It's that simple."

A reporter who must have been tailing the Governor entered the dining room and a light bulb flashed. Both Max and the Governor squinted their eyes from the sudden burst of light. "Well, sorry to interrupt your lunch."

166

"On the contrary, I'm honored by your visit. Oh, Governor, I'd like you to meet my wife, Katie."

I quickly stood, surprised at my entry into the conversation, and bumped my leg into the table, causing the glasses to shake. "Hello, Governor Glendenning, it's a pleasure to meet you." We shook hands.

"Nice to meet you too, Katie." He smiled warmly and looked directly into my eyes, a politician's touch. "Well, Good-bye, Max, Katie, enjoy your lunch."

"Thank you, we will."

Max sat down just as our food was coming. "Jeannette, I'm running short on time, would you bring our check so that we can leave when we need to?"

"Right away, Mr. Cunningham."

"You're in a hurry?"

"I'm afraid so. And it will be another late night. As you just heard, the Governor is pushing for an out of court settlement, but the Foundation won't hear of it. They don't want to kill him politically, but they want to get the issues out into the public forum. Which means I'll need a rock solid case or they'll look like litigious liberals." Max ate while he talked and barely looked up.

"Your mother called this morning," I said.

"Oh yeah?" he said, raising his eyebrows. "What did May want?"

"She was surprised to find me at home on a Friday, for one thing."

"I'll bet. She must have been thrilled to learn you'll be home now."

"Actually, she wasn't. She was curious why I would have made such a decision." I had barely touched my food, I was surprised at how distant he was growing.

"What did you tell her?"

"More than you have, that's for sure."

"Well that wouldn't be hard to do," he said, glancing at his watch as he buttered a roll.

"No, it wasn't. So that's why I told her you forced me to quit my job so that I could be your love slave and--" I stared at Max, waiting for a reaction.

"What?" he stopped eating and looked at me.

"Max, you are already back at the office. You just forgot to actually get up and walk there."

He looked at me, confused. "It's very hard for me to break stride in the middle of the day. And running into the Governor has my head spinning with new insights into this case. You know how that is, Katie. It's no reflection on you."

"I guess I do. I would just rather you let me know you've left the building. It's like when you put me on speaker phone and I can hear the pages flipping."

"I stopped doing that, Katie."

"I appreciate you taking time out to have lunch with me, but I think I should

167

let you get back to your thoughts."

"You haven't eaten anything."

"I'm not very hungry. Can I give you a lift back to your office?"

"No thanks. I'll power walk and get the blood flowing."

"Oh, by the way, Leslie's throwing a birthday party for T.C. next Friday. I told her we would be there."

"Absolutely. Is it a surprise?"

"No. Don't you think it's a little early in the relationship for her to throw him a surprise party?"

"Not from what I hear. We worked out together the other day and it sounds as if he's moved some of his stuff into her place. His wife got the house in the divorce settlement, and he's been renting a little condo over in Eastport."

"Oh," I said quietly.

"I take it Leslie didn't tell you that."

"No," I said feeling very sensitive and yet furious at myself for feeling that way. "She only had a few minutes to talk. She called me from the hospital."

"Well, don't take it personally," he said, standing up to leave. "I think your opinion is very important to her. She's probably careful about what she tells you."

"Oh, I don't think so," I said as I tried to get my purse off the back of my chair.

"Okay. That was just my amateur analysis of the situation."

"Leslie knows I don't judge her." I hated the isolation I felt since leaving the hospital.

"Anyway, that will be a lot of fun. I know today is Friday but I have to break my rule and work late tonight, and even worse, most of the weekend. I have got to be prepared for this trial. They're going to try everything they can to keep this out of court." Max was buttoning his coat and had a distant look in his eye.

"Okay," I said, trying to be supportive. "I'm sure you'll do an outstanding job. The Bay Foundation is lucky to have you."

"Thanks," He leaned down and kissed me on the cheek.

"Go ahead, I'm going to stop in the ladies room."

"Okay. See ya later, Katie," and he was gone.

When I arrived home I walked into the clean, quiet kitchen and felt strange and out of place. I wasn't supposed to be there, it was the middle of the afternoon. It felt as if I was playing hooky. Baxter loped into the room with an expectant look on his sweet face. He seemed to have adjusted much better than me to the change in my schedule. But I was appreciating my optimistic dog more and more and stopped to give him a worthwhile, full-body scratching. I sat at the table with my coat on and petted him longer that he could have wished for. His eyes sparkled up at me with unconditional love and acceptance.

I ended the scratch with a few friendly pats and realized I would need to hurry if I wanted to change my clothes before picking Jamie and Tiger up from school. I stood to take off my coat and groaned. My camel hair coat was covered in black Baxter hairs.

"Well, Baxter," I said. "Some things never change." His tail wagged a little with my words. "God, you're easy to please!" The pace of his tail wagging increased. "You're a jobless free-loader just like me," I said in a peppy voice and this time his tail was at full speed and his long, pink tongue rolled out. I laughed and gave him an extra scratch behind his ears and he padded after me as I headed toward the stairs.

The answering machine light blinked importantly as I passed the phone. There was only one call. I was tempted to ignore it, but that was risky in this new era of problems at school, so I pressed "play." The call was from a woman named Michelle who sounded a lot busier than I was and I knew immediately that she was my replacement.

Betty was thrilled to hear my voice and swore the hospital wasn't the same without me and I smiled at her familiar, raspy voice. I silently worried that the hospital may soon decide to replace her with a newer model, just as they had her desk.

"Hello? Is this Katie?"

"Yes, you must be Michelle."

"Right!" She sounded young and energetic. "Thanks so much for calling. Do you have a minute? Because I would love to ask you some questions."

"Sure," I said, not adding that I had a lot more than one to spare. "When did you start?"

"Yesterday!" she said breathlessly. "And I've been going non-stop ever since. This place is a zoo! But I love it!"

"That's good," I said quietly. "How can I help you, Michelle?"

"Well, my biggest concern is Blair. I've been working on her discharge plan and I see in your notes that she should have tutoring for a learning disability. I'm not sure how that's going to happen. Her current school has her on probation and they don't have any extra help program. And her mother still wants her to go to boarding school, but she's agreed to put it on hold and use it as a consequence if Blair doesn't follow the plan."

"It doesn't surprise me about her school," I said. "You might have to find her some help outside of school."

"Well, I'll try, but her parents aren't pushing for it. And speaking of her parents, I see that you want them to go to counseling, but they're refusing. But they should be focusing on Blair's chemical dependency, anyway, so I referred them to a Tough Love group. But everything else is in place. I've been working with Rob on a plan for her program, you know, ninety/ninety meetings and such, but the rest of this stuff is meeting some definite resistance."

"Michelle, Blair has a previously undetected learning disability which is one of the main reasons she started having problems. Set up an aftercare plan for her, but make sure it includes some sort of tutoring for her dyslexia or anything else you do will fail. Call Linda Goldman at Linkages in Columbia, she'll be able to schedule something. I know I wrote her number in the chart. Also, her parents are considering a divorce, and unless Blair knows they are in counseling and getting the help they so desperately need, then, again, her program will fail. That's how that family system operates. Those discharge plans are vital to the success of her program."

"Well, Warner was very clear with me about keeping it simple and focusing on the drugs. That's why I was questioning this other stuff. But I can see where you're coming from, with the family systems approach. I'll see what I can do. She's a tough nut, though."

"Actually, she's more like a toasted marshmallow. Crusty on the outside, but soft and mushy on the inside. Don't let her fool you. She's very scared and very vulnerable. Do what you can. And don't hesitate to ask for help. Rob has some good insights into Blair, and she made a real connection with Dolores. They'll guide you through this."

I heard a loud sigh over the phone. "I'll do what I can. I just don't want all this other stuff to distract from her program. She hasn't even completed her first step."

"I'm sure you'll do fine. Don't let them intimidate you. So, Michelle, tell me a little about yourself. Are you an LCSW (Licensed Certified Social Worker)?"

"No, not yet. I just graduated in August. I asked Leslie Sterling, the social worker from the psych unit, to supervise me so I can sit for the licensing exam in two years and she said yes! I am so excited to get this job. Both of my internships during school were in chemical dependency settings so it is really perfect."

I resisted the temptation to ask what they were paying her. "Well, you sound just right for the job. I'm sure you'll do it justice. And you're working with the best."

"Yes, I can see that. Well, gotta run! Thanks for your help, Katie. Can I call you if I have some more questions?"

"Of course. Good luck, please tell everyone I said hello." I hung up the phone and stared out the window. Tears formed in my eyes. Surprisingly, they weren't for me, but for Blair. This had been the opportunity for her family to get the intervention it desperately needed. Blair's crisis had brought all the deep-seated, serious issues out into the open. Returning a clean and sober Blair to her dysfunctional family would mean a temporarily sobriety at best. It was as effective as replacing one engine part and leaving the other dirty ones in place. Eventually the shiny, new part would be affected by the rest, pulled back into the old performance of a dirty, un-tuned engine. I was afraid for Blair. Eventually she would up the ante when her parents continued to refuse to change or acknowledge her pain. I worried that she wasn't strong enough to handle a next time.

I wiped away the tear that had made its way down my cheek and looked around for Baxter. He was predictably at my feet and I felt comforted by his presence. I patted my legs and sang, "Baxter, come on boy, want to go for a ride?" Within seconds he had gone from a deep sleep to four legged leaps into the air. "Oh, Baxter, what's wrong with people? Why can't they be more like you?" He continued to leap and I laughed through my tears. "Let's go get our girls!" He raced to the door, wagging expectantly, and I could see it would be the highlight of his uncomplicated day.

Lesson Eight: Acceptance

Acceptance in its truest form is unconditional.
It not only requires parents to accept their children
for who they are,
from their body type to their passions,
it also means accepting how having children
changes a parent's life.
The task is to understand this,
accept it,
and, eventually,
appreciate it as one's own growing and maturing.

School was still in session when I arrived so I eased the van into the line of cars awaiting dismissal and turned off the engine. Baxter was standing in the front seat steaming up the windshield. I was sorting through the mail when I heard a tap at my window. I looked up to see Sierra Ferguson, a mother from Tiger's class. I buzzed down the window. "Hi, Sierra," I said, genuinely happy to see her.

"Hey, Katie, sorry to interrupt your reading."

"I'd much rather talk with you than count my bills. How are you?"

"I'm hanging in there." Sierra and I had always been friendly with one another, but it had never gone beyond chatting at school functions or talking on field trips. We came from different worlds. Sierra and her husband were both independently wealthy, and although neither of them held jobs, they were always involved with various activities and projects. She was on the board of trustees with Max, and had always been active in the school. She was heading the new capital campaign and it was rumored that she and her husband had paid off the school's mortgage a few years ago. But despite this, I had always found her to be without airs and down to earth. Today she was dressed in jeans, tee-shirt and a suede coat.

"I saw Joe the other day in second grade," I said, recalling how he had objected to getting his name on the board. "He's adorable. I love his enthusiasm."

"I wish Mary Peterson loved his enthusiasm. She's much more likely to refer

172

to it as a behavior problem." I smiled sympathetically. "This year's off to a rough start. Mary sends a note home every other day, and Joe's been in Frances' office more times than I care to count. In fact, that's why I wanted to talk to you." She folded her arms across her chest and leaned against van.

"Careful, my van's a little on the dirty side. You don't want to ruin that beautiful jacket."

"Please! I've been cleaning out horse stalls all day. I couldn't get any dirtier if I tried. I think that's why your pup over there is wagging his tail, he's picked up the horse scent. Not that it's hard to miss," she added.

"Frankly, Baxter would like to jump into your lap, if he could, but that's not why you came over here. How can I help?"

"Joe told me that Tiger has been going to tutoring every morning, and I was wondering how you ever got Mary and Frances to agree to that."

"They don't agree, and just between you and me, I think Tiger's paying the price as a result. And it's only on a trial basis. We're going to review it at the end of the semester."

"Joe said she's dyslexic."

I sighed, "Yes, as dyslexic as they come."

"I was really impressed that you told the class. Joe thinks it's really neat that Tiger learns differently. That was a great way to handle it."

"Sierra, what's up? You seem upset."

Tears instantly began to well in the corners of her eyes and I had a fleeting thought about how much mothers hold inside, all their worries and fears, "Mary wants me to medicate Joe, she thinks he's hyperactive."

"What?" I asked, incredulous. "When did she get her medical degree? She can't diagnose that!"

Sierra looked surprised at my reaction, but relieved. She wiped away a tear that had started down her cheek. "I don't think he's hyper. I know he's not hyper. But I've watched his self-esteem slip away these past few months, and he started doing strange things like wet the bed." The strain on her face revealed how difficult it was for her to disclose such a personal thing.

"How's his school work?"

"Lousy. He can read some, but he makes a lot of mistakes, and he can't spell worth a hoot. And those prissy little girls in the class have been making fun of him."

"It's a rough class this year. But I think some of that has to do with the atmosphere in there. It's very competitive, and the kids are encouraged to tell on one another and compete for Mary's good favors. Tiger's only there a few hours a day and half the time she's standing in the bathroom." I could feel my anger rising as I thought about what these precious children were suffering through.

"Doug is dyslexic, you know. He never got any help with it." Doug was Sierra's husband. I had rarely seen him at the school and had always found him to be extremely quiet and shy.

"Do you think Joe might be too?"

"No! I mean, I don't think so. If he is it's not a bad case. But he's having a hell of a year. I don't know what to do. But Katie, I've heard through the grapevine that they might kick Tiger out of school. I'd die if they did that to Joe, after everything we've done for this school! So if I get him tested and they find out he's even mildly dyslexic, or even hyperactive, are they going to kick him out, too?"

I reddened at her words. I had no idea others were discussing Tiger's fate or that her being asked to leave was that much of a reality. I measured my words carefully. "At this point I have no idea what you should do. I think Joe needs something to change in that classroom, but I also think your fear of consequences is very real."

Sierra put her hand on my arm. "I know I can't leave him out there alone, struggling, I want to do what you're doing. But what if Tiger can't return, what will you do?"

Tears welled in my eyes from her sympathy. She was the first parent to understand our struggles. I smiled through my tears. "I don't know. I haven't a clue."

Sierra patted my arm affectionately. "I'm watching very closely. I respect what you're doing, taking on Frances like you are. Something has to change. The second and third grades at this school are like a gauntlet for our children to go through. At least the children that aren't little miss-Prissy-ass-teacher's-pet-tattle-tales!"

I laughed. "I appreciate your support, Sierra, I feel like I'm in no-woman's land."

"Think how Tiger must feel."

"Oh, I do. I do."

"Hey, maybe Tiger and Joe can get together sometime. Does Tiger like horses?"

I appreciated the change in topic. "Loves them," I said, sniffing and wiping my cheeks. "Anything from the animal kingdom. She would love to play with Joe."

"Great. We'll call soon. And just in case I have a change of heart, do you have the name of the person who tested Tiger?"

"Sure." I pulled my date-book out of my purse and wrote down Susan Chartwell's number and the number for Linkages, as well, and motioned to Sierra that the cars were starting to move.

"Thanks, Katie. Good luck with Tiger."

"Good luck to you, too." I started the engine as she trotted back to her mud-splattered Suburban.

My thoughts were racing as I edged the van to the school doors that had begun to overflow with children. When I caught my first glimpse of Tiger and Jamie, waiting patiently for their turn in the carpool line, my heart swelled. They were so beautiful, so patient and accepting of this messed up world. Joe was fidgeting in his place in line behind Tiger. I could see his thick, blond hair darting in and out. He was playfully poking the child next to him. They were laughing and happy to be out in the sun. I was glad Sierra was paying attention. Joe needed her to see his struggles.

Tiger and Jamie stood quietly. They were conflict avoiders by nature and instinctively chose behaviors that adults expected of them. I had often wondered if this behavior was learned or an integral part of their personality. Although I had behaved the same during my elementary school career, as a parent I had tried to encourage their creativity and independent thinking. And yet, there they stood, hands to themselves while the children around them squirmed and sparred with one another.

Tiger and Jamie climbed happily into the van. It was Friday, our favorite day. Once they had buckled their seat belts I pulled away from the school. "So, what will it be, TCBY or Baskin Robbins?"

"Both!" Tiger screamed happily. Jamie and I laughed and when they couldn't decide on an ice cream store, I agreed to both.

"Geez, Mom," Jamie said in surprise. "What's gotten into you?"

I laughed at her use of my phrase. "I just want to celebrate that I have two great kids." They were both silent, mistrusting of my explanation for the unexpected indulgence. "And I'm glad to be spending more time with you. Let's celebrate my not working."

Later, as we carefully sculpted our ice cream cones with our tongues, I felt a surge of love wash over me. I thought of Dolores' serenity prayer, change what I can, accept what I can't. It really was that simple. Although I longed to be back at the hospital, I was realizing the only path to serenity was to stop fighting my new lot in life, and, instead, use my strength and courage to change what I could. I would not be working, for now. I would make the best of that fact. And I had finally, albeit reluctantly, accepted that my youngest daughter was dyslexic, in the purest sense of the word. And although this distressing fact was unchangeable, it did not mean I had to accept society's manifestations of her difference. I had learned from Linda that Tiger was not doomed to a life of illiteracy and underachievement, but that she had a unique and, in many ways, gifted brain that can learn to flourish if shown how. My challenge and path to serenity was to ensure she had this opportunity, no matter how insurmountable a task it seemed to be. And along with this came the promise to myself that at some point I would return to my career. I needed to know this would eventually occur. But for now, I was at home with my daughters, and had at last found the courage to accept this with grace.

"Why are you smiling, Mommy?" Tiger asked looking puzzled.

"Sometimes, when I think about how much I love you two, I get a warm feeling inside and it makes me smile."

"Is that really what you were thinking about?" she asked skeptically.

"Scout's honor," I said holding up my fingers.

"Okay," Tiger said, and, satisfied with my explanation, returned to her bubble gum ice cream.

Suspecting Jamie shared Tiger's skepticism, I glanced at her out of the corner of my eye and said, "I was thinking something else, too."

Jamie continued licking her cookie dough. Unlike Tiger, whose ice cream had begun to travel down her arm, Jamie's smooth cone was perfectly symmetrical and drip-free. "I thought so," she said.

"I was thinking that as much as I miss working, I'm really going to enjoy spending more time with the two of you."

Jamie looked at me warily. "How much time?"

"You're going to have to kick me out of your room, how's that?"

They both rolled their eyes and looked at each other. "Dad was right," Jamie said to Tiger.

"About what?" I demanded.

"She is going loopy."

"Definitely!" Tiger agreed with an exaggerated nod.

Max worked the weekend again. I tried my best to enjoy what little time we had together, but even at home he was distracted and separate from us. We barely spoke on weekday mornings and inevitably I was asleep when he arrived home at night.

I was trying to put my acceptance into practice, but it was like breaking in a new pair of sneakers and it felt awkward and unfamiliar. My first task was to create a routine that was predictable and purposeful. I reserved my mornings for researching dyslexia and recording books on tape for Tiger. Once I dropped Tiger at school I would run errands and, when there was time, work in the garden. The gardening provided me with something to look forward to each day. I missed the constant stimulation and activity of the hospital, but so far it was nothing that a cup or two of strong coffee couldn't fix.

I enjoyed dressing up on Wednesday for my lunch with May. If felt good to be back in my more sophisticated, and certainly more flattering, clothing. May was seated at a small table by the window overlooking the harbor and stood when she

176

saw me approaching. We kissed and I breathed in the comforting, familiar scent of Channel. She was wearing a stylish cashmere twin set with a delicate string of pearls. Her hair was in a chignon and she wore a tailored pair of wool slacks. We smiled warmly at each other and sat down.

"It's wonderful to see you, May. I'm so glad you called."

"I'm glad I did too. It sounds as if you've been busy since we last saw one another. I can't tell you how surprised I was when you said you were no longer working at the hospital."

I sipped my icy water and smoothed my napkin onto my lap. "I'm sure you were surprised. Needless to say it wasn't an easy decision to make." May looked at me intently and waited for me to continue. "A lot has happened, and I've decided not to wait for Max to tell you." Alarm spread across May's composed face.

"Oh my, Katie, don't tell me." I suddenly realized what she was thinking.

"May, we're not getting a divorce!"

"Oh, thank God!" she said, and began to fan herself. She waved to the waitress and ordered us each a glass of chablis. "As long as that's not it, I can handle anything else you have to say." She was visibly shaken and I regretted my choice of words.

I rested my hand on hers. "I'm sorry, May. I didn't intend to startle you." I took a deep breath. "Why don't I just blurt it out. A few weeks ago we had Tiger tested and she was diagnosed with dyslexia. It's a pretty severe case, and I had to leave the hospital so that I can take her back and forth to a special program every day." I was amazed at how easily the words flowed from my mouth and silently congratulated myself for having come so far in my acceptance of Tiger's problem.

The waitress brought the wine and May took a delicate sip. "Now that's more like it. This I can handle. Just don't tell me you're divorcing my son."

I smiled at her. "Not a chance."

"I am the luckiest mother-in-law alive. Now, what's the big mystery? Why hasn't Max told us?"

"You'll have to ask him that. I don't know."

May began firing thoughtful questions at me. She had a unique talent for listening and following up with relevant questions. Her rapt attention enabled me to feel loved and important. "Did Max go with you to have her tested? Surely you didn't have to do that alone."

It had never occurred to me that Max should have come along. But the memory of that first drive home, the fear and sadness, I should not have been dodging potholes on the Baltimore Beltway alone. "No, I took Tiger by myself."

"Oh," May said thoughtfully.

"Max came to the last session in order to discuss the results. He was very upset."

"Yes, I'm sure he was, but he's a grown up and it doesn't sound as if his life has changed much. How is Tiger? Is this program helping her?"

"I think so." I explained the details of Linkages and my fights with Warner and the eventual decision to stop working. May was supportive and sympathetic and continued to ask insightful questions. Never once did she second guess my decisions or show disappointment in Tiger.

"It's such a relief to know there's help out there," May said as we finished our lunch and ordered coffee.

"Yes, it is," I said. May smoothed her napkin and began to play distractedly with her teaspoon. "May," I said softly, "what is it?"

She looked up at me with moistened eyes. "I don't know if Max has ever told you this, but Dusty was, or should I say, is, dyslexic."

"Dusty? Max never told me because I don't think he knows! What makes you think he's dyslexic?"

"Oh, I don't just think, I know. He had a very hard time in school. He was labeled 'lazy,' 'behavior problem,' 'slow,' you name it, he had it. But I always knew he was wise beyond his years. There was nothing slow or lazy about him. I walked him through his homework every night for years, I think that's why Max and his brothers resent Dusty sometimes, because of the time I spent with him. But it was the only way. And not until his artistic talents were recognized in high school, did he begin to have some success in school, never in academics, but as an art student. And I had to fight to get him into art classes, they wanted to put him into machine shop because he was so good with his hands."

"This is fascinating. All along Doctor Chartwell kept asking about a family history and I kept telling her there wasn't one. But there is. And Dusty's okay!"

"He's more than okay, Katie."

I sat back in my chair. "I love to hear any signs of hope for Tiger to live a happy life."

"She has a long road ahead of her. Dusty had some very hard years. And I think deep inside he's still haunted by self-doubt."

"That's my biggest worry, how to get Tiger what she needs before her self-esteem is non-existent or she falls so far behind in school she won't be able to catch up."

"You're right to worry." I appreciated her honesty. It would have been easy for her to give me false assurances, but she and I knew how difficult the next few years would be.

After several cups of coffee we noticed we were the only patrons remaining in the Yacht Club. An annoyed waitress was pushing an electric sweeper around the floor and was growing closer and closer to our feet. We reluctantly ended our luncheon and said emotional good-byes in the parking lot. I waved to her as she

178

drove away in her champagne-gold Mercedes. I felt a tremendous weight had been lifted. May's unconditional love and support were pure and unwavering. It was up to Max, now, to make peace with Tiger's dyslexia and his family.

I called Max from the car phone as I headed to the school to pick up Jamie and Tiger. I was on hold for longer than I cared to be, but eventually he answered.

"Hi Katie," he said in a hurried voice. "What's up?"

"I'm just leaving the Yacht Club."

"What were you doing at the Yacht Club? You're not that bored, are you? The next thing I know you'll be submitting your mystery meal recipes to the Junior League."

"Max!" I said, annoyed, "I was having lunch with your mother."

"Oh, right. I completely forgot. How did it go?"

"I told her everything. I told her about Tiger."

"Great. What did the old gal say?"

"You don't mind that I told her?"

"Mind? Why would I mind?"

"I don't know, I guess because you haven't told either of your parents, I assumed you were a little uncomfortable with it."

"Oh, maybe at first, but I'm glad it's all out in the open now. Look, babe, I have to run, we have a meeting and I'm already late. I'll see you tonight, don't wait dinner."

"Okay," I answered, but Max had already hung up. I stared at the phone and eventually clicked it off. As I turned down the lane to the school I began to feel very unsettled about the state of my marriage.

Lesson Nine:
A Healthy Marriage

Maintaining a healthy marriage is
by far the most difficult.
It requires
trust, communication, love and acceptance,
all within the parameters of day to day togetherness,
fatigue, illness,
children and finances.
It also requires protecting one's separateness
while offering empathy and kindness.
But it is what children need most of all.

I had reminded Max to be home on time for Leslie's party. Leslie and I had talked frequently over the past few days and she was nervous about her party. She had stressed that we be on time in order to ease her anxieties that no one would show up.

I was dressed and waiting when Max breezed in the door. Corrinne was playing with Jamie and Tiger, Leslie's number was on the refrigerator, the gift was wrapped and an appetizer and bottle of champagne were chilling in the refrigerator.

"Hey!" he said breathlessly. "You look nice."

"Thanks," I said flatly.

"I'll be back down in a flash. Time me!"

"Max," I said, "Please, I am not one of the children. I'll be waiting for you on the front porch."

"Okay. Is everything all right? Anything I should know about? We aren't fighting or anything, are we?"

"I promised Leslie we'd be on time."

"All right." Max walked up the stairs. He was accustomed to charming the world, and that usually included me. It was unsettling for him when he couldn't joke me into a good mood.

I was leaning against the front porch railing, gazing at the stars when Max was finally ready.

"Did you say good-bye to the kids?" he asked as he closed the door.

"I don't know that they noticed, but yes."

"They really love Corrinne, don't they! Hell, I love Corrinne! Too bad she's almost sixteen. That's when they get a life." Max stood next to me and looked up at the moon. "I'm sorry, Katie."

"For what?" I asked coolly.

"For whatever I've done to piss you off. It's obvious I've done something."

"I don't know that you've done anything. I guess I'm just feeling a little distant."

"You have to give me more to go on than that."

"I don't know, I can't pinpoint it. You're just, well, out to lunch all the time!"

"On the contrary, my dear," he said turning me to face him, "I've ordered in every day this week." Max smiled down at me and I could smell the faint scent of his expensive cologne. He looked extremely sexy in a washed-out, pink oxford cloth shirt and pressed, faded jeans. He was the only man I knew who looked good in pink. It enhanced his dark complexion and his blue eyes danced in the moonlight.

I looked away. "I don't want to argue. I've been looking forward to this all week."

He rubbed my arms. "Things will get better after this case, I promise."

I studied his face, I knew another, equally important case would follow. "Don't make promises you don't intend to keep."

"What if I promise I'll always find you to be gorgeous and incredibly sexy. How's that?" he said flashing me a boyish grin.

"It will do for now, I guess," I said, returning his gaze. "I'm so easy, it's pathetic."

"Speaking of easy, what are you wearing exactly?" He moved his hands down to the loose silk blouse I was wearing over a short black velvet skirt and black stockings. He untucked it and slipped his hands up inside my shirt. His fingertips discovered the lace at the top of my silk camisole.

"Max--"

"Sh," he whispered into my ear. "How long has it been?" his voice was muffled as he kissed my neck and squeezed me against him.

"If you'd get your ass home at night we might have a sex life."

He slowly slid his hands back up my body and began to unbutton my blouse. I reached for his arms to try and stop him. "Max, please, anyone could come by. Could we please just go to the car or something?"

He looked up at my face. "Really?"

"Yes, your pass was completed, but not here on the porch. Mrs. Steiner probably has her nose pressed to the window."

"Then we're out of here!" he said quickly and grabbed my hand.

It had been weeks since we had made love and I was overwhelmed with how much I wanted him. He drove to the end of street, parked the car and reclined our seats. Before long we were both sitting up trying to pull our clothes back together.

"Well, so much for silk, I am totally wrinkled," I said, buttoning my blouse.

"Come here," Max said affectionately. "Just tie it at the waist like this, and leave it unbuttoned a little. There! Now I can see that lace and your beautiful cleavage and, shit, Katie, I want you all over again." Max scooted closer and began to unbutton my blouse again.

I kissed him on the cheek and pushed him back into his seat. "Down, boy."

Max started the car and eased out of the neighborhood. He smiled the whole way to Leslie's and, for the time being, I felt peaceful and content.

Leslie opened the door before we had a chance to knock. "Where have you been? You promised you'd be on time!" She grabbed my arm and pulled me in the door. Max followed and kissed her on the cheek.

"You smell wonderful!" Leslie said to Max. She reached up and straightened out his hair, "You missed a spot," she said wryly and looked back at me. "What have you two been doing? Is that why you're late? Couldn't you have waited, I mean, after all, this is my first party for T.C."

I grabbed Leslie's arm and pulled her close. "Will you kindly keep your voice down? Besides, unlike you who gets it every night, we married folk have to seize the moment."

Leslie giggled and hugged me. "As long as you're happy. I need you and Max to liven up this party."

We locked arms and carried the champagne and appetizer into her kitchen. T.C. was at the freezer filling an ice bucket. "Leslie, dear, would you make some margaritas for the guys in the living room?" He kissed me lightly on the cheek. "Nice to see you, Kate, thanks for coming."

"Happy Birthday, Top Cat," I said, winking at him and handing him his gift.

"Katie, cut with the Top Cat stuff," Leslie said as she pulled margarita glasses down from the cabinet over her refrigerator. "T.C.'s trying to make partner and almost all of them are sitting in my living room."

"And they're all cruder and ruder than I will ever be, so relax, both of you!" I said ruffling T.C.s hair, "Just have fun."

T.C. straightened his hair and looked at me and then over at Leslie. She pulled me gently over to the counter. "Don't touch the hair," she whispered into my ear. She looked over my head at T.C. and said, "Go on back to the living room, honey,

182

I'll bring the margaritas out to you. And you should say hello to Max, too."

"Right," T.C. said trying to regain his composure. He pushed through the louvered doors and I overheard him greet Max.

"Sorry, girlfriend," I said as I rubbed a glass in salt. "We just have to get used to each other."

"Well do it quickly, okay?"

"Okay. How's the party?"

Leslie was measuring shots of tequila into a blender. "It's a mixed bag of people, I'll give it that. There are people from the firm, friends of his from his last job, which, I might add, all knew Clarissa, the ex! But they seem nice, and I invited some people from the hospital."

"Good. As long as it's not Warner or Michelle I'll be fine. Speaking of Michelle, I hear you agreed to supervise her."

"Yes, I did. I hope she isn't expecting much, though, we've been swamped lately and the hospital is starting to have us account for all our time. They want at least eighty percent of it spent in direct client hours."

"What about paper work, meetings, supervision, phone calls?"

"That's what the other twenty percent is for. I guess you have to eat and pee on your own time. I've considered inviting my patients into my office while I'm writing in the charts."

"Not a bad idea," I said laughing.

"But Michelle's all right, she's just young, and she's not you," Leslie said leaning toward me with a smile. "She really knows chemical dependency. I think she must be an ACOA (adult child of an alcoholic) by the way she talks, you know, family roles, adult child issues. But she works hard. I think she's a little nervous around the families."

"God, weren't you at that age?" I said as I sipped one of the margaritas Leslie handed me. "I can remember my first family session, I was terrified. I ran out of things to say after ten minutes. We just looked at each other. It was a disaster."

"You never told me that. That's hysterical!" Leslie piled the drinks on a southwestern style tray. "Grab those cocktail napkins, will you? Come on out to the party."

I picked up the napkins and marveled at how they matched the tray. How did she always manage to do that? I followed her into the living room.

The chairs in the living room were all occupied by the men from T.C.'s life. Leslie passed around the tray of drinks and T.C. watched her with a proud smile.

When the drinks were distributed, Leslie and I were left standing. I gently kicked Max and he jumped up to retrieve chairs from another room. "Thank you," I said through gritted teeth.

Leslie and I sat down and listened to the conversation. They were discussing

Max's case and the most recent article in *The Capital*. Max's picture had been on the front page juxtaposed to a picture of the Governor. Max was sitting on the edge of his seat gesticulating to the partner across the coffee table. He had a taco chip in one hand and a margarita in the other. After several minutes I realized I had finished my drink. I looked over at Leslie and she shrugged her shoulders. She loaded up the tray with empty glasses and I followed her into the kitchen. I grabbed a beer out of the refrigerator.

"They're having fun," I said to Leslie. "Are you?"

"I'll have fun once I know everyone else is," she said nervously. I helped her with the drinks and waited for her in the dining room where the women of the party were munching on vegetables and sipping wine. I greeted Anita, a nurse from Leslie's unit. Leslie joined us from the living room with an empty tray.

"We miss you at the hospital, Katie," Anita said. "I've been considering admitting Leslie on to the unit she's been so depressed since you left."

I laughed. "Thanks, I miss it a lot."

"How are things at home?" she asked warily. "Are you going nuts?"

"Probably," I said trying to keep things light. "It's very different from the hospital, but I've been keeping busy."

"I just don't know how you do it. My kids get on my nerves on the weekends, I can't imagine being home every day. I'd probably gain twenty pounds in a week!"

Leslie laughed, "Really, Katie, what do you do with yourself?"

"Oh, so far it's been fine." Their puzzled expressions caused me to wonder if I had a spot of vegetable dip on my face. It felt as if I needed to defend my life. After an awkward silence I said, "Did you know you could watch a segment of Martha Stewart's show at almost any time during the day? She's on at least ten different cable stations."

Leslie eventually smiled and nudged my arm. "You nut! You're not watching Martha Stewart. You had me worried there for a minute!" Anita laughed too, but I was desperate to change the subject.

We stood there for a few moments and I realized that without the usual hospital gossip, the three of us had little to say. I smiled. "Excuse me, I'm going to mingle." I stepped back from our circle and they immediately began talking about a doctor on their unit. It seems he was having an affair with one of the occupational therapists.

I walked up to a group of women who were all wives of partners from the firm. We knew each other from Christmas parties and other infrequent gatherings. "I see I've found some more party widows."

They laughed and made room for me in their circle. "Oh, who wants to talk to them anyway?" a tanned and manicured woman said.

"Really, you'd think they'd tire of work talk. We're much more interesting

184

anyway!" another woman said. Everyone laughed.

I smiled and listened politely to their conversation.

Eventually the woman next to me turned and said, "How are you, Katie? I hear you quit your job."

"That's right. How are things with you, Emily?"

"Oh, you know, busy, busy."

I smiled and nodded in agreement. "How are the kids?"

"They're great. Did Max tell you? Chandler got into the South River Academy! We're so excited! We had her tutored all summer so she'd pass the entrance test. We just heard last week. Do you know how hard it is to get into that school?"

"I've heard it's an excellent school. Is Chandler excited?"

"I think so. Kids are so funny. She's worried that she won't cut the mustard and of course she doesn't want to leave her friends. It's a challenging school and she's really going to have to buckle down, but we know she can do it. And with Chandler accepted, it will be a lot easier to get Justin in next year. You know boys, he's not quite so interested in the books."

"Actually I don't know, but that's what I hear."

"How do your girls like Chesapeake? That Frances Larson is a dinosaur, isn't she!" Emily laughed and patted my arm.

"They like it well enough." I was ready to change the subject but was saved by another woman who pulled Emily into her conversation.

"Oops!" Emily laughed. "Guess I'm needed over here!"

I headed back into the kitchen and was relieved when Leslie's louvered doors swung closed behind me. I was glad to be alone. I opened another beer and leaned against the counter. It seemed the working women were taking pity on me and the stay-at-home moms didn't have a clue what to say to me. I wasn't sure where I belonged so I decided to remain in the safety of Leslie's small but functional kitchen. Eventually I would return to the gathering and be my old charming self. I could hear my mother's voice telling me: "You think too much, Katie. Sometimes you just have to let yourself be."

I took a deep breath and was ready to join the party again when T.C. came through the doors with the empty tray. "Kate, how about some more of those margaritas?"

I looked at him in amazement. "You know what, T.C.," I said as I picked up the bottle of tequila and the shot glass and handed them to him, "why don't you guys just do shots?"

"Are we out of mix?"

"Yes," I lied.

"Well, I guess so. Maybe we should offer them beer, too."

"Maybe you should."

T.C. looked at me. "Why don't I go do that."

I watched him go and immediately started to worry that I was alienating him beyond repair. I didn't want to hurt Leslie, but just couldn't find a way to connect with her new lover. It seemed to be a theme that evening.

Max came in next. "Jesus! T.C.'s giving everyone shots of tequila. It's not even ten o'clock. Can you believe that guy?"

"Unbelievable."

"I think I'll have a beer instead. Where did you get that?"

I pointed to the refrigerator while I sipped my beer.

"Ready for another?"

"You driving home?"

"You tell me," he said as he twisted open my beer.

"By the way things are going, I would say it's a good idea."

"That's fine. I have to get up early and work tomorrow anyway. I'm going to head back to the living room. Why don't you come out?"

"In a minute," I said and watched him go. Eventually I peeked into the dining room and was glad to see the women had finally joined the men. I walked through the dining room and into the crowded living room. I wedged my way onto the couch next to Max and he nonchalantly put his arm around me and continued talking.

Everyone was toasting T.C. and encouraging him to drink more shots. Leslie sat next to him and was beaming with pleasure that her party was a success. She kept her eyes on T.C. and frequently touched his arm or leg. After one shot he leaned over and planted a wet sloppy kiss on her mouth and everyone cheered. I was happy for her and winked when she caught my eye. She winked back and gave me a discreet thumbs up.

As the evening progressed, Leslie brought out a cake. After a second look I realized it was an iced pair of breasts, a cherry atop each mound. After the singing T.C. leaned over and took a large bite out of each peak. The room vibrated with the subsequent cheers and laughter. I folded my arms across my chest in discomfort.

Leslie began to slice the bottom layer of the cake and encouraged T.C. to open his gifts. Most of them were practical jokes and drew a lot of laughs. T.C. held up a pair of silk boxer shorts and one of his friends commented that the best thing about living with a woman was the amount of Victoria's Secrets catalogs that came in the mail. I wanted to suggest to him that he could get on the mailing list without living with some poor woman, but I kept my thoughts to myself. Leslie was blushing but happy and laughed along with some of the crudest jokes. T.C. kept his arm draped around her shoulder, obviously proud of her beauty.

When T.C. had finished opening his gifts, Leslie tidied up the torn wrapping paper and sat on the floor next to his chair. "So, T.C.," she said so that everyone could hear. "Tell us how it feels to be thirty-eight?"

"Actually, if feels pretty damn good!" He said with a glossy, tequila smile. "When I stop to think about it, things are looking very good in my life! I've got a great job--"

"Hear, hear!" the other lawyers chanted.

"A sexy girlfriend," he said as he squeezed Leslie's shoulder. "I'm healthy and financially sound and a lot better off than I was at thirty, so I'd say things are looking just fine!"

Everyone chimed in with affirmative comments, including Max and Leslie. I sat silently. "I guess Katie and I could say the same, of course we hit the big four-oh this year! But life is much better than it was at thirty, right, Katie?"

Everyone looked at me and the room grew quiet. I was at a loss for words. It wasn't true for me at all. The things T.C. celebrated had taken a rapid reverse in my life. Forty was not better than thirty. I was jobless, no income, my career was at a complete standstill and at risk of losing ground, my relationship with my husband was growing more and more distant and one of my children had a severe learning disability.

"Katie," Max said, prodding me.

"Life is funny, don't you think? The way it can change so quickly and throw you off course."

The room fell silent and I noticed the music had stopped. I looked nervously around the room. "That's why it's great to celebrate the good things, right? Here's to T.C." I lifted my beer bottle in a toast.

"Hear, hear," came a more subdued chant.

Leslie looked at me with hurt in her eyes. I mouthed an "I'm sorry" and she just shook her head. "Nice one, Kate," Max whispered in my ear. I wanted to disappear. Leslie tried to get some enthusiasm for a game of charades, but the party was winding down. I had a sinking feeling that I had something to do with its change in course.

Max and I were among the first to leave. I hugged Leslie and said how much I had enjoyed her party and apologized, again, if I had put a damper on things.

"Sometimes I just don't get you, Katie."

Max slammed the car door once we had finally made our exit. He started the car and squealed out of Leslie's driveway. After several moments of uncomfortable silence he said, "What the hell's the matter with you, Kate?"

"I don't know."

"Well you need to figure it out real soon. I've tried to go along with you, ignore your moods, but this is ridiculous!"

"Just what are you referring to?"

187

"Your behavior tonight!" Max squealed around a corner.

"Max, please slow down," I said as unaccusingly as possible.

He ignored me and used every bit of horse-power he could eke out of his Saab. "You were antisocial, rude, inappropriate. Christ, Kate, Leslie is supposed to be your best friend and you're so wrapped up in yourself you can't even rise to the occasion!"

"You think I'm too wrapped up in myself?"

"Yes, I do. Leslie deserved more from you tonight. Just because you quit your job you think the whole world should feel sorry for you, well, shit, everyone has problems, you aren't the only one suffering here."

"You're suffering?" I asked him.

"Yeah, sometimes. Certainly your behavior is driving me nuts, and I work my ass off and you don't seem to appreciate it. All you do is bitch because I work late. Well, my working late happens to make a hell of a lot of money!"

"Max, please don't say anything you'll regret."

"Is that a threat, Kate?" he looked at me with anger in his eyes.

I deliberately looked forward and not at Max. "Please keep your eyes on the road, Max, you're really making me nervous."

"And see, you always have to correct me, you're always right! Well fuck that. Maybe you're wrong sometimes."

Max's anger was coming on fast and furious and I realized there was no point in arguing or defending myself. I had experienced his anger before, albeit rarely. But I was already feeling extremely vulnerable and confused and this time it seemed to cut through to my heart. "I had no idea you were so upset with me," I said quietly.

"Don't pull that hurt shit with me. Your tongue can be as sharp as a knife when you want it to be. Why can't you just admit you're wrong for once, Kate."

"I do. I was wrong tonight. I've apologized to Leslie and I will apologize to T.C."

"Oh, but not to me!"

"For what?"

"How about for embarrassing me in front of my colleagues and friends!"

"I'm sorry if I've embarrassed you, Max. I truly am."

"Shit!" He drove faster and I was terrified.

When we at last arrived home, I suggested I drive Corrinne home. Max protested and said I had had too much to drink, but that clearly wasn't so and I finally convinced him that he needed his rest so that he could work the next day.

I tried to make small talk with Corrinne about the evening and about her life. It amazed me how I could pretend everything was fine. But once she got out of the car the feelings flooded over me. I could barely breathe. I backed the car out of the driveway and started to drive. I drove and drove, without a destination, but with a strong need to keep moving. Eventually I came to a small road that led to a public landing on the edge of the Chesapeake Bay. I was relieved to find it empty. I turned out the lights of the Saab and slowly inched my way to the water's edge. I opened the sun roof, rolled down the windows and cut the engine. I leaned back and into the seat and cried until there were no more tears.

The still of the night replaced my sobs. As if in a symphony, the night came alive in a slow crescendo, awakening my senses one at a time -- the water lapping against the shore, the distinctive scent of the brackish water, the cool, damp breeze, and the wide continuous beam of moonlight reflecting off the water. I sat in the stillness of the car, my senses alive, waiting for a profound thought, but none came. I just felt confused and alone.

The last few weeks flashed through my mind all that had changed in my life. Was I really the person Max described, selfish and self-absorbed, caught up in my own problems. The thought made my stomach churn. How could that be? And if I was fulfilling my own selfish wishes, why was I so conflicted? I leaned my head back on the leather headrest and stared up at the stars framed by the sunroof, their vastness leaving me feeling small and insignificant. Where did I fit in this world? If I drove this fancy car right off the dock before me what would change? According to Max's view tonight... no, it didn't fit. However confused I felt, I knew I was not who he accused me to be. I couldn't pretend that life was rosy at forty, that much is true, and maybe that wasn't appropriate, but why had he asked? As my husband he should have known how I've been struggling, I was not the one to include in the discussion about the joys of forty. But he didn't know. May had been right. His life hasn't changed.

I took a deep breath and stared harder into the stars, searching for a sign or something to give me strength. I was never a religious person, not in the traditional sense. I had always found it difficult to pray to a Father, Son and Holy Ghost, as my Methodist upbringing had suggested, it was far too patriarchal for me. And I vowed to protect my daughters from succumbing to the extreme sexism and passivity of traditional religion. I could visualize the picture of Jesus in the sanctuary of our church growing up, long hair, fair skin and blue eyes watching over me, judging me harshly as I doodled in the program. No, not for my daughters, my daughters who had a strong sense of what was right and moral and kind. Values that came from within them, not from what they had been told was morally correct.

So what was I searching for? Was it God? Or was it something else. Was it Dolores's higher power? I closed my eyes and tried to make myself available. I craved a momentous experience. I wanted guidance, I wanted knowledge, I wanted answers. But nothing came.

I looked out at the water and stepped out of the car. I scared myself with the temptation of continuing to walk out into the water. It would be so easy. So quick. I threw my shoes and tights into the car and felt the breeze blow up under my skirt. The wetness in my panties from my lovemaking with Max still lingered, but the sensation left me feeling violated somehow. I walked to the water's edge and felt the gentle waves lapping against my feet. The water was cold but soothing. The breeze blew my blouse and skirt and hair and I stretched my arms out and wished I could fly away, be alone for a long time, so long pleasing and taking care of others. The tears began again and I welcomed them. I sat in the sand and laid back, spreading out my arms and legs. I closed my eyes and felt the sensation of the grains of sand on my skin, breathed in the salty water, and felt the cool breeze leaving tiny chill bumps on my arms and legs as it passed over me. I continued to breathe, slowly, clearing my cluttered mind, breathing away one thought at a time.

And so that night my sign did not come from the stars, as I had expected, or a lightning bolt from heaven, but from within me. As I lay motionless in the sand I felt a warmth glowing deep inside me. It must have been there since the day I was born, but I had not touched it in a very long time.

I continued to breathe slowly and although I was fearful of what would emerge, I allowed the scar tissue covering that dreaded fissure to dissolve. I had sealed off the vulnerable part of me long ago, the part of me that had needs and was childlike. It had been too risky, too scary to acknowledge its existence. But tonight, it felt risky not to.

The feelings expanded and I surprised to not be met with an uncontrollable sadness. Instead I felt overwhelmed by a strong sense of love. I felt the love of my dear, sweet father and the sense that he was nearby. I felt protected and safe and that I was no longer alone. I slowly opened my eyes and looked again up into the sky. This time I felt a oneness with the greater whole. The brightness of the stars reflected my love for my daughters, my love for my friends and family. I knew and trusted in my heart that I was a kind and loving person and deserved to be loved fully in return. And I knew at that instant that no matter what happened between Max and me, that I would be okay. I felt connected to my own, strong spirit and to a larger sense of love and spiritual presence, a faith I had lost sight of long ago.

By the time I walked back to the Saab it was three o'clock. Despite the late hour I felt energized and at peace. I knew that I could face anything and be okay. I had matured these past few months and have learned true selflessness and sacrifice. I would not trade that for anything. I felt strong and grown up.

I opened the door from the garage as quietly as possible, careful not to awaken anyone. It occurred to me that Max may have worried when I didn't return home right away. I slipped off my shoes and turned off all the lights that were still blazing. After checking on the girls I tiptoed into our bedroom. Baxter lifted his head, sensing my presence. "Some watchdog you are," I said as I scratched behind his ears. Max was snoring soundly. There were no notes or messages for me. It was obvious that he had gone to sleep immediately after I left with Corrinne. I slipped my pillow off the bed and headed for the guest room. Although I considered the effect this may have on one of our early rising children, I knew I couldn't sleep next to him, not tonight. I padded into the guest room and crawled into bed. Baxter stopped in the hallway, confused as to where he should sleep. Ever the faithful dog, he circled around three times and laid down in the hallway, equidistant from us both.

"Mommy, Mommy!" Tiger whispered as she shook my shoulder. "Mommy, Jamie's trying to make pancakes but they're all gloopy. I think she needs your help." I opened one eye to see Tiger's face very close to my own. Baxter was standing on the bed next to her, wagging his tail.

"Hey, Tig," I said. "Just give me a second to wake up. What time is it, anyway?"

Tiger picked up the portable clock next to the guest bed and handed it to me. "You know I can't tell time, Mommy."

When the hands came into focus I sat up quickly. "Shit!"

"Mommy!" Tiger exclaimed. "You said sh--"

"Tiger," I interrupted. Her eyes were so wide that I started to giggle. "I'm sorry, sweetie. I don't know where that came from, but I shouldn't have said it."

She smiled. "Maybe you should have a consequence."

I grabbed her and started tickling. "I'll give you a consequence."

"Mom!" she yelled. "Stop!"

I stopped. That was the family rule. Tickling isn't fun if the tickler doesn't stop when asked. I let go and she rolled out of my arms. I pushed my hands through my hair. "I can't remember the last time I slept this late. It's almost eleven o'clock! Are you guys okay?"

Tiger was on her back and Baxter was licking her. "Yeah, all except for gloopy pancakes." She pushed him away and sat up. "And I'm really hungry. We're all out of cereal and there aren't any more oranges."

Tiger tucked her legs underneath her and stared at me pensively. "Mommy, why are you in this room?"

"I couldn't sleep last night so I stayed up a little late. By the time I decided to go to bed I worried I would wake up Daddy, so I slept in here instead. Speaking of Daddy, where is he?"

"Beats me," Tiger said. "We haven't seen him. He was gone when we got up. He's never here on Saturdays anymore."

"Did he leave a note?"

"I don't think so. Ask Jamie. Could you come and help with the pancakes now?" she asked, tugging my arm.

"Sure. Did Jamie make coffee?"

"Coffee?"

"Just teasing," I said, ruffling her hair. "Has Baxter been out?" I pushed myself out of bed.

"Yup," she said proudly. "I let him out when I got up. He really had to go."

"Thank you, Tiger, that was very responsible of you." Tiger smiled at the compliment as we held hands and walked out of the guest room and down the stairs to a very smoky kitchen.

My first inclination was to chastise Jamie for using the stove while I was sleeping. We had a rule about using the stove or microwave without adult supervision. But when I saw her face, I immediately realized that her smoky kitchen was humiliation enough to learn a lesson from this experience.

"Is the burner too hot or not hot enough? Pancakes are tricky you know," I said as I tied my robe and walked over to the stove.

Relief spread across her face when she realized I wasn't angry. "Well, at first it wasn't hot enough, but now I think it's too hot."

I rubbed her back. "Thanks for feeding yourselves, I'm sorry I slept so late."

Jamie looked at me and narrowed her eyes. "Why were you sleeping in the guest room last night? Did you and Dad have a fight?"

"I was wide awake after Aunt Leslie's party and Daddy was exhausted. So I stayed up, but he was snoring so much by the time I went to bed that I decided to sleep in the guest room, instead of waking him up to stop snoring." Jamie looked relieved and Tiger smiled.

"It would have been nice to know where you were," Jamie said tentatively.

"I'm sorry. I didn't realize Daddy would be gone when I woke up and I had no idea I would sleep this late. Say, it looks as if our fancy new stove doesn't know how to cook up an order of old fashioned pancakes, so what do you guys say we go out to the diner and have a big old breakfast!"

"Yes!" they cheered.

"Race you to see which one of us can throw on a pair of jeans and brush her hair the fastest!" I started running down the hall, careful to let them both pass before I reached the top of the stairs.

After stuffing ourselves at breakfast, we headed back home to a quiet Saturday. I was surprised Max hadn't called while we were gone. There was a message from Leslie, however, and once Tiger and Jamie had settled into a big game of Playmobil that would probably last the afternoon, I returned her call.

"I'm really sorry about last night, Leslie. I hope I didn't ruin the party," I said sincerely.

"You didn't ruin anything, Katie. I'm sorry I gave you a hard time when you were leaving, I was way out of line. I was just so paranoid about the party that I got frustrated with you for being honest. Nice friend, huh! Anyway, you were fine, in fact T.C. credits you with making the party a success by suggesting everyone do shots of tequila. So I guess I should be thanking you."

"Not even necessary," I said in relief. "I'm just glad I didn't let you down. It was a very nice party, by the way. Does T.C. know how lucky he is to have you?"

Leslie sighed heavily. "Yes. For the most part I think he does. I just wish he was around more."

"Where is he now?" I asked, knowing the answer.

"Working. Have you been outside? It's gorgeous! Perfect, sunny, fall day. I begged him to go for a bike ride and picnic with me, but he insisted on going into the office. I was so upset I went back to bed for two hours. So what are you guys doing?"

"Waiting for you," I said matter-of-factly.

"I'm on my way," Leslie said, and hung up the phone.

I was mulching my flower beds while a fresh pot of coffee brewed in the kitchen when Leslie pulled her pale, green Mazda 626 into the driveway. Her sunroof was open and her hair was blown back. Although Leslie would have probably described herself as grungy, she looked flawless with a light layer of makeup, sunglasses, faded and pressed blue jeans, loafers and a cashmere vee-neck sweater. She got out of her car and walked over to me. "Starbucks in the pot, pour us a cup and come on back out," I called.

"Roger," she said, without breaking stride. When she returned I took off my gloves and we sat together on the weathered Adirondack chairs I had tucked in my perennial garden. We shared the foot stool and turned our faces toward the autumn sun. After wagging his tail at Leslie for several minutes, Baxter eventually settled in at our feet.

"Where are my pumpkins?"

"Playing an unbelievably fun game in Tiger's room. They have out every Playmobil set they own, the Indian village, the farm, the doll house, the western set, and, of course the cowboys are friends with the Indians and everyone's a vegetarian, even the animals. They've just created paradise only they don't know it."

"What a wonderful childhood they're having," Leslie said thoughtfully.

"I'm not so sure Tiger would agree with you," I said, immediately regretting it. "There I go again. You say something sweet and positive and I go and throw a

193

wrench in it. Maybe I am totally self absorbed."

"Excuse me?" Leslie said, lifting up her sunglasses in order to look over at me.

"Thank you for what you said, Leslie, and for the most part I would agree with you, Tiger is having a good childhood."

"Katie! You were right the first time. Tiger is going through hell right now. You don't need to sugarcoat that for me. I just thank God she has you for a mother. You need to lighten up on yourself, girl. We've been friends for too long for you to start watching what you say."

I looked over at her. "Thanks. You're the best. I was so worried I pissed you off last night. I would feel awful if I had ruined your party."

"Don't get sentimental on me or I'm likely to cry."

"I thought you said T.C. had a good time at the party. Are you two okay?"

"Yes," Leslie said carefully. "And if you asked T.C. he would tell you we couldn't be better."

"And if I asked you?"

"Good. Promising. If I'm willing to make a few compromises, that is."

"Just what compromises are you referring to?"

Leslie sighed. "I think this is where I need your help. I have some decisions to make."

I smiled. "Really? Already?"

Leslie returned my smile, but it quickly faded. "It's not like T.C. has asked me to marry him, although I know he will, eventually. Surprisingly I'm not the least bit insecure about him wanting me. I think he is very happy and is expecting things to stay on course and for us to eventually marry."

"And you?"

"Tell me, is this working all the time stuff really just about making partner, or will it get worse?"

I stared ahead. "Worse."

"I thought so."

I leaned back and smiled.

"What are you smiling about?" Leslie asked, slightly annoyed.

"Do you realize how far you've come? Not only are you no longer worried about what he wants, you're actually thinking about whether or not this relationship is the best for you! Two months ago you were afraid to hurt David's feelings even though he was walking out on your relationship."

Leslie smiled. "Has it only been two months? Well, look at me now. I have to decide how much I'm willing to compromise my idea of a relationship. Don't get me wrong, work is important. I love to work. But I want to have children. And I want my children to have a father. And I..."

"What? I'm listening."

194

Leslie looked at me nervously. "Am I upsetting you?"

"No," I said puzzled. "Why would this be upsetting me?"

"Well, I guess I'm saying I don't want what you have."

Leslie's words took my breath away. It hadn't occurred to me that I was doing exactly what she wanted to avoid. People had always envied what I had. I was the normal one, doing the right thing. It shocked me to think my best friend was trying to avoid my life's circumstances.

"Katie?" Leslie asked tentatively. "Are you okay? I'm sorry. I didn't mean to upset you."

"Just which part of my life are you trying to avoid?"

"Are you sure it's okay to talk about this?"

"You can't stop now, toots, now answer the question."

Leslie slipped her sunglasses back onto her nose and looked straight ahead. "Well, Katie, you know how much I love and admire you,"

"Leslie!"

"But I don't want to end up in a situation where the whole burden of taking care of my home and family falls on me. I don't want to be alone all the time. And I don't know if I could ever forgive my husband if he allowed for a situation where I had to leave my career when I didn't want to." Leslie looked back over at me. "And, sweetie, I guess I think that's what Max is doing to you."

"Oh."

"I didn't really see it until last night when he put you on the spot. I laid in bed this morning thinking about it and that's exactly what he did. He never should have asked you about life at forty, not if he had a clue what you've been going through. Especially when he hasn't had to change a single thing since all this started. He hasn't missed more than an hour or two of work and his life goes on just the same. Shit, even I've adjusted more than he has by staying late and covering for you at the hospital. Which you know I would do again in a heartbeat. But then to just leave you hanging there last night. Max has always been in his own little world, but this takes the cake."

"Leslie, I, um--"

"I knew I shouldn't have started this conversation. You know I love Max, I've just been noticing things more lately now that I'm in a serious relationship. And I guess I see a strong possibility for T.C. to be the same way and that's why I'm not so sure about jumping into a marriage. I love T.C., but I want a partner, not a paycheck.

"Ouch."

"Sorry." Leslie looked at me nervously, worried that she'd gone to far.

I smiled tiredly at her. "I'm a big girl. I can take it. Besides, T.C. and Max are different in a lot of ways. He could turn out to be very devoted and attentive."

195

"I think I'm starting to see that. Maybe a little insecurity in a guy is good for a relationship."

I wasn't sure what to say next. Having Leslie confirm what I'd been feeling was confusing. I watched a hawk circle over our back yard and then dive behind the house for its prey. I envisioned a little mouse, frozen in the growing shadow of the hawk, and I wished for its escape. Run for cover, little mouse. The hawk rose back into the sky and I cheered at the sight of its empty talons. I felt like Dorothy, again, watching Toto escape --"He got away, he got away!"--while she remained trapped in the castle with the emptying hourglass.

"Katie?" Leslie said with concern.

I looked over at her and smiled. "I'm glad you were open with me, Les. Please don't worry about what you've said. I'm glad you're questioning things. I envy you, starting a relationship when you have some wisdom and self-respect. It's a lot more reliable than the insecure, hormonally-charged decision-making of the young."

Leslie laughed. "I've made my fair share of those kind of decisions and you know it. But hey, if you went back in time knowing what you know now about life, don't you think you'd marry Max all over again? Or would you go for the guy in the leather jacket?"

"I would have steamy, passionate sex with the guy in the leather jacket, and then marry Max. But it's too late now. That guy's running a machine shop in central Ohio and has about ten kids."

"It figures," Leslie said. "Well, Katie, here's to us, two mature, wise women trying to save this world and mankind from itself."

I smiled at Leslie and lifted my coffee mug. "Nice toast. To us!" I said, and we clinked our mugs together and sipped the rich, comforting coffee.

By the time Max arrived home, Jamie, Tiger and I had finished dinner and were snuggled on the couch watching a movie.

"Hi, family!" he said cheerfully.

"Daddy!" Tiger and Jamie sang in unison. "Come sit with us on the couch," Tiger called to him. "We're watching a good movie."

"Be right there, Tig, just let me grab some grub and change my clothes."

I could feel myself growing tense. Max and I hadn't talked since our harsh words last night. Tiger was nestled in my lap so I waited for him in the family room.

Eventually Max joined us with some leftover pizza and a beer. I tried to read his thoughts but he stared straight ahead at the television. I was anxious to talk but decided it could wait a little longer. Max was quiet at one point I glanced over and noticed he was sleeping. I nudged him when the movie was over and gently suggested he put the girls to bed -- he hadn't seen them all week -- and he agreed.

I cleaned up the kitchen and settled into the family room, waiting for Max to return so that we could finally talk. When he didn't reappear I went upstairs and found him asleep on our bed, still in his clothes. I stared at his crumpled form. There was so much left unsaid between us. As I turned my back on our bedroom I realized the strength and security I had discovered was leading me away from Max.

I tried to plan my weekdays so that they were busy and full, but somehow, by Wednesday, the remainder of the week looked dismally empty. I was sitting on the front porch swing drinking coffee, and flipping through cookbooks. I thought I might try some interesting recipes for Thanksgiving, but cooking was Max's passion, it left me cold. I always felt depressed when hours of preparation would disappear into someone's stomach in a matter of minutes. I would rather put my creative energies into the garden where I could see and smell the results of my efforts for weeks, even years, on end. But I had exhausted the limits of autumn gardening. There was no more room for even the tiniest hyacinth bulb, the mulch mounds were already too high and if I pruned one more branch, my beautiful shrubs would be nothing but twigs. Even my sedums were drying up. My garden was ready for a winter rest.

The cookbook was flapping in the breeze and I realized I was staring at the garden again, planning where I could move some perennials before the first frost, when the phone rang. I almost spilled my coffee when I heard Rob's voice on the other end of the line.

"I hope I'm not bothering you, Katie, but you've been on my mind more than usual today, so I thought I'd call. I hope it's okay."

"As always, you show excellent judgment. How are you? It's been so long since we've talked," I said, sounding a little more enthusiastic than I knew I should.

"I'm hanging in there. It's nuts on the unit, they're packing the patients in like crazy. But they've shortened the stays so much I barely remember anyone's name before they're on their way to aftercare. The patients barely get detoxed before they're discharged. It's like a revolving door."

"Do you realize you just used the words nuts and crazy in a sentence to describe your work in a psychiatric hospital? Are these technical terms?"

"Yes, and quite accurate."

I laughed. "I can't believe how quickly Managed Care has changed things. It must be hard to watch."

"We're still doing some good work, but the family therapy department is suffering. Michelle's a good kid, but she's a purist and is missing the other dynamics in these families. And she really blew it with Blair."

"No! I don't think I want to know. Is she back on the streets?"

"Oh yeah, except I couldn't tell you what streets. She did it up right this time and ran way past Baltimore. She's either in New York or headed west to California. And she didn't leave any clues behind. Just a note that said something about getting out of her parents' hair before they sent her away. Her parents are a mess. Her mother called me the other day just to talk. Believe it or not they haven't separated yet and have been going to counseling. She says it's to talk about Blair, but you and I know how that goes."

"I certainly do. You can get at the marriage through many different avenues. They will be working on their relationship and not even know it. Blair has made the ultimate sacrifice. I just hope she makes it. She's not as street-wise as she thinks. Oh, God, I can't even think about what could happen to her."

"I know. So, on a lighter note, how are you? How's Tiger?"

"Tiger's hanging in there."

"And you?"

"Trying my damnedest to make this work. Today is a little harder than most. But your phone call has already helped."

"What are your plans today?"

"I haven't figured that out yet. I've been staring at the same page of this cookbook for longer than I care to admit."

"Do you still have Lois to help out?"

"Occasionally, but I have a hard time justifying paying her when I'm not making any money."

"Any chance you could get her to take over today?" Rob asked slyly.

"I'm not sure. What did you have in mind?"

"You just see what you can do about Lois, and then meet me in an hour at the commuter parking lot by the drug store."

"Aren't you working?"

"Nope. I took the day off. I had so much vacation time built up that Warner threatened to take it away if I didn't use some of it up by the end of the month. So, will I see you in an hour?"

"Yes," I said quickly.

It scared me how excited I felt when I hung up the phone. Lois agreed to transport Tiger and pick the girls up from school. She was excited to see them again and told me to take my time in the afternoon. I called Linkages and the Chesapeake Day School to let them know of the change in plans and then filled the tub and soaked in my favorite lavender bath salts. I powdered and puffed and took a little longer blow drying my hair. I slipped on a short, black skirt, black tights and clogs, and a black ribbed turtleneck. I appraised my figure in the mirror and approved of how the turtleneck accentuated my curves. Normally I avoided tighter fitting clothes, but today I had a strong desire to look and feel sexy. The stress of the past few weeks, and the absence of Dolores's M&M's, had caused me to unwittingly shed a few pounds, and I noticed my hip bones were starting to show a little more than I'd like, but my waist was narrow and my stomach flat and it felt wonderful. After applying a light coat of lipstick and giving my hair an extra fluff, I slipped on my tan suede blazer and headed out the door. I felt clean and pretty and I tingled with the anticipation of seeing Rob again.

I edged the van into the "Park-n-Ride" lot and drove around, looking for Rob's white, mini pickup truck. When I didn't see it I pulled into a parking space and turned off the engine. I was startled when his face suddenly appeared at my window but immediately broke into a grin, hopped out of the van and threw my arms around him. We lingered in our embrace for several moments until he put his hands on my waist and gently pushed me back and smiled down at me. "You look wonderful! God, I've missed you."

I grinned back at him. "Did you walk or what? I've been looking all over for your truck."

"It's at the rental car agency."

"Oh, I'm sorry, car trouble?"

"No," he said smiling and reached into his pocket and pulled out a set of keys and dangled them in front of my face. "You're driving."

"What?" I asked, confused.

Rob pressed the keys into my palm of my hand. "I said, you're driving."

"Rob -- "

"Sh," he whispered and guided me over to the most beautiful little, red sports car I'd ever seen. "It's yours for the day. You can take me with you or spend the day by yourself, either way, this is your car until eleven o'clock tonight."

"You're insane! If you only knew how much I needed this. But you have to come or I'm not going."

"I'm all yours." After opening the driver's side door for me, he climbed into the passenger seat and rested his arm on the open window. He placed his other arm behind my head rest and winked at me. "Now this is how I've always pictured you."

I drove and drove and drove. We traveled down the windy roads of St. Mary's County down the western shore of the Chesapeake Bay. We ate in a local bar in the Solomon's Islands and I had a beer and Rob had an O'Douls and we both had the best cream of crab soup either of us had ever tasted. We kept driving and stopping and driving and stopping. We put the convertible top down and felt the wind in our hair and by evening I could shift into fifth gear expertly around every curve. Not once did Rob correct my driving or tell me where to go. He followed my lead and gave his input only when asked. He chatted up the locals and praised my shifting. And throughout the day he reminded me of how right I looked behind the wheel of that shiny, red car.

I checked in with Lois that evening and she reassured me she was enjoying her time with the girls and to take my time. So Rob and I bought some cheese, fresh bread and a bottle of sparkling water and found a clearing on a cliff in Calvert County and watched the reflection of the sunset on the water. We were quiet for a long time, enjoying the wind, the view, and the sound of the seagulls. It was chilly so we snuggled together in order to keep warm. I was perfectly content and dreaded the idea that it would have to end. I nestled in the crook of Rob's arm and he supported my weight with his strong arms. He alternated between kissing the top of my head and smelling my hair. I nestled deeper into his chest and sighed.

"I don't want today to end," he said softly.

"Nor do I," I said with a sigh. "Thank you, Rob. Thank you for today."

"It's not over yet."

"I know, but I'm thanking you now because I feel so wonderful."

"I'm glad."

We sat in silence for a long time and Rob began to stroke my arm tenderly. He moved his finger up to my temple and gently traced the contours of my face. His touch was gentle and extremely sensuous. I shuddered at his light touch. When he stopped I leaned forward and turned to look at him. We studied each other and then I kissed him, long and hard, and with more passion than I knew I had. He held me in his arms and I felt the wind in my hair and the chill in the air. He tasted of bread and salt and of Rob, and I didn't want to stop. I felt his arms around me and couldn't get enough of his kiss, as if I had an unquenchable thirst. When he shifted and began to move me away from him I panicked, I didn't want to let go, it felt as if we had melted into one another. But eventually he pried me loose, pulled me to my feet and guided me back to the car. By the time we reached the car door I was crying.

"Katie, please don't cry," he said, his voice cracking.

"Thank you," I said into the softness of his corduroy shirt.

He buried his face in my hair. "Max is a lucky man. I hope to hell he figures that out."

"Rob--"

He lifted my face from the folds of his shirt and placed a finger to my lips "Don't. Don't say anything. I know." He openend the car door and I slid inside.

We drove slowly home and the cool night air dried my tears as they spilled from my eyes The heat I had felt had turned to a dull ache and when we arrived at the van, I clung to him once more and then said good bye.

I was relieved to find Max asleep. I washed, slipped into my pajamas and crawled into bed. I stayed close to the edge of the bed and closed my eyes, not wanting the feeling of Rob and the glorious day to drift away.

I settled back into a routine. Days were defined by the parameters of transporting and spending time with my children and researching dyslexia. Although I was frustrated with the lack of consistent literature, I continued searching and reading. And what I began to realize was frightening: much of educational policy and school curriculums were based on unsubstantiated theory, not solid research. Schools chose language arts programs based on what the administrators believed would work, not on what had been proven to educate students. This work was beginning to challenge my intellect and was, more than anything else I'd tried, helping me adjust to my new life.

But Max and I still hadn't talked. He continued to work hideously long hours. Tiger and Jamie were beyond complaining, and when Leslie said T.C. was home more, and she was glad the case was wrapping up, my fears were confirmed that there was much more to Max's absence than the desire to win his case.

He worked late Friday night, but this time I left him a note with strict instructions not to leave the next morning until we talked. By eight o'clock he was shaking me. He had already showered and was fully dressed.

"Katie, I really need to get into the office. Could you please wake up?"

I pushed myself up in bed and ran my fingers through my hair. "Okay. Just give me a minute. Are the girls awake?"

"No, but I'm not going to be able to get them up this morning, I hope you weren't counting on it. I've got to head into the office." Max was practically pacing and it pissed me off.

"Well, Max, I hate to put too many demands on you but it's fucking Saturday and I don't even know you any more so you can sit down and talk to me or, or, I don't know what!"

Max sat down. "Nice talk, Katie."

I shook my head and stood up. "This is not what I had in mind. Did you make coffee?"

"Yes. But I'm not about to talk to you if that's what you have to say."

"Look, I'm sorry. Could we just go downstairs and have a cup of coffee? I would like to start over."

"I need to get to work."

I looked at Max coolly and said as calmly as possible. "I'm not going to beg you."

Max studied me. He had the ability to put difficult issues completely out of his mind for weeks at a time when he needed to. I wondered if this was the first time he'd really thought about our situation. "Okay, let's go downstairs."

I pulled a sweatshirt over my shortie pajamas and poured some coffee into an extra large mug. It was warm for November so we decided to sit on the screened-in porch at the back of the house in order to prevent Jamie and Tiger from overhearing us. We sat in the peeling wicker chairs and kept our eyes focused safely on Baxter who was happily sniffing around the back yard.

I sipped my coffee, slowly, hoping Max would start the discussion. But he remained silent and sat stiffly in his chair. After a sufficient amount of coffee, I tucked my legs underneath me and turned toward Max. "I'm not sure how to start, I only know we are growing apart and if we want to do anything to prevent that, we need to talk."

"I don't see how my having to work long hours should be defined as us growing apart. Christ, Katie, this has been a career making case, and I'm kicking butt, and have most likely won. Why does that mean our relationship is in the crapper? Are you punishing me or something?"

Max had already shifted into a work mode and was primed to present the opposing opinion. But I had promised myself that I wouldn't argue with him, no matter how much I wanted to defend myself. I took another sip. "I guess I think it started before you got into this case so heavily. I feel like you've been slowly pulling away since Tiger's diagnosis."

"That's bullshit, Katie."

"Not to me. I don't know you anymore, Max. It seems the only thing we've been able to enjoy together lately is sex, and to be honest with you, I don't have much interest in even that anymore."

Max looked at me out of the corner of his eye. "What's this, some family therapy technique to get a rise out of me?"

"No," I said calmly. "It isn't. I'm speaking to you from my heart. I don't want our relationship to end, but there are many aspects to our lives together that aren't okay with me anymore."

Max interrupted, "Is this about you not working, Katie? Because if you ask me, that's when our problems started. I think you resent me for having a career, not to mention my recent success."

"Max, I don't resent your success or your career! One of us has to work. And as much as I miss my job, I'm surprisingly okay with the situation, for now. And I'm proud that I've put Tiger's needs first and of the kind of mother I've become. I would love to talk to you about what I've been thinking."

"You call this being okay with the situation?" Max said sarcastically.

"I'm talking about me, just me. But what about you? Is this how you want your life to be?"

"Yes. I think things are fine."

"I guess that tells me a lot." I looked back out at Baxter who was digging a large hole in one of my flower beds. My bulbs, I thought to myself. I held my coffee mug close to my face and the steam warmed my skin.

"And just what does that tell you?" Max said, the tension increasing in his voice.

"Please, Max, I don't want to argue. I'm just surprised to hear that you're fine with the way things are." I looked over at him. "I don't know where to take it from here."

Max stood up. "Well then, I guess we're finished. Because you see, I'm not all that complex," he said, holding his arms out in front of him. "What you see is what you get. And whether I should be or not, I'm fine. Now, I would like to go to work."

I could feel a tear start down my cheek but I immediately brushed it away, I didn't want Max to see me cry. But it was too late and he saw my hand out of the corner of his eye as he started to walk away. He stopped. "Look, Katie, we can talk again tonight."

"That's entirely up to you, but you won't hear me asking. I have a lot to think about too."

"What's that supposed to mean?" he asked, turning toward me. "What's this all about anyway, Katie? You want a divorce? Is that what you're trying to tell me?"

"I don't think I do. But I've changed, Max. And now I feel as if we're a million miles apart." I looked over at him, relieved that I had stopped the tears. "Despite what you think, I'm not trying to criticize or change you, Max. I stopped doing that a long time ago."

"Right."

"I have and I'm glad. It's the grown-up thing to do."

Max stood quietly for a moment. "I'll talk to you tonight."

Max turned to leave and was surprised when Tiger came running out of the French doors and jumped into his arms. "Daddy! You're here! Could you make us some pancakes? Please? Like you used to? Because Jamie doesn't make them as good as you do. I mean, she did a good job and all, no offense to Jamie, but they just weren't as good as yours. They were a little bit gloopy."

I could see Max pull Tiger close to him. He clung to her soft, little body, closed his eyes and buried his face in her hair. She rested her head on his shoulder and he rocked her gently. Holding her seemed to awaken something in him and he said tenderly, "Okay, Tiger cub. I would love to." He gave her a final squeeze and let her crawl down from their embrace. "You find the best maple syrup you can and then go wake up Jamie." Tiger skipped away and Max followed her slowly into the house.

203

After a long, hot shower, I slipped into some faded jeans and a sweater and walked downstairs. I was surprised to see that Max had not only made breakfast, but had also cleaned up. Tiger and Jamie had settled into Saturday morning cartoons and he was wiping the syrup drips off the counter.

"There are extra pancakes in the microwave if you decide you want some," Max said tentatively. "I figured that was the most Baxter-proof spot I could find."

"Thanks. I may have some in a little bit."

"Well," he said turning to me, "I really do need to go."

"Max," I said as non-accusingly as possible. "Leslie said this case was pretty much over, that both sides have presented their cases and it's up to the Judge now. Why do you have to work today?"

"Mainly to be sure I'm prepared for the verdict. I'll need to talk with the press soon, possibly appeal, but I doubt it, not with the way the things went in the courtroom, I think we have it in the bag. I just need to make sure I've dotted my 'I's and crossed my 'T's."

"I'm glad about the case, you know. I hope we have time to celebrate with your family next week."

"Next week? Why?"

I looked at him in astonishment. "If you look at your date-book you might notice the word 'Thanksgiving' on Thursday. In case you're not familiar with the occasion it's quite a popular holiday where families get together for the day, eat, talk, give thanks, it's quite a nice holiday, you might want to try it sometime."

Max looked genuinely surprised. "Thanksgiving is this Thursday? Is everyone coming?"

I sighed heavily. "I really wish I wasn't the only one who knew this but yes, even Dusty. And my mother and Aunt Matty arrive Wednesday afternoon."

"Okay. I'm on top of it."

"Right," I said quietly.

"I guess I don't even need to ask if you've planned the menu."

"No. You don't. But I've had the time so that part is okay. But I expect you to help with the cooking on Thursday, and not watch football and parades all day with your brothers."

"Well, it is a family tradition." Max began to perk up with the thought of being with his family. "I really have been out to lunch." He stood, staring out into space, deep in thought. Eventually he looked over at me. "Jamie said she was spending the night at Jessica's tonight. Why don't I pick up a pizza and be home in time for dinner? I could spend some time with Tiger, and you, if that's okay."

"Well, if you can manage it that would be fine." I was feeling leery about his new-found interest in his family. I didn't want Max to come around because I had nagged him. It had to come from him in order to have any real, sustained meaning.

And although I could see things were starting to click in his mind, I realized I was having mixed feelings about it. I had distanced from him more than I had realized.

"Katie?"

"Yes," I said hesitantly.

"I'm sorry about the other weekend. I think the tequila went to my head."

"All right."

"No, it's not all right. And it's not all right that I waited so long to apologize."

"I agree," I said coolly.

He looked up at me with concern. "I just hope the damage isn't too deep."

"I don't know."

"I know there is nothing I can say right now to make it all better, I just hope you're willing to keep talking to me about it."

"A lot has happened, Max."

"Right. Well, I'll say good-bye to the girls."

I hurried Jamie and Tiger into the van for the last day of school before Thanksgiving. Jamie had her Native American Halloween costume in a bag and her hair trailed down her back in a golden braid. I had given her some of my old eye pencils and heavy pancake makeup to take to school and she was wearing a pair of moccasin slippers. "Aren't I a little old to be in a Thanksgiving pageant?" she asked, trying to sound sophisticated.

"At least you get to be in it," Tiger said with a frown. She would have to miss the assembly. By the time I picked her up from Linkages, school would be over due to an early dismissal time. I had told Tiger the reason she would miss the program was because she couldn't miss a day of tutoring, which was partially true. What she didn't know is that her class had prepared for the pageant in the mornings and Mary had made no attempt to include Tiger in the preparations. Mary had explained to me that there simply wasn't time in her schedule and suggested I keep Tiger home that day.

"I wish you didn't have to miss it too, Tig. But you would have had to put on a dress and be a pilgrim," I said, trying to reassure her.

"I know. Why do the girls always have to be the pilgrims and the boys get to be the Indians? I wish I could be in fifth grade with Jamie."

"Mrs. Peterson is very traditional about these things."

"Whatever that means. Will you be able to pick me up, Mommy? Won't you be at the assembly?" Tiger asked with concern.

"Well, I guess I'll have to miss the assembly, won't I, because that's when you'll be finished with tutoring." I didn't think I could handle watching Tiger's class perform without her, even if it meant I would miss Jamie's part in the assembly.

"Good," Tiger said quietly.

"You're not coming?" Jamie asked in a high-pitched voice. "But I have a speaking part. I say the Native American blessing. I worked really hard on it. I can't believe you're not going to be there!"

"I am so sorry, honey. I truly am. I wish I could be in two places at the same time! I wish I could cut myself right down the middle and --"

"Okay, Mom, I get the point," Jamie said sullenly. She was fighting back tears.

"It's okay, Mommy, you can go. I'll wait in the lobby until it's over," Tiger said trying to placate Jamie.

"Thank you, Tiger. I appreciate that, but we're on a tight schedule today. As soon as I pick you up we have to go straight home because Grammy and Aunt Matty are coming."

"That's right! Yippee! Isn't that great news, Jamie?" Tiger said excitedly.

"How am I getting home?" Jamie asked, trying desperately not to cry.

"Jessica's mom. In fact, she wanted you to come over and play, but I told her you would want to be home when everyone arrived."

"Are they going to get there before I get home? Will Tiger be there and not me?" Jamie asked in disbelief. "That's so not fair!"

I tried to reassure Jamie that she would probably be home in time, but she was beyond comforting. Jamie hated to cry. She was biting her lip as she stared out the window, a trick she used to stop herself from crying, but her budding adolescent emotions were taking over and her face was turning red and blotchy.

"Do you want me to pull over, Jamie, so you can pull yourself together?"

"No," she said, sniffing, "I'm fine."

When I pulled around the circle Jamie climbed out of the van and slammed the door. I missed her customary, "Bye, Mom, I love you!" I rolled down the window to call to her but she was already inside the school.

"Poor Jamie," Tiger said sincerely as I pulled out of the school driveway.

"I agree. She isn't very happy and I don't blame her."

"You really blew it, didn't you, Mom," Tiger stated matter-of-factly.

I was flustered at her words. "I guess I did."

When Tiger emerged from her room with Jean, she ran toward me. Nothing cheered her more lately than time away from school. She wrapped her arms around my neck and said, "Let's get going, Mommy! Aunt Matty and Grammy might already be there!"

I closed my book and stood up, "Ready when you are!" We held hands and trotted out to the car.

Aunt Matty and my mother arrived shortly after Tiger and I got home and we ran out to the driveway to meet them. As I helped my mother out of the car I was struck with the unwelcome realization that she was aging. In my thoughts she was twenty years younger, but as I took her arm I could see the deepening wrinkles in her face and hands and a new stiffness in her movements.

"Hello, dear," she said warmly and held my face in her hands. I looked at her and felt a surprising wave of sadness. "What is it, Katie?"

I hugged her tightly. "Oh, Mom, I'm just really glad to see you, that's all."

"It's wonderful to see you too, my darling."

Aunt Matty was fussing over Tiger and I ran to the other side of the car and hugged her. It felt wonderful to be near her again and I squeezed her until she laughed. "My goodness!" she exclaimed. "What a grand welcome!"

Tiger and I carried their bags and Baxter led us into the house.

Once inside they settled around the table and took turns holding Tiger in their laps. They thoughtfully avoided comments about her size and questions about school, the things kids never really knew how to answer, and asked her about Baxter, bugs, and dinosaurs. I stood at the counter making them coffee and sandwiches and we all talked at once and I felt as if I were coming alive again after a long, deep sleep.

"Katie, darling, have you lost weight?" my mother asked as she watched me moving around the kitchen.

"Oh, maybe a little, Mom. Who knows, I don't really pay attention."

"Well I do and you're too thin. But you didn't have any to spare, honey, you've always been just right. Nice and curvy and huggable. Isn't your Mommy huggable, Tiger?"

"Yup," Tiger agreed as she sat comfortably in Aunt Matty's lap.

"Thank you, both, but there's no need for concern. I'm healthy and I don't have any intention of losing any more. Please, Mom, let's talk about something else." Aunt Matty observed us carefully.

A car door slammed and was I grateful when my mother and Aunt Matty hurried out to meet Jamie in the driveway. They made a tremendous fuss over her and she was beaming by the time she came in the door.

"Hi, sweetie! How was the pageant?" I asked, kissing her lightly on the cheek.

"All right, I guess," she said quietly.

"Your mom tells us that you read the Indian blessing," Aunt Matty said as she came in the door behind Jamie.

"Uh huh. I researched it myself."

"Well, what if you said it for Thanksgiving dinner, tomorrow. How would that be?"

I was amazed at Aunt Matty's insights. "Well, it would be all right with me.

Is it okay with you, Mom?" Jamie asked tentatively.

"Absolutely! I would love it! Have a seat at the table, Jamie, Grammy and Aunt Matty just got here and I'm making lunch for everyone."

Jamie plopped her heavy book-bag on the floor and snuggled into the breakfast nook with everyone else. My mother brought out presents, more American Girl doll goodies, and Aunt Matty delivered books and a kit for making tornadoes in a bottle. I smiled when I saw that each of Tiger's books was accompanied by a cassette recording. I was warmed by the love in the room and realized how much I had needed this visit. The burden of raising my children in a creative and loving atmosphere had been resting solely on my shoulders and I was grateful to see them experiencing unconditional love from someone other than me.

Max arrived home on time and was genuinely happy to see my mother and Matty. He gave them bear hugs that lifted them off their feet and although they protested vociferously, it was obvious they loved it. Mine was a solidly female family and I relished how much my mother and Aunt Matty enjoyed Max. He teased them and made them cocktails and hors d'oeuvres and asked them about their lives. The conversation was lively and full of laughter and Jamie and Tiger delighted in every word. They were enjoying a house full of people and levity as the stress of the last three months began to ease away.

My mother tucked Jamie and Tiger into bed and had fallen asleep while reading to them. Her attempt to revive herself failed so she kissed me good night and waved to Aunt Matty. Max followed, saying he wanted to get a good night's sleep for tomorrow, and guided my mother gently up the stairs. "You must be tired, too, Aunt Matty, after your long drive. Please don't stay up on my account," I said.

"On the contrary, I'm wide awake after Max's coffee. I may be awake all weekend."

I laughed softly. "Well, then, it sounds as if you could use a nightcap. Don't you like a little sherry in the evening?"

"That would be perfect, dear. Will you join me?" she said and started to push herself up out of the sofa.

I hopped up and patted her arm. "I think I will, but please, sit, I'll get them. You put your feet up and relax."

"Only if I can stop jittering! I feel like I could run a marathon."

Aunt Matty and I sat quietly when I returned with our sherry. We were next to each other on the sofa and watched the fire Max had started for us.

"Jamie reminds me more of you each day," Aunt Matty said, breaking the silence.

"Really?" I asked, surprised, "I always think of her as being more like Max."

"Oh, I see that too, but she's very observant, always thinking."

"Sounds more like you."

She turned toward me and smiled. "Maybe so, maybe so."

"So, what exactly have you been observing?"

She patted my leg, "I've been watching you, my dear." Aunt Matty paused, choosing her words carefully. "You look as though you're carrying the weight of the world on your shoulders. And not only are you too thin, but your face is tense and lined." I was uncomfortable with her words but knew I could never satisfy her with casual reassurances. "Your mother sees it too, you know. She wanted to stay up and talk to you, but just couldn't keep her eyes open."

"I don't know what to tell you. I suppose I feel like I have been carrying the weight of the world these days. So much has happened."

"It certainly has. Learning about Tiger, trying to find her help, leaving your job. I guess what I didn't expect, though, was that you would be having problems with Max."

I looked at her in surprise. "What makes you think Max and I are having problems?"

"It's not my business, but you two seem very distant from one another. I don't think I've ever seen you like this before. It worries me, sweetie, what's going on? I mean, if you feel like talking about it," she added.

I sighed and took a sip of my sherry. "It's hard to say. He's been very distracted lately, working constantly. We hardly see each other, that's part of it. We don't do well when we don't communicate. But it's more than that. In a nutshell I guess I feel as if he's abandoned me during all of this. I've basically been handling everything alone. It's been so hard," I felt the tears begin to form in my eyes and Aunt Matty rubbed my arm. "But the crazy thing is I think I've come through it okay. I'm feeling very strong and clear about myself and the choices I've made."

"And what about Max?"

"I don't have a clue. He doesn't say. He knows I like to talk things through, but I think somehow talking to me stirs up his own upsetting feelings, so he either avoids me or gets angry."

"Sounds as if you have it figured it out. But he'll work through this, don't you think?"

"I hope so," I said as I blew my nose. "But he hasn't yet, and the longer he ignores the problem, the more distant we become. I don't know how long I can wait for him to get his act together."

"He will, just give him time."

"Shoot, Aunt Matty, how much time? While he sits in his comfortable denial I'm carrying the burden for us both. I'm raising our children alone, making decisions about them alone, sacrificing my career alone, managing our home alone. I don't want to be the patient, dutiful, willing to put myself last, wife. I don't believe in that! And I don't want my daughters to be raised that way, either."

Aunt Matty watched the fire, her kind face deep in thought. "I've never been married, so I hesitate to give advice, but I know people, and I guess I have faith Max will come around. I see why you're losing patience with waiting. But he's a smart man. And he loves you, Katie, very deeply. I just hope you can hang in there."

"I'm trying but it's wearing me down. It's like the last scoop of ice cream on an overstuffed cone. It's starting to tip and melt and make a big old mess. I'm just so tired of compromising. I mean, I can do it when it comes to the children. I can even do it up to a point in my marriage. But it's gone too far," I paused and stared into the fire. I looked at Aunt Matty thoughtfully. "Do I just have unbelievably high expectations of people?"

She chuckled. "Well, dear, I suppose you do, but it's also what make you so special. And for the most part, I think it's a good thing. Your expectations bring out the best in people. And I believe in my heart that eventually they will bring out the very best in Max."

I rested my head on her shoulder and she stroked my hair. "But what you need to do for the next few days," she said softly, "is relax and enjoy your family and let your worries take a vacation. Let your mother and I help and love you and love your wonderful family."

A tear crept slowly down my cheek as I listened to her soothing words. "Who takes care of you?" I asked softly.

"I don't think you heard me, dear. I said, let your mother and I help you, and here you are asking about me."

"Oh, I have every intention of letting you take care of me, this feels wonderful, but I was just wondering, who takes care of you?"

"Well, if you must know, your mother and I help each other in every way. And, believe it or not, you do, sweetheart. You are very supportive and kind. I count on you a lot. And your sisters are too, in different ways. They help out with the everyday practicalities, you know. All in all, Katie, I am a very happy woman. I love my family and thank God for giving me this life. It is not what I would have chosen for myself, but it's one that I love and am grateful for."

I sighed and took a long, deep breath. "I'm so glad you're here. You have always been there for me, you know that? I can still remember the day you walked into the living room after Daddy died. I have never been so happy to see anyone in my entire life. I was so afraid you would go away again. As long as you were there, Mom would function, get out of bed, take care of us a little, but I was terrified that if you went away, she would go back to staying in her room all the time. The day you moved in I knew I was going to be okay. I knew I could get on with my life and stop worrying about whether or not Mom was going to make it. You gave us our lives back. I will never forget that."

"Well, I certainly hope not," she said jokingly. "It was a turning point in my life, too."

"Any regrets?"

"None," she said with certainty.

"I think, for the first time in my life, that I understand that completely."

"That's good, my dear," she said as she stroked my hair. "That's good."

The next morning I awoke early and tiptoed downstairs to start the turkey. The house was quiet and I was glad for the time alone to anticipate the day.

I pulled the turkey out of the overflowing refrigerator and almost dropped it. I had forgotten how heavy it was. I peeled off the wrapper and shuddered at the sight of the bloody turkey filled with organs and "giblets." I decided to make a pot of coffee before I continued with my task. I was pouring my first cup when my mother crept quietly into the kitchen.

"Good morning, dear. Getting an early start?"

"Actually, I was sitting here thinking about becoming a vegetarian again."

"That's nice," she said, accepting the mug of coffee I handed her. She pushed up the sleeves of her robe, "Mind if I help?"

"No!" I said with relief.

She smiled and began to scoop out the unwanted pieces of the turkey. I cringed at the sight of the slippery organs and was shocked when she put them into one of my sauce pans.

"Mom, what about salmonella?"

"We're going to simmer them for the gravy, and perhaps for Baxter, if he's a good boy."

"You sure are a depression baby, use everything, don't let anything go to waste, even turkey livers!"

Mother chuckled and asked for the stuffing. I proudly removed a large pot of homemade sausage stuffing from the refrigerator. I knew my mother considered me to be the least domestic of her three daughters and I often felt defensive about my abilities around the house when she visited. Although she was never critical, I would sense an air of disapproval when Max would do most of the cooking or I would order out during a visit.

"How does it look?" I asked tentatively.

"Did you make this yourself? Why, it smells delicious. And there's extra. That will come in handy."

"Thanks, Mom," I said in relief. "It's from the *Southern Living* cook book you gave me for Christmas. I think it's pretty good. I burned some of the bread, but I think I got those pieces out." I stood next to her and helped her scoop the stuffing

211

into the chest cavity. "So, Mom, how are you? Had any dates worth telling about?"

"Worth telling about? No. I went out with Stan Parker a few times. Remember the Parkers?"

"Sure," I said as I poured us more coffee. "Cliff was in my class. He wasn't bad looking as I recall."

"His dad isn't hard on the eyes, either, and after Sarah died earlier this year he asked me to dinner."

"And?"

She smiled. "It happens every time."

"What?"

"By the second date I knew every ache and pain he'd ever had and how many colds he'd had that year." I laughed. "Why do men feel the need to tell women all their ailments? Needless to say that was our last date."

"You heartbreaker. Did you let him down easy?"

"I don't think he was too broken up because he married Doris, his next door neighbor last month."

"No way!" I laughed. "Doris must be a better listener."

"Either that or hard of hearing. But honestly, Katie, I haven't much interest any more. I guess if someone really great came along I'd consider a relationship, but I'm happy with my life, and I'm pretty set in my ways. Matty and I are good company for one another. There's something to be said for longevity in a relationship. I really value the relationships I have with people who knew me before your father died. They know the complete me. It adds depth to a relationship to have known someone at their best and their worst. I don't feel like I have to try so hard with Matty, for instance, to be perky or interesting like I do with the men I've dated." She expertly spooned my stuffing into the turkey. I was leaning against the counter watching her.

The wisdom of my mother's words penetrated my thoughts. I considered Max and all we've been through. She felt my eyes upon her and looked over at me. I smiled. "I never looked at it that way before."

"So, as I was saying, I haven't really been looking for any dates, but I wouldn't pass up a date with Tom Selleck if he should ask."

"At least you're not picky," I said, teasing her.

She laughed and elbowed me in the side. "You know what I mean."

"I'm just glad you're happy. How's your health? Any depression?"

"No. I don't think so. But leave it to you to just jump right in there and ask."

"How many times do I have to tell you, depression is a disease that has to be monitored and sometimes medicated, just like diabetes. It's nothing to be ashamed of. Believe me, the people who don't take care of it are the ones that suffer."

"Well, Katie, I think I'm fine. I still have trouble sleeping, but that's probably more due to my age, than depression."

It had always believed that my mother had never completely gotten over the death of my father, even after thirty years. My memory of her before his death was of an extremely kind and happy woman. She was patient and content and from what I remember, madly in love with my father. Aunt Matty had confirmed this, and there are pictures of them together that bring me to tears. There was a sadness in her after his death that kept my sisters and me at a distance from her. I always knew she loved me, but she would sink into black moods that lasted for weeks during which I would barely see her. Although she would make it to work, she would come home and go right to bed until Aunt Matty would force her to eat dinner and say good night to us. Eventually she began to date. She was an attractive woman, and men never stopped expressing an interest in her, but she kept them at a safe distance. And not once did we ever expect to have a step father. She remained loyal to my father.

I will always regret the evening I shouted at her, "Daddy would have remarried and gone on with his life!" I was in my early twenties and studying social work and thought I knew, well, everything. She had been shocked and deeply hurt, and although I knew I was right, very few men can stay single for long, I had misunderstood the essence of my mother. She was proud of her ability to stay true to their love.

We have come a long way since then. I eventually learned to accept her choices and respect the tragedies she had suffered. "I'm glad you're feeling good, Mom, you deserve it," I said as I put my arm around her small waist. "Now, if you would just stop getting older everything will be fine."

"Ah, If only we all could, Katie. I better wash my hands. I know how worried you are about salmonella."

"Well, can you blame me, Ma? I've got Max's entire family coming for dinner. Shoot, they're used to having a cook, or at least Max, prepare their meals. And I just saw this big warning on the *Today Show* about turkeys and salmonella and wouldn't it be just typical if the small town girl from Ohio who can't cook worth a hoot managed to poison them all on Thanksgiving!"

Mother's spontaneous guffaw tickled me and I poked her in the side. "You're going to wake everyone up," I teased.

"How late did you and Matty stay up?" she asked through her laughter.

"Not too late. We had some sherry and enjoyed the fire."

"Did she talk to you?" Mother asked pointedly.

"Yes," I said, refusing to take her bait.

"About what?" she said, losing patience and tact.

I turned to look at her. "She told me that you were concerned about Max and me and we had a good talk."

"And what did you conclude?" she asked as she dried her hands on a paper towel.

"Mom, I've been through a very hard time these past few months, and it's been hard on my marriage, too. But I haven't given up on it, either. We just have some work to do. I can't guarantee anything, but Aunt Matty helped me get some perspective about being patient. And I'm feeling a little better."

She smiled. "Good. That's what it takes. And as much as I miss your father every day, we had our share of hard times. But what none of us realize when we're caught up in the middle of things is that time passes, and the good times and the love return. If only couples could see that, instead of getting stuck in the misery of the moment."

"You are a very wise woman." I leaned over and kissed her on the forehead. "Are you shrinking, woman?"

"Possibly, but I'd rather refer to it as my bones settling."

We laughed and I looked her sincerely in the eye. "Mom, thanks for coming out. I know it's hard on you to ride in the car for so long, and I know Megan counts on having you at her house for Thanksgiving. It means a lot to me that you made the effort to come."

She put her hands on my cheeks and smiled. "I knew you needed us, Katie, and that's what mattered."

"But how did you know? I never told you."

"That's the great thing about family, you don't always have to ask. And I know you well enough to know that you would never ask, even if your house were burning down."

"I think I may be outgrowing that."

"Well, that would be fine by me. You have always been the tough one, the one I didn't have to worry about, but sometimes that made me worry all the more."

"Really?"

"Absolutely!"

There was a shuffling behind us and we turned around simultaneously to see a sleepy Tiger standing in the doorway.

"Well, hello, sleepyhead!" Mother said walking over to her. "Did I wake you up with my laughter?"

Tiger looked up at her. "I'm not sure, but, maybe."

Mother scooped her up, as we were all prone to do, and carried her over to the breakfast nook. They sat next to each other and she rubbed Tiger's back as she slowly woke up.

"Sometimes I wish I could give Tiger a cup of coffee, it's so hard for her to wake up in the morning," I said after a few moments.

"Oh, no you don't!" Mother said disapprovingly. "She'll come around."

"Hey, Tig," I said as I looked down at the sauce pan full of giblets. "Ever see the inside of a turkey?"

Tiger immediately perked up and came over to the sink. "Whoa! That's the inside of a turkey?" She instinctively began to pick up the different parts and let them slide around in her hands. "What's this?" she asked her Grammy. Mother came over to the sink and began to explain each part as Tiger picked it up in her hands. She was fascinated and unaffected by the blood and slimy texture, studying each part with a scientist's detachment. Eventually she put them back in the saucepan and I scrubbed her hands. "Poor Tom the Turkey," she sang.

"Are you thinking about becoming a vegetarian, too?" I asked her.

"No. I just feel bad for Tom the Turkey."

"You would make a great Buddhist," I told her, more for the benefit of my mother, than Tiger.

"Still not taking these children to church?" she asked over the *Washington Post* she had begun to read at the kitchen table.

"No, Mom, I don't want to mess them up. I think they are both the most moral and 'Christian' people I know. And Tiger has a real sense about the connection humans have to all life. I think she's an evolved soul. Who knows, maybe she'll reach Buddha-hood in this life time."

"Whatever that is," she retorted.

"This is a child who won't let me kill a tick when I pull it off Baxter. She believes in the value of all life. She's a Buddhist, she just doesn't know it."

My mother rolled her eyes. "Well, you were raised a Christian, and so was your husband, and you should get these children to a church. But it's none of my business," she said as she continued to sip her coffee and read the paper.

I laughed as I loaded the heavy turkey into the warm oven. "But at least you don't have an opinion about it, do you, Ma?"

"No. Of course not. You run your life, and I'll run yours."

I laughed and Tiger laughed, too, enjoying our teasing of one another.
Jamie was next to awaken, followed by Max, and finally, Aunt Matty. We all lingered in the kitchen, drinking coffee and eating cantaloupe and fresh bagels with cream cheese. We passed around the newspaper and Aunt Matty read Tiger the comics. We joked with the girls and drank several pots of coffee. At ten, Max looked up at the clock and reminded us that his family would be arriving in less than an hour and we all scrambled toward the showers. Meanwhile, the baking turkey filled the house with a comforting aroma.

I was spraying on a little perfume when I heard Max calling to his family in the driveway. I had styled my hair and put on a simple, short black dress with black stockings and a string of pearls Max had given me for our fifteenth anniversary.

By the time I made it down to the kitchen, May, Max Senior, Dusty and Max's brother, Justin, were standing in the kitchen hugging Tiger and Jamie and kissing my mother and Aunt Matty. Baxter was in the middle of it all, acting as if he was the reason for their visit.

"Katie! How are you?" Justin yelled as he lifted me up off the ground. "Gosh, it's great to see you! Your house looks great. What a kitchen!"

"Thanks, Justin. I'm glad you like it, and I'm glad to see you, too. I'm sorry Lily couldn't make it, we'll miss her," I said as I headed over to May and Max. Lily was Justin's wife. They had been married for five years and were childless by choice. They were doctors and consumed by their careers. But they doted on their nieces and I knew at some point they would be ready to devote some of their endless energy to children of their own.

"Well, she could have time off during Thanksgiving or Christmas, so we chose Christmas. You see, she can't schedule her surgeries like I can, she's still a peon of an intern. And babies don't care what day it is when they decide to come out, anyway. In fact, they prefer holidays and weekdays. They did an exit poll."

Everyone laughed and Max slapped Justin on the back. I walked over to Dusty and hugged him. "Hi, Katie, it's good to see you," he said softly.

"Mm, it's great to see you too, Dusty," I said, enjoying his embrace. "I'm so glad you could make it."

"Wouldn't miss it!"

I greeted May and Max and they quickly became engaged in conversations with my mother and Aunt Matty. They asked all kinds of considerate and well informed questions of them, and they all genuinely enjoyed the chance to talk with peers at a family gathering. I felt blessed with the room full of kind and interesting people.

While we were all milling about in the kitchen, I noticed that Dusty had taken Jamie and Tiger upstairs. I tiptoed up the steps and found them in Tiger's room. Dusty had brought them each an art set from FAO Schwartz. Paper was all over the floor as he showed them how to use the oil pastel crayons. I had always wondered why art sets included those crayons. All they did was crumble in the hands of an inexperienced artist, but Dusty was showing them how to blend colors and use their hands freely. Tiger and Jamie were mesmerized by the ease with which he sketched a drawing of Baxter, who was panting heavily in his face.

"Did you guys thank Dusty for that wonderful present?" I asked.

They all looked up, surprised by the interruption. "Yes, Katie, they were the epitome of politeness, but more importantly," he said smiling, "they are also quite talented." Dusty had a unique ability to connect with Jamie and Tiger on their level. He was sitting with his legs crossed and a piece of his brown hair hung down in his eyes. He was attractive, but in a different way than Max. His features were softer and he was more gentle in his movements. He had straight brown hair and matching brown eyes. He was dressed in washed out khakis and a button front shirt that you could only find in Soho, loafers and no socks. Jamie and Tiger were riveted to his every move and as much as I wanted to watch Dusty draw, I decided they should have him all to their selves.

"I look forward to talking with you later, Dusty. Can I bring you something in the mean time?"

"Have any Pellegrino?" he asked.

"Something like that."

Max had served drinks and snacks to everyone during my absence. He had brought in extra chairs as everyone was gathered around the kitchen table. Justin was entertaining them with a story from Johns Hopkins. He was a surgeon, recently promoted to the head of his department. They were all laughing hysterically and I was reminded of how wonderful it felt to be among this family. I walked up next to Max at the butcher-block island and offered to take a plate of his hors d'oeurves to the table. "It's great to have everyone here, isn't it?" he asked me.

"Yes, it is."

Before noon, Blake and his wife, Meredith, arrived from Charlottesville, Virginia. They apologized for being late, and although Blake was as loud, if not louder than his brothers, a breeze of tension followed them into the kitchen. Everyone greeted them and the hubbub grew to another crescendo. I approached Meredith and told her how glad I was to have another daughter-in-law around. She smiled stiffly and let me take her coat. Meredith and I had never been close the way Justin's wife and I were, but we had always managed to find common ground. She was an accountant and very successful in her career, but for the last six years, she and Blake had suffered from infertility and the stress showed in her face. Meredith had always carried herself with an air of elite sophistication which kept her at a distance from most people, but I could see the lines of stress in her otherwise flawless skin and hoped she would be able to absorb some of the warmth and love this family had to offer.

May stood to welcome Meredith and put her arm around her affectionately. "How are you, dear?" she asked.

Meredith smiled tentatively. "Oh, as good as can be expected."

Max brought her a chair and she handed me the pie she was carrying. May guided her over to the table and my Mother and aunt Matty greeted her. They had already started asking her thoughtful questions about her new home and her job, so I went over to greet Blake. It was a Cunningham trait and I shouldn't have been surprised when he picked me up and spun me around, but I was. "Well if it isn't old Katie, the only good thing that ever came out of Ohio!"

I straightened my dress and laughed. "I'm sure my mother and Aunt Matty won't take too much offense at that!"

"Oops!" Blake said, loudly. "I beg your pardon, Joan and Matty!" He walked over to the table and shook their hands.

"Well, it's okay, we were born in Kentucky," Aunt Matty said.

"Oh, that's much better," Blake said and burst out laughing. "As long as you're not Indians fans, then we'll be fine." Blake looked hard at Aunt Matty. "Now I remember. You are an Indians fan!"

"And they outplayed the Orioles all season long, as I recall."

"Oh, man, I'm sorry Max, but I'm going to have to leave. Come on Meredith, we're out of here!"

Meredith looked over at him with feigned tolerance on her face. But Blake was animated and ignored her pointed expression. He slapped Max on the back. "Sorry, Bro! But you had to go and marry the enemy."

May and Max Senior were beaming at their sons' interaction and the rest of us laughed along.

"Katie, you said I was the loudest person you know, but come on! This guy could announce the Orioles games without a microphone," Max said.

"This, coming from my meek and mild older brother!" Blake cried. "By the way, 'Mr. Big Shot,' front page of the Post? Unbelievable!"

"That's right, Max," Justin joined in, "Way to go. Kicked the Gov's butt, didn't you. You made headlines in the Sun, too. What a hero!"

Max smiled at his brothers' compliments. Although they were competitive in their play, family loyalty took priority and they dispensed praise with an ease and generosity of spirit that bestowed a rare gift onto the lucky recipient.

Eventually everyone settled back into conversations. Blake went upstairs to see Dusty, but Meredith stayed rigidly in her seat. My mother and May joined me in preparing the final touches for dinner. Mother made the gravy and May tossed the salad. I asked Meredith to mash the potatoes and then stopped myself. "Oh, Max, dear, you know how I hate segregated parties, so could you get your butt over here and mash these potatoes! Meredith's been on the road all morning and could use a rest."

"But, Katie, it's not segregated, Aunt Matty is right here next to me!" Everyone laughed but Max hopped up and pointed Meredith back to her chair.

Max stood next to his mother. "Haven't I done a good job getting everything ready? I've been cooking all week."

"Yeah, right!" Justin called from the table. "And I made that pie I carried in!"

"Max," May said calmly, "I love you very much, but I do not believe that you did much of anything to prepare this lovely dinner."

"Ouch!" Max said as Justin and his father laughed.

218

May kissed Max on the cheek and smiled.

"I'm going to check on the girls," Aunt Matty said as she stood up from the table. "I haven't seen them all afternoon. Would you like me to get them washed up for dinner?"

"That would be wonderful," I said. "We should be ready to eat in, oh, say," I looked over at Max's potatoes, "ten minutes?"

"Sounds right," Max said. "You know, little brother, since I'm doing all this work, it means you, Dusty, and Blake are on clean up duty!"

"I like the sound of that," Mother said, joining in the fun.

Aunt Matty winked at me. "Dusty's been up there all afternoon, I wonder what they're up to." She walked up the stairs with a playful bounce in her step.

"What going on up there?" Max asked. "Mom, what's Dusty doing with Jamie and Tiger?"

"He brought them a present and he wanted to show it to them. He was very anxious to see them, he said he had a lot of questions for Tiger."

Max looked at her, puzzled. "Like what kind of questions?" The room grew quiet and even Meredith was interested in this conversation. May looked at me and I realized I had never told Max about Dusty. I had intended to, as soon as I had found out, but he had cut our conversation short and I hadn't had the opportunity to bring it up again.

"Why don't you ask him yourself, dear," May said tactfully.

Max was quiet for a moment and studied his mother. "I guess I know better than to pressure you to tell me."

"Your brother is a grown man, Max, he can speak for himself," she said.

"No shit, Mom. Well, these potatoes should be nice and starchy by now, who's ready to eat?" he asked.

Appreciating the change in subject, I led everyone into the dining room and showed them where to sit. Eventually Dusty, Jamie and Tiger came downstairs and we were all seated. We had put every leaf in the infrequently used table and Max and I were backed up to either wall of our intimate dining room as we sat at the heads of the table. Everyone grew quieter and more proper as the mood created by the candlelight, crystal, china and glorious food spread before us took affect.

"It's absolutely beautiful, Kate," May said warmly. Everyone voiced a consensus.

"Shall we bow our heads?" Max asked.

Jamie looked over at me in desperation, "Oh, Max, wait, Jamie is going to give the blessing today. I completely forgot to tell you."

Max looked up in surprise. "Oh."

Jamie looked worried, "I don't have to, Daddy."

"Oh yes you do," May said.

"I agree. I've been looking forward to this all day!" Aunt Matty chimed in.

I stared hard at Max, he was the only one who could make this work. I willed him to look at me and at last he noticed and a look of recognition spread over his face. "Why of course, Jamie, would you like to stand up so that we can all hear you?"

"Well..." she hesitated.

"Jamie, stand up!" Tiger whispered. "Everyone is looking at you."

Jamie took a deep breath and scooted her chair back. She looked beautiful. Her golden hair reflected the candlelight and her skin had that flawless glow of the young. "It's an Indian blessing," Jamie said timidly. "I wrote it myself after I researched it for school."

"Great!" Dusty said, impulsively, "Way to go, Jamie!"

Jamie smiled proudly at her uncle's encouragement.

> *O' Great Spirit,*
> *We celebrate the renewal of all things that grow and feed us,*
> *We celebrate the connectedness of all living things,*
> *the song of the bird,*
> *the fur of the buffalo,*
> *the speed of the horse,*
> *the meat of the deer,*
> *We celebrate the land, the sky, the sun and the rain,*
> *for it is all strong and beautiful,*
> *We celebrate the colors and the beauty of the earth,*
> *for it is old and everlasting,*
> *We celebrate, you, Great Spirit, for looking upon us*
> *with kindness and generosity,*
> *We celebrate every dawn, for it is a sacred event,*
> *and all those who stand on this earth,*
> *for they are sacred, too, and should be treated as such.*

"Amen," chorused the subdued voices surrounding the table.

No one spoke while the sentiments of Jamie's blessing lingered. Eventually I leaned toward my mother who was seated next to me. "Now how am I supposed to take these children to a sterile Protestant Church after that?" I said in a loud whisper.

Faces turned our way. "It would just be nice if they knew what the inside of a church looked like," she retorted

"I know what a church looks like inside, Grammy!" Tiger spoke up. "I went to one once."

The table exploded into laughter and Tiger beamed, unsure exactly what the joke was, but seemingly confident that it wasn't at her expense.

I watched my guests before I began to eat and was relieved to see that everything seemed to taste all right. Conversations broke out around the table and Tiger brought some laughs with her giblet story, at least from everyone but Meredith, who looked on with disapproval. Meredith was from a wealthy, southern family and had never warmed to Tiger's earthiness. I suggested to Tiger that she change the subject and she looked hurt.

Dusty patted her on the back. "We dyslexics like things messy and gooey, don't we Tig."

The room fell silent. Max and his brothers stared at Dusty. Max Senior stared at Tiger and Tiger looked around the table nervously. "Since when have you been dyslexic, Dusty?" Max asked.

"All my life, big brother, since when didn't you know that?"

"None of us knew that, Dusty!" Justin chimed in. "And for that matter, since when is the Tiger dyslexic? I talked to you last week, Max, and you never mentioned it."

"So did I!" Max Senior added. "I had no idea."

"Did I do something wrong?" Tiger asked, worried.

"God, no!" Dusty said, adamantly. "You are just perfect, and you should shout it from the rooftops if you feel like it."

"Dusty... Mom... what's going on? Did you know this, Katie?" Max asked.

"Not until recently, but, yes, I know about Dusty. You didn't call it dyslexia, though, did you Dusty?"

"Not until later," he said.

Max looked thoughtful. "That explains so much! Of course. That's why you spent so much time with him, Mom." Max looked at his mom and then over at me, his face revealing the depth of his understanding. "And all this time I thought he was your favorite."

"I am," Dusty said with a straight face. "I'm Dad's favorite, too."

Everyone laughed nervously. "I was too out to lunch to have a favorite," Max Senior said. "Which, from what I recall, Max, is just what you didn't want to be."

Max looked at his dad. Although his father said it in a joking manner, Max took it to heart. I resisted the urge to jump in and protect him. Something was happening here that needed to occur.

"Are you still dyslexic, Dusty?" Justin asked. "I mean, do you get cured for that?"

Dusty looked at Tiger. "No, Justin, it's just how my brain works. Unfortunately it isn't something talented doctors like you can fix. Some say it's a disability, but I've managed just fine."

"It's probably why you're such a talented artist," Aunt Matty added.

"Whoa," Blake said, shaking his head, "what a dinner!"

"No kidding!" Jamie chimed in, enjoying the lively discussion.

"It's funny how life repeats itself, I mean, with Katie not working now and having to help Tiger," May said.

"Hold on, you're not working anymore, Katie?" Blake said. "Since when?"

Everyone stared at me. None of Max's family seemed to know, not even his father. "No, I'm not," I said. "I know it's unusual in this family, but it's true."

"Damn, Max, you haven't told us anything!" Blake said. "Did you know any of this, Meredith?"

"Of course not," she said seriously. "Katie, why did you stop working? I can't imagine. I mean, you have your Master's degree. How can you stand it?"

"It was hard at first, I admit, but I'm okay, now. I really am," I said. "But I'm not ready to be teased about it yet!" I added quickly, looking at Blake and Justin.

"That's what the doctor told you, Meredith. To cut back on work," Blake said. Meredith shot him a look. "He said the stress in her job could be contributing to her inability to get pregnant."

"So he told you to quit?" I asked, incredulous.

"More or less," she said stiffly.

"But weren't you just made a partner at the accounting firm?" Max asked.

"Yes, I was. But what Blake failed to mention is that the stress in both our jobs could be contributing to the infertility. And that Blake is not only running his stock brokerage firm, he is also teaching night school and is president of the Chamber of Commerce. Should I go on?"

"My goodness!" my mother said. "When do you ever see each other?"

"Good question, Joan," Meredith said angrily.

"Well!" Justin said. "Maybe you're not out of a job – Katie, looks as if our family could use a family therapist right about now!"

"I don't know about that," May said tactfully, "but I do think Blake and Meredith have a lot to deal with. It must be so hard for you, dear," she said to Meredith.

Tears welled in Meredith's eyes from May's kind words. "We've had three in vitro procedures and none of them have taken. I feel like such a failure."

May patted Meredith's back. "It happens to a lot of couples just like yourselves, but maybe the doctor is right about stress, maybe if you just stop trying so hard for a while, you'll get pregnant."

"And maybe if you spent some time together, Blake," Max Senior added, "you'll actually have a chance to try it nature's way!"

"What do you mean, Grandpa?" Tiger asked.

"Nice going, Dad," Justin said.

"I'll tell you later," Jamie said. She was hanging on to every word.

"What this family needs is to communicate better and to spend more time together, don't you think, Katie?" May asked.

"I really do, May," I answered softly.

Meredith was wiping her eyes and glaring at Blake. He mouthed an "I'm sorry" to her but she didn't respond.

"Who wants pie?" I asked.

The brothers were true to their word and cleaned up after dinner. Even Max Senior chipped in, although his help consisted mainly of sitting at the island laughing with them. As I was clearing the table I overheard a lot of talk about baseball, politics, their various jobs. I thought to myself how extremely interesting, good looking and funny they all were. What a room full of talent. And yet, what had just happened at dinner?

I poured coffee and brought it out to the women who were sitting on the screened-in porch. Tiger and Jamie were running around outside with Baxter. I set down the tray and passed around the cups and saucers. "They say turkey is a soporific. Is anyone else sleepy?" I asked as I took the last cup and curled up in a wicker chair.

"Very," Aunt Matty said. She was stretched out in the chaise lounge, smiling.

"Well, I think that's my fault for keeping you up so late."

"And I wouldn't have it any other way," she said warmly.

"That sounds nice," May said. She was sitting in an old antique hard wood chair we had put out on the porch. The paint was peeling but it was solid. She was sitting upright, ankles crossed. "I look forward to having some company tonight." She smiled at Meredith.

"Oh, May, I don't know. Didn't Blake tell you? I think we're going to go back to Charlottesville tonight. I know he was looking forward to spending some time with everyone, but we have a lot to do tomorrow, and, well, I think it's best."

"Oh," May said, politely. "Well, you know what's best for the two of you." She resisted the urge to say more. I was amazed at her grace. Meredith looked down and shifted in her seat. There was an uncomfortable silence.

The tension was interrupted by Tiger who let the screen door slam as she came onto the porch. "Who wants to go with me and Jamie to take Baxter for a walk?"

"Oh, great idea!" Aunt Matty said, clumsily pushing herself out of the chaise. "Anyone else care to join us?"

Meredith looked at Tiger but didn't speak. May noticed and looked over at Tiger. "I think I'll stay here with your Aunt Meredith, sweetheart, but thank you for inviting me."

"Grammy?" she asked.

"Oh, well, why not," my mother said as she stood slowly. "I need to work off all that turkey and stuffing!"

"Goodness, Joan, you don't have anything to work off!" May said to her.

Mother patted May's shoulder. "It all just shifts to the wrong places, doesn't it?"

"I'm afraid that's so!" May laughed in agreement.

The three of us watched them leave and the silence fell upon us again.

"Meredith," I said cautiously, "do you want to talk?" May smiled and looked over at Meredith.

Meredith stared straight ahead but tears began to well in her eyes again. "I don't know what to say."

"I know it's not like you to talk about your personal issues, Meredith, but we're family. And it looks to me as if you have a lot going on," I said, pushing a little.

Meredith looked over at me. "I don't have any sisters, Kate, so I'm not used to confiding in anyone. And I'm an only child, if I don't have children, that's the end of the line for my family!" A tear began its descent down her enviable cheek bone.

"What about adoption, Meredith?" I asked.

"That's what Blake says, but I don't want to do that. I'm not ready to stop trying. I read all those articles about people adopting babies and finding out they have learning disabilities and all kinds of things! I just want my own."

Meredith was oblivious to the impact of her words, but I felt as if I'd been punched in the stomach. But May knew immediately and winced. She looked over at me sympathetically.

"Excuse me, Meredith," I said. "I don't mean to interrupt, but I think I need that walk after all." I stood, avoiding her eyes. "Besides, maybe it's best if you and May have some privacy to discuss this, I was wrong to pry." I walked purposefully out the screen door and it slammed behind me, as well. I walked around to the front of the house and saw the walkers several houses away and decided I would be better off with some time alone. I sat on the front porch steps and tucked my knees up close and hugged them.

The wooden porch floor creaked and I looked up to see Dusty coming out of the front door. He had a kitchen towel over his shoulder. "Mind if I join you?" he asked.

"I'd love it."

He sat down on the step next to me. "Ah!" he said as he cracked his knuckles and then leaned back on his elbows, his long, thin legs stretched before him. "This is such a great house. I love this neighborhood with the mature trees and shaded sidewalks. It's such a nice change from the city."

I smiled at Dusty. He had a peaceful look on his flawless face. "It's good to be reminded of that, I guess. Because there are times when I ache for the hustle and bustle of the city." I paused. The wind rustled the remaining stubborn dry leaves that were left on the trees. A cool breeze passed though our hair and one of Dusty's brown locks fell to his forehead. "How are you, Dusty? Are you happy?"

Dusty brushed the hair off his forehead but the stubborn strand fell down again. "I'm as happy as anybody can be, I guess. I've been selling some paintings and one of the major galleries is hosting a show of my work next month. I can't complain about that. I'm lucky to be able to earn a living doing what I love."

"Yes, you are. But you deserve your success, you're very good at what you do."

"Thanks, Kate. I appreciate that." Giving up on his hair, Dusty leaned forward and pulled up a blade of grass and began to twirl it around in his fingers.

"Well, I have to ask," I said playfully, "who's the lucky woman I've been hearing about?"

Dusty smiled. "Her name is Rosie. We've been seeing each other for almost a year now. It's good."

"I'm glad. What does she do?" I asked. "Oh! Why do I do that? I swore when I stopped working that I would stop defining people by their jobs!"

Dusty laughed. "Jesus, Kate, give yourself a break. It's a legitimate question. She obviously has a job or she wouldn't be living in New York. Well, and dating me, that is. She's a writer, free lance, and she's good. Her articles have been in *Vogue*, *Harpers* and she's working on a special piece for the New Yorker right now. But, Katie, just because you're not working, it doesn't mean you're no longer a family therapist. It's still 'what you do.'"

"I know, but that question still annoys me."

"Yeah, but so do all those politically correct questions, like 'Do you work outside the home?' 'No. I only work when I'm indoors.'"

I laughed, "I guess the intention is good, it's just we've gotten carried away with it. But I really don't think we should define people solely by how they earn a living."

"True enough. But Justin's right about our family needing therapy. What a dinner! How did the men in this family get to be so out to lunch?"

"I was going to ask you the same question. What's your read on it all? You grew up with them."

"I don't really know. I guess we were all encouraged to be successful, work hard, prove ourselves. It's not that we weren't loved or anything, there was just such a big emphasis on work and success."

"I guess that's why you're all such slouches!"

"Yeah, right," Dusty said chuckling. "But in all seriousness, it's the other stuff that we're not very good at, the emotional stuff. Maybe it's knowing we're lousy at feelings and empathy that drives us to go the extra mile in our jobs. We've got to be good at something."

"You say we, Dusty, but I think you're different from your brothers. You really connect with Tiger and Jamie. You don't just joke with them, you talk to them, get to know them. You treat them as people, not just kids to tease and then ignore," I said.

"Thank you, Kate. I try. But they are people. And they have tremendous insights. I mean, that blessing Jamie said, wow! If only a few more people in the world thought that way, this world would be a much better place."

"I agree. I just hope she can remain true to her feelings and beliefs and not be swept away by the status quo. There's so much pressure here to have the latest and best of everything. I don't remember it being that way in Ohio."

"She has some hope with you as her mom."

"I don't know about that. I used to think kids needed to be molded and instructed, but Jamie and Tiger have such wonderful instincts and compassion, I've decided my job is to just make sure I don't screw them up in some way."

"Well, you certainly haven't done that." Dusty laughed. "So, I don't know what's going on with Blake, or Max for that matter. I don't know why they have their heads up their backsides. Their families are going through some major deals here, and they're living their lives at work."

I stared ahead. The feelings about Max began to creep into the pit of my stomach again.

"I'm sorry if I upset you, Kate. It's really none of my business."

"You haven't upset me, Dusty."

"I think it's me that's upset her," Max said from behind us as he let the front door close behind him. Dusty and I whirled around from the unexpected interruption.

"Hey, Bro," Dusty said uneasily. "How long have you been standing there?"

"Long enough to hear you mention where my head's been lately. Scoot over, Katie," he said as he squeezed between us on the step.

"Sorry about that," Dusty said sheepishly.

"No need to apologize. You're right. That's exactly where I've been keeping my head."

"Well, you came by it naturally, that's where Dad's head has been most of his adult life."

"No argument there," Max said. "I think it's a family disease. Meredith's on the back porch crying and Mom was out there with her. Blake was watching the football game until he noticed Meredith wasn't around. When he found her on the porch, Mom pushed him down into one of the chairs and told him he had to sit there

226

and listen to his wife and then came inside. Heavy stuff."

"Good for May," I said quietly.

"Why don't you remove your head, Max? It is possible, you know. You have a fantastic family. I want to take your children back to New York with me. They're unbelievable."

Max looked over at Dusty and studied him. "You make it sound so easy. But what you seem to have forgotten is that I'm clueless in these matters."

"Someone once told me, the key to getting along with people is asking questions. If you don't know what to say or how to connect with someone, ask them a question," Dusty said.

I looked at Max. "Wasn't it you who said that?"

Max smiled at Dusty. "Have you always been a smartass? Oh, that's right, you have."

"Maybe, but I'm serious, Max. I think your wisdom would apply to your relationships with your family, as well."

Max grew quiet. He was obviously thinking about what Dusty had said. He looked down the sidewalk and watched Jamie, Tiger, Aunt Matty and my mother growing closer. Baxter was ahead of them, sniffing and pulling on the leash in Jamie's hand. He watched them for several minutes and without breaking his gaze said, "What's it like to be dyslexic, Dusty?"

I held my breath. Very good question, I thought to myself.

Dusty took his time answering. "Well, big brother, it's a gift, but it's also a tremendous burden. I think my artistic talent, and I use the term loosely, is probably a result of being right brained and processing things a little differently than most people. But it's hell when you're trying to navigate the world of language. And when you're a little kid like Tiger, that's what the world is: a world of words that you can't read or understand. You feel like an alien. You feel like you don't fit in anywhere and that the whole world is leaving you in its dust."

Max kept staring.

"I'm sorry if it's hard to hear, Max."

"Hearing it isn't half as hard as living it."

"That's right," Dusty said. "Good answer."

Max chuckled. "Okay, here's another question for you."

Yes! I thought to myself.

"How was it, with Dad, when you were growing up? I mean, with the learning disability?"

"Hell," Dusty said tersely. "It was hell. I know you guys thought he spent more time with me, but that wasn't how it was. He didn't know how to handle my failures in school so he would either yell and call me lazy, say I just wasn't trying hard enough, you know, or he would ignore me, give me the silent treatment. And he compared me to you guys, not intentionally, but he did. I didn't really amount to anything in his eyes until I came into my own in sports. That's why he went to all my games, because he finally had something to be proud of."

"So what was it like? How did you feel?" Max asked Dusty.

"Well, I guess I felt like I was a loser. Thank God for Mom. She hung in there with me, she fought the schools, and she came between Dad and me, defended me. It helped a lot, but I still felt like I wasn't as good."

Max turned to look at Dusty. "I'm sorry, man, I had no idea."

Dusty reddened with the intimacy. "You ask good questions."

"Thanks," he answered. Then he looked at me and said, "I know this doesn't change anything for you, but it does for me. I'm sorry. I have been staying away since Tiger's diagnosis. I didn't realize it, but I just didn't want to deal with it. I'm great at cheering them on and being proud, but, shit! I didn't know what to do with a disability. I still don't."

"Neither do I, Max, I'm just taking it one day at a time."

"Right," Max said, "But I am sorry. I think I'm starting to get it."

When the walkers returned they came up onto the front porch panting and happy. Max had gone out to meet them and had swung the girls around in the yard for a while. I walked Aunt Matty and my Mother into the house and Max and Dusty followed behind, each with a child on his shoulders. "Watch the door jams!" I called back.

Everyone else had gathered in the family room to watch football. Justin was stretched out on the floor, May and Max were in the chairs, and Blake was sitting next to Meredith on the couch, his arm around her affectionately. Meredith's eyes were red but she was smiling a little. I was glad to see they had talked.

Baxter ran over to Justin, panting from the walk, and started licking his face, he loved to find people on the floor. Justin started yelling and laughing and overreacting and everyone laughed. I brought in more chairs and Max went into the kitchen and came back with a case of cold beer. He handed one out to everyone and accepted no refusals, even Meredith was denied her usual glass of white wine. "We're going to watch some football and everyone has to drink beer."

"What about us?" Tiger asked.

"For you--root beer floats!"

"Yum!" Tiger said enthusiastically.

"Hey Tiger," Jamie said as she snuggled up next to her Uncle Justin on the floor, "We're watching the Lions! Hey, Dad, are they playing the Chicago Bears? Get it? Lions, Tiger and Bears!"

Everyone groaned at her eleven-year-old sense of humor and Justin started tickling her. "Who said anything about you being allowed to be funny?" he teased. "I've got enough competition as it is in this family, I don't need another jokester to out-do me!"

Jamie's laughter was so genuine that no one could suppress a smile.

For the rest of the afternoon, we cheered the Lions and drank cold beer and laughed. Each person grew funnier as the day wore on, challenged by the wit in the room.

Eventually the game ended and Max's family collected their things and prepared to leave. Meredith and Blake had decided to stay in Potomac after all, and May was thrilled. Justin was going to stay there too, and would drive back to Baltimore the next morning.

It was an emotional goodbye and we all agreed to meet in Potomac for Christmas at May's insistence. "We need to work on that communication and now's the time to start," she said.

Everyone told my mother and Aunt Matty how much they had enjoyed their company and I could see they truly had. Tiger and Jamie were hugged and kissed and squeezed, by everyone, that is, but Meredith. She had said good-bye to me in her usual way and I realized that she had no idea that she had offended me earlier. I decided to overlook it and assume she was just too caught up in her own distress to realize what she had done.

May made a special effort to hug and kiss me. "It was outstanding, Kate. Everything was perfect. You have such a knack for making people feel at home. That's a rare talent and you make it seem effortless."

I blushed with May's compliment. "Coming from you, that means everything. Oh, and May, excellent work with Meredith and Blake. If you ever decide to start another career, you might want to consider family therapy."

May smiled. "Coming from you I'll take that as a real compliment!" We both laughed. "But really, Katie, aren't all mothers family therapists?"

"I guess the good ones are, aren't they!"

"Yes."

I felt a sadness as their cars backed out of the driveway, almost a homesick feeling, and I was disappointed the day and the fun had to end. Max put his arms around my Mother and Aunt Matty and guided them back to the family room. "The night is young, ladies. I'm going to tuck in the little rug rats and then I'm going to fix you an after dinner drink that will knock your socks off, or whatever you're wearing. What do you call those things? Trouser socks or something?"

"They get your point, Max!" I said, laughing.

"You sit down too, toots, I'm going to make yours a double!"

While Max was saying good night to Jamie and Tiger I changed into some leggings and started a fire. My mother had also changed into a stylish robe, but

229

Aunt Matty had been comfortable all day in a pair of gabardine pants and a sweater. Max went straight to the kitchen and we could hear the blender. "Anyone ready for a cold turkey sandwich with mayonnaise?" he called.

"Absolutely!" Aunt Matty called. My mother and I declined.

Max passed around the drinks and plopped down on the couch next to me. "What a day! Whew! Do not attempt to adjust your television, you have entered the Family Zone! Do do do do, do do do do! What a bunch of whackos we all are!"

"Now, Max, you have a lovely family!" my mother said, laughing at his joke.

"We may be lovely, but we're whacko. What were you talking about before I so rudely interrupted?" he asked.

"I was asking Aunt Matty about her Orton-Gillingham training. I start mine next week and Aunt Matty just finished hers."

"You're taking a training next week?" he asked.

I looked at him.

"Well this is embarrassing!" he said. "Here's yet another thing I don't know," He looked over at my mother and Aunt Matty. "Drink up, ladies, this could get a little messy."

"Max, I'm not going to chastise you about this. We can discuss it later."

"Good. I'd much rather talk with Matty and Joan than about my shortcomings, anyway."

"I'd rather talk about your beautiful children," Aunt Matty said. "Tiger said she likes her tutor and I looked at some of her work samples, this tutor knows what she's doing. She's where she needs to be."

"That's good to hear," Max said.

"And then, of course, there's Jamie."

"What about, Jamie?" Max asked.

Aunt Matty grew serious. "I think she may be in trouble."

Lesson Ten:
The Importance of Siblings

It has become a commonly held
belief in this society that it is natural for siblings
to argue and fight with one another.
This is a false assumption
and a destructive one.
Siblings, not unlike suckling pigs, fight
when there isn't enough nourishment to go around.
Young piglets are calm and peaceful when there is a sufficient number
of teets. But when there are more piglets than teets,
the scuffling and scrambling begins.
Such is the world of siblings. When each child is
receiving sufficient love and attention and consideration,
there is no need for fighting or competition for what their
parents have to offer.

My mother and Aunt Matty left early Sunday for their long, drive home. Aunt Matty had been unable to articulate her concerns about Jamie, just that she noticed something wasn't right. I watched Jamie closely but failed to detect any signs of distress.

Max continued on his course of becoming more involved, and I began to feel a tremendous relief at his participation in our family again. He promised to be home in the evenings while I took the training and agreed to be responsible for contacting Lois if he couldn't make it home in time. Nonetheless, I put Lois on red alert. I didn't want to miss a minute of the training.

The trainings gave me something to look forward to every evening. Linda's enthusiasm for for her work continued into her classroom, and I tried to absorb every word she uttered. There were nine other women in the class, all training to become tutors. Being the only parent enabled me to learn from the other trainees, as well as Linda. It was also a small enough group that I could ask specific questions about Tiger's learning style and I began to feel hope for the first time that she might learn to read.

By the time I got home, the children were asleep, and usually Max as well. But he was enthusiastic about his time with the children. He was the only parent on duty and was rising to the occasion.

On Friday, I dropped Tiger at Linkages and headed home to do some reading Linda had recommended. I was cleaning up the breakfast dishes and wiping the counter tops when the phone rang.

"Hello, Kate. This is Frances Larson."

"Hello, Frances," I said, finding it easier to be friendly now that I knew Tiger was getting help. "Is it time to set up that conference already?"

"Well, actually, we need to be doing that within the next few weeks, but that isn't why I'm calling."

"Oh," I said, puzzled. "What is it, Frances? Is everything all right?"

"I'm surprised you're asking me that, knowing that Jamie hasn't turned in any homework in three weeks!"

"What?" I asked, feeling my knees grow weak. "What are you talking about, Frances, of course she's turned in her homework. Jamie always does her homework."

"Not anymore. And in addition to that, she's been given detention for misbehaving in gym class this morning. That's why I'm calling, to tell you that she'll be staying after school."

I sat down hard, onto one of the tall chairs at the island. Jamie? Not Jamie! Not now! "What do you want me to do, Frances? Do I need to come over there?"

"No. That won't be necessary. But you will need to sign a piece of paper every night telling us that you've checked her homework."

"Of course. I'll do that and more. But, Frances, do you have any idea why this would be happening? I mean, is there a problem at school?"

"Frankly, Katie, as far as we can tell, things are fine at school, but I would expect you to know these things. But her behavior today was unacceptable and we need to nip this in the bud before it gets out of hand."

I bristled at her words. "Of course, Frances, I'll take care of it."

"Thank you, Katie."

"Good-bye, Frances."

I clicked off the cordless phone and put my head in my hands. Aunt Matty had been right, of course. I racked my brain to think of signs that something was wrong. She had been upset about my missing the pageant, but seemed to get over that once everyone arrived for the holiday. But Jamie hadn't turned in her homework for three weeks! This had started long before the pageant.

Tiger and I waited on the playground for Jamie to finish her detention. Tiger was swinging slowly, and I sat motionless in the swing next to her. Tiger looked worried about her sister and kicked her white canvas sneakers in the loose dirt under the swing.

"How long does detention last, Mommy? I've never known anyone who had detention before."

"Mrs. Larson said it would be about half an hour. Jamie should be out soon."

"Are you mad at Jamie, Mommy?"

I looked over at Tiger and smiled. "A little. But I'm more worried than angry. This isn't like Jamie and I guess I need to find out what's bothering her."

"It's like Jamie a little bit."

"What do you mean, Tiger? Why would you say such a thing?"

Tiger began to retract her words, "Oh, I don't know. It's no big deal."

"No, Tiger, Please! Tell me what you're talking about. I can't help her if I don't know what's wrong."

"Well," Tiger hesitated. "She's been a little bit mean, lately."

"Mean! To you?"

"Yeah, a little."

"What has she been doing?"

"Well, not letting me in her room. And she calls me stupid sometimes if I don't understand what she's saying. And the other night when she had Jessica over, they were leaving me out and telling me I was a baby and stuff."

I tried not to overreact, but the "stupid" enraged me. "Tiger, why didn't you tell me before? It is absolutely not okay that she did those things to you."

"I don't know, I guess I didn't want her to call me a tattletale."

"But Tiger, there are times when it's good to keep someone's secrets, but there are times, especially if someone is hurting you, that you need to tell an adult. And this is one of those times."

"Okay, that's why I'm telling you now."

"Right," I said, trying to calm down. "Right."

"You already said that, Mommy."

"Right, I mean, Tiger!" I reached over and tousled her hair.

Jamie emerged from the heavy school doors and let them bang behind her. She was dragging her backpack through the grass and had a defiant look on her face. She didn't say anything as she approached us, no apology, no explanation, not even hello. I wasn't sure what to say first, that she should pick up her backpack instead of dragging it, that she needs to do her homework, or ask her what she did in gym to warrant a detention. I said hello to her and then stood up and led the way to the van.

We were quiet on the way home. Jamie stared out the window and I stared

233

straight ahead. I was feeling so angry with Jamie that I dared not speak to her now, for fear I would say something I'd regret later. Tiger was perched on the middle seat, looking nervously between us. She hated conflict, especially between family members. When she could no longer tolerate the silence she said, "Mommy, why aren't you talking to Jamie?"

Leave it to Tiger to get to the heart of the matter. "It's not that I'm not talking to Jamie, Tiger. I'm just thinking. I have every intention of talking to Jamie, and if Jamie has something to say for herself, I would be happy to talk to her now, but I think it's better for everyone if I just do a little thinking."

Jamie continued to stare out the window. But Tiger wouldn't give up. "Mommy."

"Yes, Tiger?" I asked, trying to not sound annoyed.

"Are you going to yell at Jamie for getting a detention?"

I sighed. "I don't think that would be very helpful, do you?"

"No," she said matter-of-factly, "But it feels like you're going to yell."

I looked at Tiger through the rear view mirror. Her intuitions never ceased to amaze me. But her words enabled me to gain perspective. Being angry with Jamie was a symptom of something underlying this problem. Why was I so angry? I knew how to handle behavior problems. Jamie had pushed the limits in the past, just never at school. And then I knew. My anger with Jamie was about Tiger, and her precarious position at school. If Jamie became a problem at school, then they would be twice as likely to kick Tiger out. I wanted, depended, on Jamie, to be the perfect student to help our case with Frances Larson. She was an asset to her school with her academic abilities and high test scores. I sighed deeply and smiled back at Tiger.

"Jamie, we need to talk about what's been going on at school, but I'm going to let you choose when, we can talk now, or later. If it's going to make you too anxious to wait until later, then we should talk now. But if you need some time to cool off and think about what you want to say to me, then we can do that too."

"I don't need any time to think about it because I don't have anything to say to you!" she said through gritted teeth.

"Jamie, Mommy's trying to be nice!" Tiger said.

"Stay out of it, you spoiled brat!"

"Jamie Marie Cunningham, that's enough!" I yelled spontaneously.

"Well there's a surprise," she said sarcastically. "Take her side for a change."

Tiger had a hurt look on her face and I felt furious at Jamie for making her life harder than it already was. Tiger was hanging onto her self-esteem by a thread and the last thing she needed was for her sister to turn against her.

"Tiger is not the problem, here, Jamie. She's only trying to help. If you don't want her to help, then there are more appropriate ways for you to tell her that," I said, trying unsuccessfully to maintain my composure.

Jamie continued to stare out the window.

I turned into our street and thought how quickly the ride home had been with the distraction of our arguing. I needed some perspective. "Jamie, I'd like you to go to your room when we get home, I'll be up to talk to you in five minutes."

"I'll gladly go to my room, but I'm not going to talk to you!"

"Jamie Marie," I said, starting to heat up again, "I will be up to talk to you whether you want to or not." I pulled the van into the garage and Jamie was in the house before I turned off the engine. She threw her backpack on the floor, grabbed a soda can and ran up to her room. I looked back at a miserable Tiger. I patted her leg, "Don't worry, honey. Jamie and I will work this out. We're having a problem now, but we'll work it out."

"I'm not so sure, Mommy. It doesn't look good. Jamie is really mad."

"I know, but we love each other very much and we'll work it out. That's what families do."

Tiger crawled slowly out of the van. She left her backpack and opened lunch box on the seat next to her. She was already out of her shoes and left them in the van as well. I started to call to her to come back and get her belongings, but didn't have the energy. It was easier to carry them in myself.

Tiger turned on the television, which was unusual for her on a sunny day, but I let it go, it was Friday.

I hesitated to talk to Jamie. I didn't understand her defiance and I was worried she wouldn't open up to me. After fifteen minutes I walked slowly up the stairs to her room. Her radio blared an inappropriate song through the closed door. I knocked but she didn't answer. I knocked again, harder, and called to her. After waiting a few moments I took a deep breath, expressing more anger toward Jamie was not going to help the situation.

"Jamie!" I called, increasing my volume, but careful not to sound annoyed.

The radio snapped off. "I'm not talking to you if you're going to be all mad."

I took a deep breath. "Jamie, please, we need to talk. Now open the door."

Jamie opened the door and stood in the open space, blocking my entry. "I'm listening."

"If you would like to talk somewhere else, fine, but either let me in this door or come into another room. I want to talk to you, Jamie, and I'm doing my best to stay calm, but I need for you to meet me half way."

"I don't want to talk to you because I know you're mad. You haven't even asked me my side of it. You assume I'm guilty. You are so quick to judge me. You think you know me, but you don't!" The tears began to trickle from her eyes and I could see she was debating whether to slam the door in my face. I stepped back, just in case.

"Of course I want to hear your side. Please let me in so we can talk." I paused. "Come on, Jamie, stop being so stubborn!"

Slam.

Shit.

I was sitting on the screened porch when Tiger opened the door and said, "Mommy, Aunt Leslie's on the phone."

"Thanks, Tig." I took the phone from her and put my hand over the mouthpiece and whispered, "Any sign of Jamie?"

"Nope," she said sullenly. "Nothin."

"Okay, thanks."

"It's happy hour," Leslie said.

"Not in this house," I said flatly.

"Oh, Max in the dog house again?"

"No, it's Jamie."

"Jamie!" she asked in surprise. "Now that's a little hard to believe. She's perfect! That child is from another planet she's so together"

"I know. But something's up. She's suddenly become the adolescent I've been dreading and she's not talking. She's pissed at me. I really think this one is about me."

"Not just being paranoid, girl?"

"I don't think so, not this time."

"Well, I've already invited myself over once, and you didn't say anything, do I have to ask again?"

"You don't have to ask, you know that. Come over. I'm pouting on the back porch."

"Great. I'll bring my pout. I have a very effective one, I've been working on it for years. Besides, I can't wait to get out of this hospital. But I better take these shackles off first, they're really starting to bind."

I laughed. "They're letting the slaves out for the weekend?"

"Just the underpaid ones."

"See you soon."

Leslie arrived carrying a six pack of good beer and a bag of taco chips. "Wilma, I'm home!" she called. I came into the kitchen to greet her. She was wearing a light-weight wool suit with a short, pleated skirt. She kicked off her pumps and hung her jacket over the back of a chair. "No hair, Baxter. No, hair," she said, wagging her finger at him.

236

I laughed. "Is that a new command?"

"Well, it's worth a try." Baxter was wiggling all around her, oblivious to her words.

Tiger ran out to meet her and jumped into her arms. Leslie hugged her and swung her around before she put her down. "Aunt Leslie, I'm glad you're here. Mommy and Jamie are having a fuss."

"So I hear," Leslie said seriously. "What should we do?"

"I don't know, I've tried everything I could think of, but nothing seems to help. They just get mad at me."

"That happens, doesn't it? But at least you tried. Pop open a couple of brewskies, Katie, I'm going to say hi to Jamie. Want to come with me?" she asked Tiger.

Tiger looked at me warily. "I better not. Jamie's sort of mad at me too."

"Okay, sweetie. I'll be back down in a few minutes. Don't eat all those chips, I'm starving!"

I milled around in the kitchen, wondering what Jamie would say to Leslie. But the kitchen was clean and I had no intention of cooking, so I put some chips in a bowl for Tiger and carried the rest out to the porch. I munched on them as I waited.

Eventually, Leslie plopped down beside me. She put her feet up on the footstool and took a sip of her beer.

"Don't snag your stockings," I cautioned her.

"Oh, who cares."

I looked at her in surprise. "You do, as I recall."

She glanced over at me and smiled. "Well, I sort of do, but not enough to move my feet."

"So?" I asked.

"She seemed fine with me. I think she knows I would tell you anything she said, though, so she didn't give me much to go on. Isn't it great we don't have to worry about confidentiality in the rest of our lives? I keep so much to myself in this job I feel as if I'm going to explode sometimes. Can't you just see it, I would explode, and all of these secrets would come flying out on little pieces of paper and would be spread all over the place."

"Feeling a little stressed, Les?"

Leslie laughed. "Nothing out of the ordinary."

"Back to Jamie."

"I don't know, Katie, I really don't. She was as sweet as can be. She let me sit on her bed and we talked about some of her friends and she showed me the stuff your mother brought her for her dolls. That's about it. She seemed a little sad, though. I think she wants to come down, but her pride won't let her."

"You're probably right. Thanks for talking to her."

237

"I didn't do it for you, babe."

"I know, at least I think I know, whose side are you on, anyway?"

"I haven't decided yet. I think I'll plead Switzerland."

We sipped our beers and munched on chips and enjoyed the crisp autumn breeze. "Katie," Leslie said tentatively. "Can I ask you something?"

"Sure," I said.

"Are you having an affair with Rob?"

I choked on my sip of beer. "No! No, Leslie, I'm not! Why do you ask?"

She looked at me seriously. "It's none of my business, I know, but I'm worried about you. Don't screw up your marriage, Katie, affairs aren't worth it, believe me, I know."

I took a deep breath and decided it would feel good to confide in Leslie. "Is kissing an affair?" I asked cautiously.

Leslie hesitated, I was confirming her fears. "It depends."

"Yes, there were tongues."

"That's not what I meant!" she said adamantly. "Affairs are about emotions as much as they are about sex. Are you in love with him?"

"No. I mean, yes. Well, sort of. I love him, dearly. He's special to me in many ways. We trust each other, we respect each other, we kicked butt on that unit! And we've been there for each other. And he's the only one, besides my Aunt Matty whose four hundred miles away, whose been there for me these past few months." I stopped myself and looked over at Leslie. "I mean, you've been there, too."

"No I haven't, Katie. Go ahead and say it, we're being honest, here. I haven't been there, and I still probably don't quite understand what you've been through. I was so caught up in T.C. that I didn't pay attention. It wasn't until his birthday party that I started to get it. Shit, I was feeling sorry for myself that you left the hospital. How self-centered is that?"

"But it's no excuse to kiss Rob."

"Maybe not, but maybe it is. I'm glad he's been there for you." Leslie sipped her beer and stared at the trees, the breeze blew back her hair. "Are you sure you didn't have sex?"

"Scout's honor,"

"Did you want to?"

"What do you think I am, dead?"

"He's is a sexy little thing, isn't he!" Leslie laughed.

"Oh, lordy!"

"Of course, this coming from a woman married to Max the hunk! It's not fair for you to have them both. Have you told Max?" she asked, turning serious again.

"No." I grew quiet. "I will, I know. But I don't really know what I'd say."

"You'd be pissed as hell if he was kissing a co-worker."

"I know. I'd be pissed if I knew he was attracted to a co-worker, although I guess that happens all the time, I just don't like to think about it."

"Tell me about it," she agreed.

"But I'm going to have to agree with what you first said. This is about emotions and feelings. If there has been a betrayal to Max, then that's what it is."

"Oh, Katie, hasn't he betrayed you? By abandoning you through all of this, physically and emotionally?"

"Well, it's not about paybacks or revenge or evening the score. It's just about, well, whew, I don't have a clue. But I'm glad you asked. It's a relief to talk about it."

"I saw him today in the cafeteria. He's such a great guy. He's so down to earth. He's the least full of bullshit man I've ever met. Can he kiss?"

I shivered with the memory. "Yes."

"Oh, Katie, you poor dear," she said patting my leg. "Just don't blow it with Max or my last hope for the institution of marriage will be dashed. I'm counting on you."

"I'm counting on me too, Les. I want to stay married, and I want to stay married to Max. If I can say that after a day with Rob, then it must really be true."

"This calls for another beer. Do you need to feed your children?"

"They have chips."

Leslie laughed. "Oh, well then, that's a relief!"

Leslie returned and reported that Jamie was watching TV with Tiger and seemed to be okay.

We clinked our beer bottles together and I put my feet up on the footstool next to her. "So, what are you and T.C. doing this weekend?" I asked her after a few minutes of silence.

"Well, we might shop for a ring."

"What?" I screamed. "Leslie, that's great!" I leaped up to hug her. She hugged me back and then sat back down.

She sat quietly and I stared at her. "Don't bowl me over with your excitement, there, Les. What's the deal? Aren't you happy?"

"Yes. I am. But I have mixed feelings. I mean, I want to marry him, we're happy together, and everything."

"So what's the problem?"

"Well, there isn't one, really. I'm still attracted to him, and we're very compatible, in fact sometimes it seems as if we've been together for years. But, you know, marriage is great, and I've wanted it for so long, but I've realized lately that it isn't the goal. It's just part of the process. Does that make any sense?"

"Very much."

"Remember when you were in your twenties? That's what everyone talked about, weddings. Who was marrying who, what the weddings would be like, it's like that was the end all, to have a wedding. But you've only lived such a small percentage of you life at that age. Now that I'm almost forty, a wedding is really just a ritual to go through so that I can continue on with my life."

"Well, it's a nice ritual, right? With matrons of honor and cute little bridesmaids?"

Leslie laughed. "Come on, I'm thirty-eight. This is the second marriage for both of us. Granted, my first one was so short it doesn't even register on the marriage scale, but I'm no blushing bride." I looked at her with my eyebrows raised. "Okay! You can be in the wedding." We both laughed.

I pumped her with questions about the proposal, dates, and I threatened to go buy a bridal magazine. "So what about children? Tiger and Jamie need some more 'cousins."

"Well," Leslie hesitated, "we've talked about it. He said it's fine with him, but I would like to see him want them a little more than he does. But maybe that will come in time. I don't know, I desperately wanted a relationship, and I'm really happy we're together, but some days I miss my independence. Everything is going to change."

I patted Leslie's hand. "You don't have to change, you know. You will still be you, you don't have to give up your individuality just because you're married."

"That's going to be harder than I thought. I hope I've never been judgmental of you, Katie, about your choices." Leslie said looking over at me. "Have I?"

"Absolutely not." I smiled at her. "Cheers, Leslie, to you, to being a great person and a wonderful friend and to not ever compromising that!" We clinked bottles.

"I'll drink to that," she echoed.

Max came home and found us on the porch and was appropriately thrilled with Leslie's news. He called T.C. and invited him over and then went out for pizza and champagne. In the meantime, I convinced Jamie to make a truce with me so that she could join in the fun, and that she could be mad at me again tomorrow. She agreed and was relieved to let go of her angry stance. Eventually she even played with Tiger, and, at least for the evening, everything was good.

I could smell Max's pancakes as I dressed. He had brought me a cup of coffee in bed and announced that he wouldn't be going in to work today. Although I was leery of the 'new Max', and wondered about his attention span for life at home, I had decided to give him a chance. It was what I hoped for, after all, and he did bring me the coffee.

I slipped on a pair of khakis, a thick turtle neck sweater, warm socks and padded into Jamie's room. I rapped lightly on the door and peeked in without waiting for a response. She was lying on her back, hands behind her head, staring at the ceiling.

"Hi," I said quietly, "Can I come in?"

Jamie continued to stare. I stepped inside and walked over to her bed. Baxter had followed me in and jumped up on the bed between us. He stood over Jamie, wagging his tail and licking her face. She turned her head from side to side, trying to avoid his relentless tongue.

"You don't have to let him do that, you know, honey."

"Well, I can't get him to stop!" she said, continuing to try to avoid his licks. I grabbed his collar and pulled him off the bed. When he tried to jump back up I put my leg in his way.

"No, Baxter!" I said sternly.

Jamie sat up in bed. "Well you don't have to yell at him. He was just saying good morning."

I looked at her, incredulous, I had been trying to help her. Baxter looked at me indignantly with his expressive, brown eyes and trotted slowly out of Jamie's room. She looked down at her hands, the tension between us began to rise without the distraction of Baxter.

"Jamie, what happened yesterday? Why did you get a detention?" I asked her as gently as possible.

"It wasn't my fault!"

Okay, but what happened? What wasn't your fault?"

"I talked back to Mrs. Miller."

"That was risky," I said surprised, "She's one tough cookie."

"She just thinks she's tough, but I hate her!"

I resisted the urge to lecture her about hating, respecting her teachers, etc., and decided to try and open up the communication so that I could learn what was really bothering her. "She really made you mad, huh?"

"She is so unfair!"

"She treated you unfairly when she gave you the detention?"

"No, well, yes, but she has favorites. It drives me nuts. She's so mean to Kelly, she always picks on her and embarrasses her, just because she's slower than everyone else."

"Was she picking on Kelly yesterday?" I asked, trying to get her to focus.

"Yes. She was so mean! Okay, here's what happened," Jamie scooted up the bed and crossed her legs. "Kelly had this really pretty dress on that had buttons going down the back and she couldn't get it unbuttoned. Well, she got really upset because she was afraid she'd get in trouble for being late for gym so I offered to help her. Well, then we were both late and when we came out of the locker room Mrs. Miller told Kelly she had to run a lap for being late."

"But not you?"

"Right! Just Kelly. So I told her what happened, about the buttons, and she told me to stay out of it. Well, if you ask me, I think she just thinks Kelly is too prissy so she picks on her. Anyway, I decided I wasn't going to sit back and watch this injustice any longer!"

"My goodness, Jamie, what did you do?" I asked nervously.

"I told Mrs. Miller she was prejudiced!"

"Oh my. What did she say?"

Jamie looked down. "First, she really yelled. It was sort of scary, I mean, she was really close to my face. I was afraid she was going to slap me or something. But then she made me go to Mrs. Larson's office and I stayed there through the whole class. After that, Mrs. Miller came up to the office and told Mrs. Larson what happened and that's when they gave me the detention. And while I was in detention, I had to write a letter apologizing to Mrs. Miller."

I was amazed that Jamie had behaved this way. "Well, Jamie, I'm glad you stuck by your friend, but you know, there are other ways to right the wrongs in this world."

"I knew you would side with her, I don't even know why I told you!" Jamie started closing up again.

"Jamie, that's not all that's going on with you. Mrs. Larson said you haven't done your homework in weeks."

She looked up at me defiantly. "What do you care?"

"What do you mean, I care a lot."

"Well, you didn't even notice. You would never have known if Mrs. Larson hadn't called you."

"I certainly would have noticed when your report card came home. But Jamie, you've always done your homework, and you're a good student. I thought that was important to you."

"How would you know what's important to me? Why don't you go bother Tiger, that's all you care about anyway!"

"Jamie! You know that's not true."

Jamie's face reddened and her eyes began to tear, "Oh, yes it is! How can you say it isn't?" She climbed out of bed and turned to look at me. She looked much younger in the oversized tee-shirt she had worn to bed, and my heart ached as she struggled to keep from crying. "That's all you talk about, dyslexia, dyslexia, dyslexia! It's all you care about. You take Tiger's side in everything. She's all you talk about, think about, do anything about. So don't tell me that you don't have a favorite, because you do! You're no better than Mrs. Miller." Jamie, humiliated by her tears, scanned the room for an escape route. "Get out of my room!"

I was horrified at Jamie's words. And yet they rang true, I hadn't been paying attention to Jamie, but not because I didn't love her as much as Tiger, because she didn't seem to need it. "Oh Jamie!" I said softly, tears welling in my eyes. "Oh, please, don't ask me to leave, not now, I can't."

Jamie stood with her arms folded to control the shaking from her sobs.

"Jamie, I'm so sorry!" She looked at me and I could see the relief in her eyes. "You're absolutely right, I have been so caught up in Tiger's dyslexia that I haven't paid enough attention to you. You're right! I was wrong to do that, I guess I just assumed you were fine, but that was so wrong. You deserve my attention whether you're fine or you're not fine." I stood up and walked over to her. "Jamie, darling, I'm sorry." I looked in her eyes and then pulled her toward me and wrapped my arms around her. She began to sob even harder, but I was thankful she didn't push me away. I held her for a long time, she sobbed into my shoulder and I rubbed her back gently. I cried, too, and kept whispering how sorry I was into her ear, and how much I loved her.

"Breakfast is ready!" Max bellowed, interrupting our embrace. "Everything all right?"

Just then Tiger's little face appeared under her dad's arm. "Did you guys make up?" she asked hopefully.

I looked over at her and smiled. "I think so." I looked at Jamie, "I hope so."

"Yippee!" Tiger squealed, jumping up and hitting her head on Max's biceps.

Jamie brushed her tear-dampened hair from her face and sniffed. "Would everyone please get out of my room so I can get dressed?" she asked, but her tone was different, she was smiling.

"Of course, we'll wait for you at the table," I said, stroking her hair. I looked over at Max and smiled. "I'm hungry."

"You better be, because Tiger and I have been cooking up a storm."

After breakfast, Max and I lingered at the table, reading the paper and finishing our coffee. "Max," I said as I stared out the window, "as much as I would love for the four of us to spend the day together, I think we need a one-on-one day."

"Today? But I was hoping we could all be together. I can't remember the last time I was home on a Saturday."

I glanced at him sideways and pushed my readin glasses further up the bridge of my nose. "I am more than aware of that. Max rolled his eyes. "I guess that's why I'm suggesting this. They've had to share one of us for months. I think they could use some time alone with a parent."

Max folded the newspaper and gathered the sections. "Who do I get?"

243

"Tiger and I spend a lot of time in the car. I think Jamie and I should do a little shopping, maybe have lunch together."

Max contemplated my suggestion. "Maybe Tiger and I could go for a bike ride on the trail." He looked over at me and added quickly, "Yes, dear, I will make sure she wears her helmet."

One-on-one time was a family policy Max and I had begun not long after Tiger was born. Whenever one of our children was out of sorts we would find time to be with them separately. I referred to it as their emotional wells being empty and needing a refill. The indicators, such as when they were having difficulty sharing or being kind to one another, would tell us that it was time for us to fill them up, and for the most part, it would work wonders. Once reunited, they would immediately run off and play together, happy to see each other again, and more cooperative with one another than before. I was frustrated with myself for not seeing the need for this before. Of course Jamie had been feeling shortchanged.

Jamie reluctantly agreed to spend the day with me. She was withholding, at first, and as much as I grew frustrated with her aloofness, I knew she needed me to continue to pursue her.

We shopped a little, but the stores were crowded and noisy. I bought her a dress for the "holiday" pageant and teased her that I might not make it to the performance. She rolled her eyes but was able to laugh. We finally decided to abandon our shopping and get out of the crowds and were happy to find a table by the window at California Pizza Kitchen. The waiter had shown us to our seats and handed us each a menu. I smiled at him and said thank you, but noticed Jamie looked concerned.

"What is it, honey?"

"Well," she looked up at the waiter shyly, "could I have a children's menu please? And some crayons?"

"Oh," he said politely, "no problem." He winked at me as he walked away.

Jamie's face reddened. "I just like their spaghetti and meatballs, and, well, it's boring to sit here if you don't have something to do."

I smiled at Jamie, happy to see the younger side of her eleven-hood. "I agree."

Once the waiter returned with the crayons, we managed to play five games of hangman, six games of tic tac toe, and draw our own renditions of Baxter with the limited color selection. While we waited for our lunch, I could sense Jamie was letting her guard down more and more as the day wore on and I began to feel relieved that I hadn't lost her.

On the way home Jamie sat next to me in her father's clean car. "So," she said with some hesitation, "does this mean I'm not really grounded?"

244

I looked over at her. "No. It doesn't."

"You mean I'm still grounded, even after I explained to you what had happened?

I felt myself regret the change in conversation, but knew I had to remain firm. "Yes, honey. You're grounded for the weekend for talking back to Mrs. Miller, and you have lost your phone privileges for the week for not doing your homework."

"But, Mom!"

"And," I said, interrupting her protest, "You will not be permitted to use the phone until you have finished your homework, and I've checked it, through the end of the semester."

"Why?"

"Because, honey, that's the deal. I'll take your phone out of your room, and return it next week, and then, each evening, after I've checked your homework."

"Mother, and if you would please stop interrupting me, you admitted yourself that you were wrong, so why do I get punished?"

I glanced over at her, F. Lee Bailey reincarnated, I thought to myself. "Jamie," I said clearly, "I was wrong to pay less attention to you because I was preoccupied with Tiger, totally wrong. And I feel very bad about it, and I have every intention of not letting it happen again, even if things get worse with her situation. The problem for you, however, is how you handled your feelings. It's never okay to neglect your responsibilities, no matter how you're feeling about something, or someone else. And it's also not okay to say what you did to Mrs. Miller. There are a lot more appropriate ways to make your point then to show disrespect and be critical."

Jamie sat quietly. I was expecting an outburst, and was surprised when she said calmly, "How else could I have gotten my point across to Mrs. Miller? She was so unfair to Kelly!"

"Well, let's see, you could have explained to her as calmly as possible what had happened."

"I tried," Jamie said earnestly, "but she wouldn't listen, she never does. I think she's been teaching too long."

"That may be true, but that part is out of your control. So, if she didn't hear you when you said it calmly, perhaps you could have let it go and..."

"But I was so angry!"

I smiled at her, "I'm sure you were, it sounds as if she wasn't being fair. So if you have a legitimate point, how can you get it across without letting your anger get in the way?"

"That's what I'm asking you."

"Well, what do you think? You're the budding lawyer. How else could you have handled it?"

Jamie thought hard. "I could sue her."

"Ha, ha," I said, a little worried. "Try again."

What if I wrote her a letter, explaining my point of view? I could even send a copy to Mrs. Larson. That's what you and Dad do."

"Great idea! It would be like writing a letter to the editor of a newspaper or magazine. That's a great way to express your point of view in a healthy way."

Jamie was grinning with pride.

"I'll tell you what, If you write the letter, I'll consider giving you back your phone privileges a little earlier, as a reward instead of a punishment."

"Cool," she said quickly.

"And," I added, speaking more softly, "Jamie, in terms of me, it would have been hard, but it would have been much better for you to have tried to tell me how you were feeling, than to get my attention in a negative way, because in the end, all that does is hurt you."

Jamie stared out the windshield. "I know," she said quietly, "I just wasn't sure you would listen. And all you talked about was dyslexia, and read about dyslexia, and talk to people about Tiger."

"I'm sorry I made you feel you couldn't come to me with your problem, honey, I truly am."

Jamie sat quietly for a few minutes. "Well, am I still grounded?"

I growled and looked over at her, "Yes, you are."

"If you say so," and I was surprised to see a small smile on her face. I reached over and stroked her arm and was relieved when she didn't tell me to stop. Jamie had less tolerance for physical closeness than Tiger, who craved it. But as we neared our house, I began to realize that my setting limits on Jamie was enabling her to feel better. She must have been feeling out of control with her behavior and her strong feelings, and these limits gave her a sense of when she had gone too far, and in turn, a sense of safety. She was relieved to be reigned in. I silently promised myself to never hesitate to step up to my role as parent again, especially now that the harbingers of adolescence were upon us.

When we arrived home, Max and Tiger had prepared a wonderful dinner. Tiger was proud of her contribution. She loved cooking and creating her own concoctions. But Max had managed to direct her creativity toward a delicious ratatouille and Jamie and I raved about how delicious it was. After dinner, Jamie and I offered to clean up while Max and Tiger started a fire. Then Jamie brought out the Monopoly game. Tiger was hesitant to play at first, feeling insecure about reading the cards and counting her money. She finally agreed to play when we promised we would read together and double check all banking transactions. Jamie was relieved, it was her favorite game, and I could see she appreciated that we didn't lower our standards again to a quick game of Candyland, a game neither Max nor I could tolerate for long, but which required no reading.

It was a wonderful, relaxing evening, and although Tiger spent more time having her dog play as it rounded the board, she managed to stay interested enough to last the entire game. Meanwhile, Jamie and Max negotiated and bargained over every property and at every turn, and when at last Jamie was victorious, her cheeks were rosy from the excitement and challenges of the game.

Max and I returned to the fire after spending extra time tucking in Jamie and Tiger. I felt warmed by their affection and contentment from us spending a relaxed evening together as a family. They were once again in the same bed, and although I didn't encourage this practice, I had begun to see it as a barometer for how our family was faring.

Max and I cuddled on the couch and ate popcorn and drank tea. We were tucked under the afghan and watching the fire. After a few moments Max spoke, "Katie,"

"Yes."

"Are you still attracted to me?"

"Of course," I said tentatively.

"Seriously, Katie, I mean it."

"Oh," I said, growing uncomfortable.

"What I'm asking you, is, are you still attracted to me, I mean, if things were better, would you be interested in me, because, I have to tell you, lately, you seem a little distracted."

"When did you notice that?"

"What kind of question is that?"

"Well, I guess I feel as if you have only recently tuned in, and now that you have, you think I'm distracted. But maybe that is a result of you not being around."

Max sighed, "Perhaps, I don't have a clue, and I sure as hell don't want to figure it out now, I guess I was just looking for a little reassurance, you know, that I was still the guy for you."

I debated a long time about whether to tell him about Rob. "I love you, Max, and I sincerely want things to work out, and, lately, I'm beginning to think that they will. There are things we should probably talk about at some point, you know, about what each of us has gone through these past few months, but not yet. We're still on shaky ground, let's wait for the after shocks to abate, what do you think?"

"Well, to be honest with you, 'I love you' was enough. I don't know what the rest of that mumbo jumbo was about. 'I love you, Max' was what I was fishing for."

"Oh." I said reddening. "Well, I do. I love you Max. I really do."

"Oh, Katie," he said, scooping me up in his arms and burying his face in my neck. "I needed to hear that so much! I love you and I have been so terrified of losing you." The urgency in his voice touched my heart. "I have been so afraid I had fucked up beyond repair. Please tell me that isn't true! I don't think I could live without you, without our family!"

I hugged him back and stroked his hair.

We held each other for a long time and I was relieved at how wonderful it felt. Eventually we climbed the stairs to bed and as we held eachother and I felt the warmth of his body and breathed in his familiar scent, I was comforted with the knowledge that I was still deeply in love with the man I had married.

It was conference day. Although the semester didn't end until after the Christmas break, Frances had requested we meet a few weeks before the end of the term. When she had told me this my heart sank. She had an agenda, I was naive to hope it would be any different than her original plan.

Max had offered to come along and I was relieved. We arranged to meet in the school parking lot the afternoon of the conference. Lois had agreed to take Jamie and Tiger home from school and offered to take them for ice cream and then exchange Christmas presents. Jamie and Tiger had chosen a delicate picture frame for her and had placed a picture of them with Baxter in the middle and wrapped it that morning. I was relieved to know I wouldn't have to face them immediately following the conference.

I was standing outside the van, despite the chill in the December air, and began to pace as it grew closer to the meeting time. Please don't be late, Max, I wished to myself, not today. I didn't need any additional stress that might shake my composure. After waiting as long as possible, I kicked some dirt and swore at him under my breath. I started to walk toward the door when I heard the unmistakable hum of the Saab as he downshifted through the gates. His tires squealed as he rounded the bend. He jumped out of the car and grabbed his suit coat. "Hello, dear," he said in his charming way, pretending he hadn't been hurrying. "Little nip in the air, wouldn't you say?"

I tried not to smile. "You don't want to know what I was just thinking."

He put his arm through mine when he reached me. "You're quite right about that, I have no interest, whatsoever."

Frances, Mary, and Joan were in their designated seats. I had a sense of foreboding when I saw the slight trace of a smile on Mary Peterson's face. We greeted one another and Max waited politely for everyone to sit before he seated himself. There was some small talk about the weather and the possibility of snow and then Frances cleared her throat and began the meeting.

"Well, I have a progress report that Mary has prepared for you," she said as she handed us each a copy of two typed paragraphs. "Mary has evaluated Trisha's progress since our last meeting and compared it to the rest of the children in the class. And, as you can see, Trisha is way below average, and in fact, is not performing at all."

I swallowed hard, fighting back the swell of emotions stirring in my gut. "Let's cut through the pleasantries, Frances," Max said firmly. "What have you decided?"

"Don't you think it's important to understand how Trisha is progressing?" Mary said defensively.

Max looked at her and then back to Frances. "Well, Frances?"

Mary looked disgusted, but Frances seemed to know Max was right, we all knew what was coming. And neither of us was interested in hearing Mary's evaluation of Tiger's "progress."

"All right, we have decided that Trisha is not appropriate for this school. We don't think she should return to the Chesapeake Day School next semester. In fact, I don't think she should return after the holidays."

I kept staring at the paper. "And what does the board say about this, Frances?" Max asked.

"Max, you know perfectly well that I run this school and decisions of admission are solely up to me. But if you must know, John Brady, the President of the Board of Trustees, is fully aware of my decision and supports it completely."

Max looked over at me, he wasn't sure where to take this meeting.

"So," I said, gathering my composure, "that's that. Good-bye, Tiger?"

"Please, Kate," Frances said. "We agreed to give it a try and I think we have been more than accommodating to Trisha's tutoring schedule, but she still isn't reading, or spelling, or even adding for that matter. We just can't accommodate her disabilities, or allow her to continue to disrupt the class anymore than she already has with this ridiculous schedule."

"No, that much is true," I said quietly. "And I must say, I'm not surprised at your decision, just disappointed. But what I'm wondering, is what about the other students in this school who are dyslexic? What happens to them?"

"We don't have any other dyslexics in this school," Joan spoke up.

"Really?" I said, trying not to heat up. "Well, you should know that you do. Twenty percent of the population is dyslexic, and since you screen for intelligence, your percentage is probably higher. But, for now, my concern is for Tiger, and although I don't have any idea where she will go to school, I believe in my heart that anywhere will be better than what she has experienced here. I just hope the damage that has been done to her self-esteem is not irreparable."

"Katie," Max said, cautioning me.

I looked at him and then back at Frances and her teachers. "It's true, and I would think as educators you would want to know how your teaching methods affect your students. But in the meantime, I hope you know that we will continue to support Jamie and the school, and I know you are professional enough to keep their school experiences separate."

"Of course, Kate, Jamie, who by the way has been doing much better lately, will not be affected by this decision."

I sighed, I was losing steam, the fight was over and I knew anything I had to say would fall on deaf ears.

"Of course you know that we will not be paying for next semester," Max said.

"No, I understand that. This is a mutual agreement, you will not be billed."

I looked at Frances, "This is not a mutual agreement."

"Well," Frances was flustered, "I mean the contract, you won't be expected to pay, that's what I mean."

"And of course that will be in writing?"

"Yes, of course," Frances said.

I needed to get out of there and stood quickly. "Okay, I guess that's it, good-bye."

Max jumped up, surprised at my abrupt departure, "Katie, hang on there." He shook everyone's hand again and said, "Well, I guess this meeting is adjourned! Good-bye, ladies."

I was leaning against the van by the time Max caught up with me. "Christ, Katie, what if I wasn't finished?"

"I'm sorry," I said through my tears, "I just couldn't keep it together any longer, and I didn't want them to see me cry."

Max put his arms around me. "I know, I guess there wasn't anything left to say, it just seemed so quick and abrupt. That's it, Tiger's out of there."

I started to cry even harder at his words. "Max, what are we going to do? Where is she going to go to school? What do we tell her? She'll only blame herself!"

"Oh, boy," Max said with a deep sigh. "Oh, boy."

I heard the school door open and pulled away from Max. I looked over to see Joan and Mary leaving the school with their purses and canvas school bags. They looked to be normal teachers, middle-aged women with kind faces, the image that comes to my mind when you think of "teacher." And I knew they weren't unkind people. What was causing them to reject Tiger? And how could they live with themselves, knowing what she was going through? I knew in my heart that Tiger could remain in that classroom if only they were willing to try some new things. I knew that Tiger did not have to continue to feel punished for learning differently. It seemed that the only thing standing between Tiger and this school was her teacher's unwillingness, or perhaps, inability, to learn new ways of teaching. Was that too much to ask? That she know, or learn, a few ways to engage Tiger's brain?

250

There were twenty students in her classroom. That is a lot. Perhaps it was too much to expect. But then I thought of Joe. He wasn't excelling. And he was most likely dyslexic, too. And how many others? How many children are failed by our educational system? And, what if every school taught language arts to children with Orton-Gillingham? Then no one would fall through the cracks. And perhaps, even successful students like Jamie, would have a better mastery of the English language.

"Katie, stop staring at Mary and Joan," Max whispered.

"Oh. I didn't realize I was."

"Do you want to go have a drink or something?" Max asked, he was rubbing my arm affectionately.

I smiled at him. "No, I don't think so. Max, we're going to have to tell Tiger about this."

"I know," he said reluctantly. "At least it's Friday and we have some time to think about it."

"True. But the word will be out by Monday. For all we know they'll have that new girl in her seat. We have to be able to tell her where she'll be going to school."

Max looked at me. I was glad he was there and was engaged in the problem, but he didn't have a clue what we should do. This one was up to me.

"Can you pay Lois? I have a stop to make on the way home," I asked him.

"Sure, but where are you going?"

"I'll be home as soon as I can, why don't you order a pizza?" I said as I unlocked the van door.

Max looked perplexed. "Katie-- "

"Bye!" I called, "I'll explain later!"

When I reached Linkages I was relieved, but not surprised, to see that Linda Goldman's car was still in the parking lot. When I entered the waiting room I saw several mothers reading magazines, waiting for their children who were in the various rooms being tutored in Orton-Gillingham. I smiled at the ones who looked up and felt a tremendous comfort at their presence. They were helping their children too. This was a good place.

I edged through the sea of crossed legs and peeked into Linda's half open door. She was on the phone, talking cheerfully, and taking notes on a yellow legal pad. She looked up and I waved. She excused herself from her phone conversation. "What's up, Katie?"

"I'm sorry to interrupt, Linda, but I'm in a bit of a crisis, do you have a minute? I don't mind waiting."

Linda smiled. "Of course, it could be a while though, I have a parent conference that I'm already running little late for, but we can talk after that. Is that

251

okay?"

"That's great, thanks. I'm going to run over to that Starbucks across the street and I'll be right back. Can I get you a latte?"

Linda's face lit up. "Yes!"

"I'll bring it in to you, and perhaps a little chocolate dipped biscotti?"

Linda gave me a thumbs up and we both smiled. I closed her door behind me and felt as if a tremendous burden had been lifted. I had no idea what was going to happen, but I knew this was the right place to go looking for answers, in this modest little office, full of battle weary parents and children.

As I passed through the crowded waiting room again I said, "Who wants a latte? I'm buying!" Everyone looked up in surprise. "Come on, it's Friday afternoon!"

A few laughed, one spoke up, "I would love one!"

"You're on," I said. Eventually I got a few more orders and felt happy that the mood in the room was beginning to match mine. When I returned with the tray of coffees, I took off the lid and said in a loud voice so that Linda would hear, "Here's to Linda Goldman!" and we all toasted our paper coffee cups. "Hear, hear!" they echoed. I could hear Linda tittering in the next room and soon saw her shining face in the doorway.

"Here's to Orton and Gillingham!" she said as I handed her a steaming cup. We all smiled and raised our cups once again.

"Here's to chocolate and coffee!" another, very tired looking woman said, and the room broke into laughter.

By the time Linda finished her parent conference, the waiting room had emptied and I was alone. I didn't mind the wait, I knew Linda was taking time with this parent as she did with everyone. She was thorough and kind. She said good-bye and the woman smiled at me and thanked me for the coffee. Linda waved me in after her.

"So, Kate, what's the crisis?" she asked with concern.

I looked at her and was surprised when my eyes welled with tears. I grabbed a tissue quickly. "Whoa, I don't know where this is coming from." Linda waited patiently for me to regain my composure. I blew my nose. "Well, they've finally done it. They've kicked Tiger out of school."

"I was afraid that was what you were going to say," she said kindly. "What's their reasoning?"

"Oh, no surprises, Tiger isn't performing, the tutoring was too disruptive."

"Would it help if I talked to them? Because Tiger is doing very well, it's just a matter of time before the reading kicks in."

I smiled at the good news. "I appreciate the offer, but I think Frances made up her mind long before today, she was just going through the motions in order to cover herself. I think she's already replaced Tiger. Anyway, she's out as of the holidays."

"Really?" Linda said in surprise. "What are you going to do, Katie?"

"That's why I'm here. I don't want to stop tutoring, and I don't want to send her to the public school, I think she would fare worse there than at Chesapeake Day, so what can I do? Any chance you could open a school in the next few weeks?"

Linda looked at me thoughtfully. "The idea isn't as farfetched as it may sound."

"Really?" I asked.

"Well, it certainly won't help Tiger right now, but Anne Arundel County is becoming less and less cooperative with our program, for virtually the same reasons as the Chesapeake Day School, they say it's too disruptive, and that their special ed program is adequate. But it's not, they're cutting funding like crazy, and they're not using any multi-sensory techniques, they're just slowing down what they're doing in the regular classroom. And you and I both know that isn't the problem. It's how you teach, not the speed. You saw that when you visited, didn't you? So, anyway, you're not working, want to help?"

"Help what, Linda?"

"Help me start a school," she said. "What do you say?"

"I'm not an educator, what could I possibly do?"

"You know more than you think, plus you know people, and you've walked in their shoes. You could do a million things, help me raise money, be a liaison to the community, help with admissions, family therapist, coffee gopher, you name it!"

I laughed. "I'll give it some thought. But Linda, I still don't think it should have to come to this -- a separate school just to educate the twenty per cent who don't fit into the mold. It's not right."

Linda smiled. "I know, Kate. And I've been fighting the system for twenty years and I just can't watch the devastation anymore. So, this is my solution. I even have a site picked out and it's perfect. And I'll need help with fund-raising. Anne Arundel is cutting back on everything, including funding children for special schools. But I want a school people can afford."

"That's wonderful, Linda."

"But back to Tiger," she said. "What are you thinking?"

"I'm thinking I wish your school was up and running today." We laughed. "But for now, could Tiger be tutored here full time? What if this were her school, it would be like home schooling, but she would be here with one, or perhaps, more than one of your tutors."

Linda looked thoughtful. "What if I checked to see if one of our tutors could come into your home the other half of the day, how would that be?"

"Fine," I said, filling with hope. "And I could help in any way I could,

253

provide materials, take her on field trips. But I can't teach her."

"No, even though you took the training, you're right not to try. What about socially? She would be very isolated."

"I hadn't thought about that, I don't know. I guess I could involve her in some more activities, you know, Brownies, art classes, soccer team. And it's only for half a year. It's better than what's happening now, being excluded at school and punished by her teacher."

"I'll see what I can do on this end," Linda said. "You do what you can and let's see if we can't pull a curriculum together for Tiger."

I stood up and spontaneously hugged her. "Thank you, Linda Goldman!"

Linda laughed and hugged me back. "Oh, you can thank me now, but I have plans for you, Katie. You and I will make a great team. This is going to be a wonderful school, you'll see."

"You're really going to do this, aren't you," I said seriously. "This is more than just a good idea."

"Absolutely. I haven't told many people about it, but I'm going to do it. And you're going to help me. I can see it in your eyes."

"I'll give it some thought. But if anyone can pull this off, you can. And I can't think of anyone I'd rather help more."

Linda smiled. "I like the sound of that." She reached over and handed me a packet of information. "This is confidential, but I want you to read it. It's the charter. I've been pulling a board together. We need legal counsel, too, any chance we can pull Max off the Chesapeake Board?"

"After today, yes!"

"Read this, Katie, and share it with Max. If you're willing to help me, I have plenty for you to do. I want to open the doors in September, and I want Tiger to walk through them with pride."

My eyes began to tear up again. "Okay, let me know what you come up with about a tutor for the afternoons, I'd like to tell Tiger this weekend, are you confident enough for me to do that?"

"Yes. You tell her, I have several people who would love to work with her."

"Great. Good-bye, Linda, thank you."

"Thank you, Katie, I'm glad you're on board!" I laughed nervously as I closed the door behind me.

When I arrived home, I found Max, Jamie and Tiger spread out on the family room floor. They were watching a movie and the pizza was on the top of the entertainment center, out of Baxter's reach. "Hey!" Max said when I walked in. He started to stand but I waved him back down.

"Just let me change into something cozy and I'll come and join you."

Max looked at me curiously. "You seem to be in a good mood."

"I am, considering."

"Good," he said sincerely.

I changed into my favorite pair of leggings and an oversized sweatshirt and tucked my hair into what little ponytail I could muster. Once back downstairs I helped myself to a cool piece of pizza and sat down on the floor. "I could warm that up for you," Max offered.

"No thanks, I like it cold." Tiger noticed me on the floor and while still watching the movie, inched her way over into my lap. I looked down at her and stroked her silky hair. I could see her body relax with my strokes and I felt a rush of love and protectiveness for her. I looked over at Jamie and whispered, "How did it go with Lois?"

"Fine." She flashed me a quick smile and went back to watching the movie.

When it was over we continued to sit on the floor and were all still caught in the mood of the movie. Eventually Tiger broke the silence, "I don't know if I like that movie."

"Why's that, honey?" I asked her softly.

"I don't know, it makes me feel too much. I feel like I could cry or something."

"Me too," Jamie said, hopping up and heading for her room.

"Jamie," I called to her before she reached the steps, "Before you go up to your room, Daddy and I have something to tell you."

"Are you pregnant?" she asked and came running into the room.

"Pregnant?" Max and I said in unison. "Jamie," I said in exasperation, "You know Daddy had a vasectomy, we're not having any more children."

"Well," she said, "You can't stop a kid from hoping, can you?"

"Don't you have enough siblings to share with?" I asked her teasingly.

Jamie put her arm around Tiger, "Me and my sis don't mind sharing!"

"Yeah!" Tiger chimed in. "So, can we have a baby brother?"

"No!" Max bellowed. "No, No, No!" Jamie and Tiger flinched at his booming voice but were relieved when he broke into a grin. He grabbed them each around the waist and began to wrestle with them. I debated about calling a time out but decided to clean up the dishes while they got it out of their systems.

When the yelling died down I rejoined them and handed Max a cup of hot tea. "Can we have our family pow wow now?"

"That rhymes, Mom," Tiger said, and I was thankful she noticed.

"Oh, yeah, you had something to tell us," Jamie said, "I forgot. So, why are you acting so weird?"

Max and I looked at each other. "Well, the reason I'm, I mean, we're acting so weird is we had a conference at school today about Tiger." Tiger's expression changed immediately from happy to terrified. I took a deep breath, "and, it seems that they don't know how to teach to Tiger's dyslexia so they suggested," I was choosing my words carefully, speaking more slowly than my usual cadence. "They have suggested Tiger go to school, well, somewhere else."

"What?" Jamie screamed. "Why? They can't do that!"

Tiger's eyes filled with tears. "You mean I can't go to school there? But Mommy, where will I go to school? Will Jamie still go there? Mommy!"

I grabbed Tiger and hugged her and I could see Jamie's distress so I looked at Max and nodded my head to Jamie. To my relief he took the hint and touched Jamie's hand softly, "Come on over by me, Jamie," he said and he pulled her gently toward his lap. She plopped down, tears forming in her eyes as well.

I stroked Tiger's hair and told her that it was not because she wasn't liked or that she wasn't a good student, but that they didn't know the techniques that her tutor did and that she would be tutored full time for the rest of the year. "It will give you a jump on everyone else, and give you a chance to catch up, at your own speed and in your own way." I explained about the afternoons at home and that we would make a special effort to invite her friends over and involve her in lots of activities.

"I don't want to go to that school if Tiger isn't welcome there," Jamie said adamantly.

"I respect that, darling, I really do."

"Me too," Max added.

"But for the most part that has been a good school for you and I think you should stay. Your friends are there and you are doing well. But if that changes, then there is no doubt in our minds that we'll take you out as well. And who knows, if we get Tiger up to speed, she might return, if she wants, that is."

Everyone grew quiet, absorbed in our thoughts. Eventually Tiger and Jamie asked a few more questions. They were worried and sad and we huddled together on the floor for a long time. "Mom," Tiger asked after a long silence.

"What, honey?"

"Does this mean I'll be able to go to school in my socks?"

We all burst into laughter, probably louder than was warranted, but were relieved to be laughing. "Not fair!" Jamie yelled in mock protest and Tiger smiled.

Eventually we walked them up to their rooms. Max stayed close to Jamie and I could hear them talking in her room. I walked Tiger into her room after she brushed her teeth so that she could change into her jungle animal pajamas. "Can I sleep with Jamie tonight?" she asked.

"It's all right with me if it's all right with Jamie," I said as I walked around her room, picking up toys and clothes from the floor. "Hey, Tig. Did Lois give you a

Christmas present this afternoon?"

"Oh, yeah," Tiger said and stopped putting on her pajamas midway in order to go get it for me. She picked up several books, handed them to me and continued to pull her shirt over her head. "They're about a girl and her dog, Mammoth. That one's called *Mercy and Mammoth and the Best Day Ever*. It's pretty good. Mercy likes nature, like me, and she likes to be outside. So does Mammoth."

"Mammoth is the dog, I presume," I said playfully.

"Yes, Mom," she said rolling her eyes.

"Did Lois read it to you?"

"No, we didn't have time." She pulled down her shirt and flipped her hair out of the neck line.

"So how do you know what it's about?"

"I read it."

I looked over at Tiger, saddened she felt the need to pretend with me. "You mean you looked at the pictures?"

"No, Mommy, I read it! Listen." Tiger sat cross-legged on the floor, the small book in her delicate hands. "One day, when the sun had climbed high into the sky, Mercy and her very large dog, Mammoth..." she read slowly.

I could barely see through my tears as I picked up a startled Tiger in my arms and burst into Jamie's room, "Max, Jamie, Tiger's reading!"

* * * * *